LONE STAR

LONE STAR

The Extraordinary Life and Times of Dan Rather

Alan Weisman

John Wiley & Sons, Inc.

This book is printed on acid-free paper. ∞

Copyright © 2006 by Dandi Productions, Inc. All rights reserved

Published by John Wiley & Sons, Inc., Hoboken, New Jersey
Published simultaneously in Canada

Design and composition by Navta Associates, Inc.

For general information about our other products and services, please contact our Customer Care Department within the United States at (800) 762-2974, outside the United States at (317) 572-3993 or fax (317) 572-4002.

Wiley also publishes its books in a variety of electronic formats. Some content that appears in print may not be available in electronic books. For more information about Wiley products, visit our web site at www.wiley.com.

Library of Congress Cataloging-in-Publication Data:

Weisman, Alan, date.
   Lone Star: The extraordinary life and times of Dan Rather / Alan Weisman.
      p. cm.
   Includes bibliographical references and index.
   ISBN-13 978-0-471-79217-8 (cloth)
   ISBN-10 0-471-79217-9 (cloth)
   1. Rather, Dan. 2. Television journalists—United States—Biography. I. Title.
   PN4874.R28W45 2006
   070'.92—dc22
   [B]

                                                         2006009366

Printed in the United States of America

10 9 8 7 6 5 4 3 2 1

To Diana, Daniel, and Jeanne,

For their love and their infinite patience

When I got them north Texas blues
Thought I'd paid all my dues.
Then them south Texas blues
Told me, son, you ain't through.
Had them east Texas blues
And them west Texas blues too.
I've done all I know to do
Tryin' to lose, tryin' to lose
These Lone Star blues.

—Delbert McClinton,
"Lone Star Blues"

Contents

Illustrations follow on page 110.

Acknowledgments

My thanks to all of my former colleagues who gave me their time, their insights, and their encouragement throughout this process. A nod also to those television beat writers who willingly went back through their files and their memories to provide their unique perspectives.

To my lifelong friends Don Ryan and Steve Friedman (the great photographer, not the former NBC News executive), my thanks for your help and support.

To executive editor Tom Miller and his colleagues at Wiley, a thumbs-up for their time, effort, patience, and skill.

And a special thanks to my agent, Sharlene Martin, for taking on a first-time author and tolerating (barely) all the nonsense that goes with him.

LONE STAR

Prologue

By all accounts, the memorial service for Peter Jennings at New York City's Carnegie Hall on the morning of September 20, 2005, was an elegant and moving affair. Yo-Yo Ma and Wynton Marsalis performed, along with a corps of bagpipers from the Royal Canadian Mounted Police in a nod to Jennings's roots.

The guests were the elite of the broadcast journalism business; they included Ted Koppel, Barbara Walters, Diane Sawyer, Katie Couric, and a cortege of corporate heavies and movie stars. Jennings's longtime friend the actor Alan Alda described the former ABC anchorman as a mix of graciousness and candor: "We're left now with just a little bit of snow at the bottom of the screen."

Also in attendance was Daniel Irvin Rather, the former CBS News anchorman, the former managing editor of the *CBS Evening News*, formerly one of the most powerful figures in broadcast journalism, and the former heir to the legacies of Murrow, Cronkite, Sevareid, Collingwood, and a long list of legends who had invented television news. He was now the former Dan Rather.

Twenty years earlier, at an equally somber event, Rather and many of his CBS News colleagues had milled about lamenting the sad state of

affairs that had befallen their company and its once-mighty news organization. At the time, the company was in the throes of an ownership struggle, a tense if not hostile relationship between the News Division and
management, and a change to a softer on-air product that rankled the
hard-news veterans—with more layoffs on the horizon. There was an
overwhelming sense that something unique and treasured had been lost
for good. "We weren't attending Charles Collingwood's funeral," said 60
Minutes's Don Hewitt at the time. "We were at our *own* funeral." Now,
with Peter Jennings gone, Tom Brokaw retired, Dan Rather banished to
the sidelines, and Ted Koppel halfway to good-bye; with the Viacoms,
Disneys, General Electrics, Time Warners, and News Corps controlling
the airwaves, the satellites, and the cable systems; and with bloggers and
podcasters expounding through the prism of their own political and social
perceptions, Hewitt's remark covered an entire industry. Now, they were
all at their own funeral.

After two hours, the audience filed out, some people to power
lunches, others back to work. Rather returned to the office, which used to
be known as the Ford building because it once housed a Ford dealership
on the ground floor. Now it features a lavish BMW dealership with
gleaming Beamers and their $75,000 stickers parked throughout, mock-
ing the masses who can afford only Fords.

The building is home to 60 Minutes and what used to be 60 Minutes
Wednesday, the spinoff of the venerable magazine show that had been
canceled several months earlier. I had been a producer on the staff of 60
Minutes Wednesday and was among those let go, just a few weeks shy of
my fifty-fifth birthday. Despite more than thirty years in the TV news
business as an executive producer, a senior producer, and a producer,
much of it at CBS, I was neither angry nor bitter. Given my age and
salary level, I was not surprised to be among those terminated. Most companies that are cutting back prefer a younger and cheaper workforce—
experience is simply not as valuable as it used to be.

I had anticipated the cancellation of 60 Minutes Wednesday (origi-
nally called 60 Minutes II) even before the 2004–2005 TV season had
begun. While the broadcast had been praised by most critics and had

performed reasonably well in the ratings through its first five seasons, changes in management and much stiffer competition made it a likely target for elimination. The show was drawing the oldest audience of any program on the CBS prime-time lineup, and CBS's top programmer, Les Moonves, wanted what advertisers wanted—young and younger.

Although there were already nails in the coffin of 60 Minutes Wednesday, the final spike came pounding down on the evening of September 8, 2004, when the show opened with a report by Dan Rather alleging that some thirty years earlier, President George W. Bush had used his family's influence to avoid the Vietnam draft. When serious questions were raised about documents used to support the story, questions that could not be adequately answered, CBS was eventually forced to retract the story and publicly apologize to the president and to the viewers.

In the ugly fallout, the story's producer was fired and three top CBS executives were forced to resign. At least some people at CBS believed that Rather should have been fired as well, but in many respects he ended up taking the hardest hit of all: irreparable damage to a career that had lasted for fifty years. Not only would he be forced to give up his anchor chair on the CBS Evening News, a chair in which he had delivered the news for twenty-four years, he would be branded forever as at best a dupe and at worst dishonest and unethical.

When I thought about how Rather had come to CBS so many decades earlier, how far he had risen, how overwhelming the odds against his success were from the beginning, and the unprecedented power he had held for so long at CBS News, I realized that the Dan Rather story was one hell of a story. Many books have been written about CBS and CBS News, but none have been written about the man who was its standard-bearer for almost a quarter of a century. Rather himself, with the help of several different writers, has recounted parts of his life and career in several books, but the perspective, of course, was always his. To many of even his closest colleagues, he has always been an oddity, a puzzle—where did Dan Rather the person begin and Dan Rather the persona end?

To his legion of critics, both inside and outside CBS, Dan Rather is a phony—a man whose sincerity is contrived, whose motives are suspect, whose entire career has been more a performance than a calling, and whose private life has been another ruse. To his many admirers, he was the true heir to the patron saint of television journalism, Edward R. Murrow. Rather's childhood hero represented the man Rather had always longed to be: scholarly, brave, hardworking, unflinchingly honest, a speaker of truth to power.

B efore Rather became the CBS anchorman in 1981, the nightly network news was delivered by men who—at least, on the tube— appeared to be exactly who they purported to be: Chet Huntley and David Brinkley, Howard K. Smith and Harry Reasoner, John Chancellor, and, of course, Walter Cronkite. These men were easy on the eyes and the ears and managed to be both human and professional at the same time. What you saw was what you got. No agendas were perceived by viewers and no tension was on the air, real or contrived. As Jack Webb used to say, "Just the facts, ma'am," and with Brinkley and Reasoner you got some wit thrown in for good measure.

Even as a reporter, though, Rather was different and the viewer could sense it. As journalist Sally Bedell Smith told me, "With Dan, you just never knew what was going to happen." Perhaps it was the clipped east Texas accent or the way he stood ramrod straight, holding the microphone stiffly under his chin. Perhaps it was the way his smile seemed forced even when it was genuine. "I am not—never have been—a natural smiler," he once wrote.

When he became an anchorman, these eccentricities were magnified. He sometimes appeared to be an anchor playing an anchor, and tension seemed to vibrate through the screen. As radio talk show host Don Imus once said, "I want to be watching when he cracks." Over the years, Rather attained a reputation for being what his colleague Andy Rooney once called "transparently liberal." He had an agenda, critics said, and it was anticonservative, antibusiness, antiauthority of every stripe, and, worse, anti-American.

Despite these alleged shortcomings, Dan Rather won every award there is to win in broadcast journalism, and, as anchor, he kept CBS Evening

News number one throughout most of the 1980s. He revolutionized the role Walter Cronkite had largely created by taking the anchor out of the anchorman chair, traveling to virtually every war zone and hellhole on the planet and risking his life on numerous occasions for a story. He interviewed just about every world leader who came and went on his watch. He compiled a body of work that was distinguished by any measure.

Throughout much of CBS News, the announcement of Rather's retirement as anchor was met with both sadness and relief. The Rather years had not been easy on the News Division for a variety of reasons, at least some of which were beyond his control. As anchorman, he was the public face of the company; his image was CBS's image, and with Rather that was a mixed blessing. When he was out from behind the anchor desk, battling the winds of a hurricane or going one on one with a hostile witness, the rank and file was proud that he was "their guy." He was tough, he studied hard, and he showed up early and stayed late. But then there were those other moments, those twilight episodes that made some people suspect that their guy wasn't all there. Like his shouting match with a sitting Vice President Bush. Or his vanishing act the night a tennis match ran over into his airtime. Or his "Ratherisms" on election nights: "This race is as hot and tight as a too-small bathing suit on a too-long ride home from the beach." Or his sign-off with coanchor Connie Chung to Bill Clinton after an interview: "If we could be one-hundredth as great as you and Hillary Rodham Clinton have been in the White House, we'd take it right now and walk away winners."

Those public moments made people embarrassed, and since one never knew when another of those moments would occur, Rather's career became a white-knuckle flight for most of his colleagues. His actions often triggered a chorus of disbelief: Why did he do that? Why did he say that? What was he thinking? I can't believe he . . . et cetera. These episodes in turn led to convoluted explanations and occasional apologies.

By the early 1990s, after a decade of Rather in the anchor chair, an ever-growing portion of the audience said that it simply did not like him and did not trust him. In one recent survey, Rather's negative ratings were

25 percent higher than those for either of his network news rivals. (The only TV news personality to score even worse was Katie Couric.)

Nat Irvin, a media professor at Wake Forest University, said to radio host Ed Gordon, "I never watched him. The guy never smiled. He never looked like he was happy. He looked like he was always struggling in the shadow of Walter Cronkite. But he never impressed me as being a liberal." Of course, he had impressed most conservatives that way. Rather claimed not to know the genesis of that belief, but most critics say it began with Watergate and Rather's famous — some would say infamous — exchange with the embattled Richard Nixon. "Are you running for something?" asked Nixon, as Rather stood to cheers and jeers during what was supposed to be a news conference. "No sir, Mr. President," he replied, "are you?" To Nixon haters, it showed guts. To Nixon supporters, it showed arrogance and disrespect. Should Rather have just ignored the Nixon remark and asked his question? Perhaps. But Rather felt that the president was baiting him, and his response just popped into his head.

"Keep in mind, we were dealing in milliseconds," Rather wrote in his book *The Camera Never Blinks*. "When the President said, 'Are you running for something?' I thought to myself, 'Well, I don't quite know what he means by that.' If I had been allowed half a day or even half a minute to think, my response *might* have been different. But in those sand specks of time I only had long enough to think, 'Well, you don't want to stand there simply mute.' So I said, '*No sir, Mr. President, are you?*'"

The exchange triggered a ton of mail to then CBS News president Richard Salant, with about half demanding that Salant either fire Rather or extract an apology from him and the other half praising the correspondent and CBS for having hired him. Among the latter group was a woman from North Carolina who threatened to streak naked through Salant's office if he took any disciplinary action against Rather. To this, the dignified Salant responded, "For the first time I am tempted to take Rather off the air. Up to now, I have been adamant, but that is because nobody has offered to streak through my office if I did so. Oh, well, I will have to get Satan behind me. Not even the tempting prospect of my own personal streaker will cause me to abandon Dan."

Nevertheless, the exchange branded Rather for life as an antiestablishment lefty. It didn't matter that CBS had been tagged as a liberal network since the days when Edward R. Murrow took on Joseph McCarthy and the anticommunist witch hunts. Or that some people referred to it as the Colored Broadcasting System during its coverage of the civil rights struggle.

Correspondent Morton Dean, who spent ten years with CBS News, says that no amount of reasoning can convince many people that Rather in particular and reporters in general are not antiestablishment and unpatriotic. "In a little over a year, I gave three speeches in Dallas," Dean told me. "And, of course, to them, I'm red meat—a Northeastern Jew who worked for a major network. And even if I'm not asked, I bring it up anyway because I love the reaction: I say that although Dan Rather was never my best friend, he was a damned good reporter, and I don't buy what you folks say about his being a liberal. And God—the reaction! They go nuts! I also say Dan probably would've made the same mistakes had he gone after a Democrat and a liberal instead of George Bush."

"I've always prided myself in being fiercely independent," Rather has said on numerous occasions, "maybe too independent. I don't back up. I don't back down. I'm hard to herd and impossible to stampede."

And now? As former CBS News president Edward Joyce told me, "Brokaw goes out a hero, part of the greatest generation. Poor Peter dies, tragically. And Dan goes out like a whipped dog."

Few of us in life receive the justice we feel we deserve. Jack Kennedy once famously said, "Life is unfair." Yet those realities should not change or distort the record. If Dan Rather dropped dead tomorrow, the tainted Bush story, which has come to be known as Memogate, would be in the first paragraph of his obituary. This book is an attempt to take a few steps back from Memogate and examine the whole picture—the scope and breadth of Dan Rather's life, career, and times. If he mattered enough to be watched by untold millions of people for fifty years on television, then his story matters enough to be told as fully as possible, and because of the many controversies in which he had been involved, this was no easy task.

When I contacted people who have known and worked with Rather over the years, many of his and my former colleagues — including every member of the current CBS management — declined to speak. Don Hewitt, for whom Rather and I had worked at 60 *Minutes*, laced into Rather in a phone conversation with me, calling him, among other things, a "coward" for not having resigned in the wake of Memogate. "When push came to shove, where the hell was he? And Mike Wallace, Morley Safer, Ed Bradley, Steve Kroft, and Lesley Stahl never lifted a finger to help those people who got fired because of that story. Let's face it: it was a 'get Bush' story, plain and simple. If the story had been about John Kerry, don't tell me they wouldn't have been more careful." When I asked Hewitt for an interview for this book about Rather's career, however, he paused and said, "I don't want to get involved." When push came to shove, Hewitt took a pass on discussing the man he had just called a coward.

Fortunately, many former colleagues willingly went on the record and told me of their experiences and feelings about Rather, including former executives Van Gordon Sauter, Ed Joyce, Bill Small, and Sandy Socolow; correspondents Mike Wallace, Morley Safer, Morton Dean, Bob Pierpoint, Richard Threlkeld, Richard Wagner, and Roger Mudd; and a host of producers and writers. I have also drawn on the writing of some of the great CBS executives who have passed away, including Richard Salant, Bill Leonard, and Les Midgley. TV critics who followed Rather's career for decades also gave of their time, including Pulitzer Prize–winner Tom Shales, who told me, "We keep saying it's the end of an era every time a tree falls in the forest. But this really is. It's not just the end of the Dan Rather era. It's the end of the era of dominance by network news. He was a giant, and I don't see any giants on the horizon. I hope I'm wrong."

As for Rather himself, he wrestled with my request for cooperation for months. Finally, at the urging of some of his friends, he told me he had to decline. He still hoped that CBS News would extend his soon-to-expire contract, and he felt that cooperating with a book that was in any way critical of CBS would not be in his interest. "There's nothing in this for me," he said. Of course, CBS had no intention of keeping Rather; one anonymous executive told the *Washington Post* there was "no room" for the former anchorman at *60 Minutes* or anywhere else in the News Division. Friends described him as hurt and confused by this treatment. Referring to management's desire to turn the page and move on, Rather told a reporter, "They talk about wanting to break with the past. Look at the Murrow film. I don't want to break with that past." Rather was speaking of George Clooney's stirring film about Edward R. Murrow, *Good Night and Good Luck*, which Rather told the *New York Times* he had seen five times in theaters, most recently alone.

Shortly before he and CBS formally parted company in June 2006, Rather revealed that he was considering an offer to join a fledgling TV channel called HDNet, bankrolled by dotcom billionaire Mark Cuban, who had also invested in the Clooney film. The venture, Rather said, would give him a chance to do what he called "real news" again.

Despite all that has happened, Dan Rather still believes he can erase the stigma of Memogate if he's given the chance. He still believes he can go out on his own terms.

In Anthony Harvey's brilliant film *The Lion in Winter*, the three sons of King Henry are locked in a dungeon for plotting treason against their father. They expect he will execute them. As they hear approaching footsteps, Richard, the oldest and toughest, says to his brother Jeffrey, "He'll get no satisfaction out of me. He isn't going to see me beg." "Why, you chivalric fool," says Jeffrey. "As if the way one falls down matters!" Richard stares straight ahead and replies, "When the fall is all there is, it matters." Right now, for Dan Rather, the fall is all there is, and it matters.

1

Thanks for the Memories

The only man who wasn't spoilt by being lionized was Daniel.
— Herbert Beerbohm Tree

In November 2004, CBS CEO Les Moonves and Dan Rather agreed that Rather would step out of the chair one year short of his twenty-fifth anniversary as the *Evening News* anchorman. The Bush Memo-gate controversy provided Moonves with a convenient excuse to do what he wanted to do anyway: go younger. After all, Rather had just turned seventy-three, and the *Evening News* had been in third place for a decade. Talk of succession had gone on for years, but CBS News was so thin on talent, there was no one to replace Rather. When Moonves told reporters that he no longer wanted the "Voice of God" to deliver the news, he knew, as did everyone else at CBS News, that there was no one on the roster with the gravitas to affect the Voice of God even if he had wanted one.

For Moonves, Rather's report on Bush's National Guard service was the camel that broke the camel's back. Rather had been involved with controversies before, but the firestorm from this one was simply too hot to handle. The outrage triggered by the report was curious because it was not a new story. The same allegations about young Lieutenant Bush had been reported over and over again since at least 1999. The response from Bush was always the same: "I was honorably discharged."

This time, Rather and his producer, Mary Mapes, had believed that they could revive and advance the story by showing documents they claimed would corroborate the charges. The four pages of documents, actually photocopies of documents, were memos allegedly written by then Lieutenant Bush's Air National Guard commander, now deceased. Their origin was unknown, and the source not always truthful. Without the memos, what they had was largely a rehash.

The story was rushed onto the air September 8, 2004, out of fear that other news organizations might have the same documents, and the skeptics began weighing in and weighing in heavily. When the documents were placed on the CBS News Web site, so-called bloggers quickly declared that they were fake. They wrote that the type style used could only have been made on a personal computer, which was not available back in 1972. There were also questions about the terminology used in the memos that some Guardsmen said would never have been used in an official memo.

This was serious stuff. It was bad enough that Rather had had a memorable on-air contretemps with the president's father during the 1988 presidential campaign, but this scandal played directly into the hands of conservatives who believe that the press in general, CBS News in particular, and especially Dan Rather are liberal lefties to the core. When all was said and done, Rather, Mapes, and their superiors at 60 *Minutes Wednesday* simply could not prove that the documents were copies of genuine originals.

The end game was numbingly predictable. First, stubborn denial, followed by grudging acceptance, followed by a mandated public apology, followed by a fresh burst of denial, followed by the denouement: Rather's final broadcast as anchorman on March 9, 2005. Although Moonves, Rather, and official CBS spokespeople insist that Rather's early exit had absolutely nothing to do with the Bush story, no one believes it.

"That last day in the studio," an observer told me, "management was really sweating bullets that nobody was going to show up. It was supposed to be an incredibly emotional moment. But the feeling was more like 'Go away . . . go to your room.' Because that Bush story was such a colossal wound. We play a very high-wire act here, don't we? We walk the tightrope. And he pushed more people off that tightrope than I care to think about."

Although at least one TV Web site stated flatly that "Dan Rather holds the dubious distinction of being the only network anchorman that people vaguely expect to go berserk on the air," the technicians and the staffers in the control room that night were reasonably sure that unlike the terminally depressed anchorman of *Network*, there would be no Howard Beale moment at the end of the broadcast.

In fact, Rather was downright eloquent. "Not long after I first came to anchor chair," he said, "I briefly signed off using the word *courage*. I want to return to it now in a different way. To a nation still nursing a broken heart for what happened here in 2001 and especially those who found themselves closest to the events of September 11, to our soldiers in dangerous places, to those who have endured the tsunami and to all who have suffered natural disasters and who must find the will to rebuild, to the oppressed and to those whose lot it is to struggle, in financial hardship or in failing health, to my fellow journalists in places where reporting the truth means risking all, and to each of you . . . courage. For the *CBS Evening News*, Dan Rather reporting. Good night."

The cartoons jumped off the pages of every major newspaper and magazine, their bite eliciting more of a wince than a smile. From the *Tampa Tribune*, a sketch of a graveyard with a talking tombstone: "This is a CBS News bulletin . . . the report of the death of our credibility has been grossly exaggerated!" The tombstone is marked CBS News. From the *Orlando Sentinel*, a harried secretary hands a note to her boss at CBS News. Secretary: "Here, it's Dan Rather's resignation." Boss: "How do we know it's authentic?"

Conservatives across the country acted as if the Soviet Union had collapsed a second time. Several CBS radio affiliates canceled Rather's daily commentaries. Some called it a victory for "the people's journalists," the bloggers. On right-wing Web sites, one could find a lengthy list of Good-bye Dan parties, scheduled for the night of his final *Evening News* broadcast. "The Independence Institute of Denver will break out the tissues at Jackson's Hole Sports Grill as we say a tearful farewell to legendary anchorman and beacon of journalistic integrity, Dan Rather. Retirement gifts and party favors for the first 48 people."

Former CBS newsman Bernard Goldberg, who had once used his friendship with Rather to secure a hefty new contract, listed him as number twelve among *100 People Who Are Screwing Up America*. Osama bin Laden did not make the list. From the *National Review's* Jonah Goldberg there was this outpouring of ecstasy: "Why is Dan Rather doing this to himself? Why would he let this happen in the first place? There can be only one plausible answer: Ours is a just and decent God. Second, and more important, if we, as Americans, cannot take a moment to relish the comeuppance of the most enduringly pompous partisan yutz in Elite Journalism, then the terrorists will have won. . . . This story is really God's own piñata: You can bash it from any angle and nothing but sweet, sweet goodness flows out."

Perhaps such bile from the right wing could be expected, but if Dan Rather thought he might receive kindness from his longtime colleagues at CBS News, he was mistaken. Mike Wallace, whose famously checkered career has included the secret videotaping of a fellow journalist, an unfunny racist crack about Hispanics caught by an open microphone, and his complicity in a seriously flawed documentary about General William Westmoreland and the Vietnam War, told the *New Yorker* magazine, "He's a superb reporter, and dead honest. But he's not as easy to watch as Jennings or Brokaw. He's uptight and occasionally contrived." (To which one columnist replied, "Mike, may all your foxholes be lonely ones.") Walter Cronkite, who still believes that the anchor chair should have been retired with him in 1981, said, "It surprised quite a few people at CBS that they tolerated his [Rather's] being there for so long." On NPR, Cronkite added, "There was a kind of mystical self-promotion in things that Dan did. He seemed to be consciously amplifying his role as anchorman rather than simply the reporter of the day." Cronkite later tempered his remarks, describing Rather as a "victim" who had trusted his producer too much. Other CBS veterans, speaking anonymously, reveled in what they saw as his payback for wielding far too much power for too long.

All this made Tim Goodman of the *San Francisco Chronicle* boil. "You can take your CBS backstabbers who found in Rather's last hours of weakness a chance to rise up and join the chorus of haters . . . and give them all a great big prize for bravery. And yes, that includes Walter Cronkite." This sentiment was echoed by Victor Navasky in the *Nation*: "Yes, Dan Rather and his *60 Minutes II* colleagues ought to feel embarrassed, but so should his *60 Minutes* colleagues who seemed more eager to exonerate themselves from having anything to do with those tainted documents than to support their colleague, who has anchored CBS News with passion and professionalism for twenty-four years."

Former executive vice president Bill Small told me that he discussed the internal warfare with the venerable Frank Stanton who, along with William Paley, had created CBS from nothing. "He's ninety-eight years old now and bedridden," Small said, "but his mind is still clear. I said, 'Frank, they're beating up on him.' And he said, 'They shouldn't be doing that. He's part of the family.'"

Support for Rather also came from a few unexpected sources. Bill O'Reilly, the rottweiler of right-wing FOX News, defended Rather's right to be wrong. "Dan Rather is guilty of not being skeptical enough about a story that was politically loaded. I believe Rather, along with Andy Rooney, Walter Cronkite and other guardsmen of the old CBS News, is liberal in his thinking. . . . But holding a political point of view is the right of every American and it does not entitle people to practice character assassination or deny the presumption of innocence. Dan Rather was slimed. It was disgraceful."

It didn't seem to concern Moonves or anyone else at CBS that the network had no transition plan and no vision about what a new *Evening News* would be. It appeared that Moonves simply wanted Rather out and the sooner the better. In examining the causes of Memogate, many press followers, including Carl Bernstein of Watergate fame, described it as an "institutional failure." That may be true, but over the years Dan Rather had become the institution itself. His aggressiveness and zeal were exacerbated by a system that he himself had largely constructed, with the help of timid and sometimes encouraging managements.

As if to underscore Rather's new place in the CBS News pecking order, he was not even informed that longtime friend and fellow Texan Bob Schieffer would be replacing him temporarily on the *Evening News*.

"They haven't even asked me what I thought they should do with the *Evening News*, nor do I particularly think they should," he told Larry King on *Larry King Live*. "It's their decision to make."

When King asked how he felt as the Bush story unraveled and the criticism mounted, Rather replied, "It's never pleasant. But you know, among the many things that my late father—God rest his soul—said was 'Don't whine, don't complain, and don't fall into a trap of saying it's bad luck or good luck. Stand up, look them in the eye, and tell them what you know. Tell them what you don't know.' And I tried to do that. I'm not a victim of anything except my own shortcomings. And it didn't feel terrific. There certainly were days when I felt I had been put to bed wet. But I always get up the next morning and say, 'You know what? This looks like a great day to me even during what other people might say were the worst of times.'"

King asked, "Do you think the Republicans, the right-wing Republicans, were after you?" Rather responded, "No. Again, I'm not a victim of anything."

But Dan Rather doesn't really believe that. In fact, in the days that followed his final broadcast as anchor, he began to sound somewhat like his old nemesis, Richard Nixon, taking personal blame for personal flaws but quickly pointing out that, as Henry Kissinger was fond of saying, "even paranoids have enemies."

"A man is not finished when he is defeated," Nixon once said. "He is finished when he quits," and that is Rather's philosophy as well. The Nixon-Rather comparison has been pretty much flogged to death in recent years, but there are those who dispute it. As one veteran producer said, "Nixon was a crook and a liar. Dan Rather has principles. I can't think of Nixon and Rather in the same sentence."

As Rather cleaned out his *Evening News* office, he came across drawers full of touchstones, tchotchkes, and every manner of memorabilia that had piled up over the course of his anchor career. He dusted off a piece of framed embroidery once sent to him by a nun. "Be thou a soul to fullness grown. . . . Arise to gain thy dreams. . . . Today's trials were meant to make you young." There would be more than just cardboard boxes leaving with him. He would be taking part of a culture with him as well, even though some people would say that culture had left a long time ago.

Now he was anxious to get back to reporting, telling reporters that he felt his best work was still ahead of him. Yes, he truly believed, you *can* go home again.

To an interviewer, Rather recalled one of his favorite stories: the last at bat of the mighty Ted Williams, who hit a home run, circled the bases, and trotted through the dugout tunnel, as legend has it, into the parking lot, where he drove off into history. But the analogy is not apt. After all, the Splendid Splinter was a blue-blooded specimen—a can't-miss prospect who had size, strength, and a knowledge of the fine art of hitting that went well beyond his years. In contrast, as a prospect, the young Dan Rather was more like the young Pete Rose. No power, no glove, no arm, no speed—just a buzz cut and some ungodly hustle. And that's about all Rather had had when he left Texas on his way to "the show."

2

Never Stay Down and Never Quit

Man, I did love this game. I would have played for food money. Shoot, I would have played for nothing.
— Shoeless Joe Jackson, *Field of Dreams*

Hᴵˢ childhood was not exactly like *Tobacco Road*, but it was close. The Rathers were not poor, but they were just getting by. It was the Depression, and it was no better in east Texas than any-where else. At least, Rather's father, Daniel, nicknamed Rags, had a job, which in those days made him a member of a minority group. But it was a backbreaking, mud-covered, sweat-soaked job digging trenches and laying pipeline for the Texas oil industry just as his father had. He was known as a company man, fiercely loyal to his coworkers. His wife was a sometime waitress and full-time homemaker.

Their first son, Daniel, was born on Halloween, October 31, 1931, in a small town called Wharton, but he grew up outside Houston in a place called the Heights Annex. The Annex part made all the difference, because the Heights still exists, while the Annex does not. The Annex was separated from practically everything else in Houston, a real estate development that never developed. In the 1930s, it consisted largely of vacant lots, dirt roads, and a scattering of small houses that included 1432 Prince Street. The nearest bus stop was a mile and a half away. The nearest market was a three-mile round trip. The Rathers kept the basics nearby: a cow down the street, chickens in the backyard, and a vegetable garden in a vacant lot.

For recreation, Rags taught Dan to hunt and fish—squirrel, rabbit, deer and ducks, fresh water bass, sea trout, and redfish. The family, which would soon include a brother and a sister for Dan, often visited the Heights Boulevard, which Rather, in his book *I Remember*, referred to as "our Champs-Elysées." There they found, among the faded Victorian mansions and the vacant opera house, the Heights movie theater. Tickets were five cents apiece. For that, you got a short, usually a to-be-continued cliffhanger, a cartoon, a newsreel, coming attractions, and a feature.

Dan was never ashamed of being from the Annex, but the fact that he hadn't grown up in a more cosmopolitan setting where he could have met young people from different classes and ethnic backgrounds and experienced more varied diversions was always on his mind. It made him feel inferior—or at least lacking.

The Heights produced more than its share of future Hall of Famers. There were race-car legends A. J. Foyt and Bobby Waltrip, flamboyant trial attorney Richard "Racehorse" Haynes, and the world's most famous firefighter, Red Adair.

There was occasional violence in the Rather neighborhood, largely the result of frustration over joblessness and poverty. The kids picked up on this, and young Rather had to put up his dukes to defend his choice corner from which he sold newspapers. There was also a local gang that preyed upon Rather and a friend, administering regular beatings. The friend's father suggested that he teach them to box, and he did, much to the chagrin of Rather's mother. Rather learned some stick-and-move riffs and some slick footwork, but, most important, he learned the importance of getting up after you've been knocked down. "In a boxing match," the father told him, "roll to your knees, watch the count, stay down until your head clears. But in a street fight, Dan, get up quickly. *Never stay down.*" This lesson, once learned, would never leave him.

Yet he could not get up when hit by rheumatic fever. Over a period of five years in his early teens, he was often bedridden with the debilitating and then incurable disease. One stretch lasted eight months, in which he was forbidden to get up except for trips to the bathroom. The Rathers rearranged their tiny house so that Dan's bed was next to the window that looked out on the dirt road in front of his house. He watched the seasons change through this window, saw his friends going to school and playing games, and daydreamed about playing football, which is like an organized religion in Texas.

He dreamed about all sorts of things but wasn't sure if he'd even get the chance to live a normal life. He used to say, "You never have as much time as you think you have for whatever you want to do, whatever you want to be, whatever you want to accomplish." His parents were told that even if he was lucky enough to return to school, his heart would be damaged. No doubt this thought must have crossed his mind: if I ever get out of this bed, I will never lie down again.

His parents wouldn't lie down, either. Rather's mother, Byrl, waited tables, sold encyclopedias door to door, answered phones at a construction office, and sewed upholstery and slipcovers, anything to improve the family's income. Rags wanted to improve the income, too, but he also wanted to improve himself. He took a correspondence course in electricity and was proud when he passed. His first project was building the motor for a huge overhead fan that would cool the tiny house in the hot summer months. The monster worked all right—just a little too well, practically pulling the wallpaper off the walls. Rags promised a few adjustments, but in the future he opened the doors to the house when the fan was on to keep it from sucking the furniture off the floor.

Years later, Rags mastered the intricacies of the slide rule and could work it just like the real engineers he called "those institute boys." Of Rags, Rather wrote, "Father's marathon struggle with the slide rule was another of many examples that hammered his most heartfelt motto home to me. He always joked that he wanted these words inscribed on his tombstone: 'Don't quit.'" And indeed, his self-education led to a few promotions that at least got him out of the trenches.

So now there was "Never stay down" and "Don't quit," both of which became part of Rather's makeup. He had come to believe that the real heroes were those who didn't just accept their lot in life but strove mightily to improve it. You don't fold early. You find ways to stay in the game because you just might end up winning it.

"I had an optimistic outlook about things," Rather told a profiler from Washington's Academy of Achievement. "But I could be shy about some things, too. I remember the William G. Love elementary school band. It became clear quite early on that I was not musically inclined. They started me on several instruments, all at which I immediately failed. And this did things to my confidence. Even at an early age I recognized that the wood block was about as low as you could go in the Love school band."

When Rather was nine, his father, now a lineman for the pipeline company, was called out on a stormy night to fix a break in an electrical line. He took his son with him, spent hours finding the break, and then climbed up the slick pole. He fell some twenty-five feet, first hitting a barbed-wire fence and then landing in a heap on the ground. Bleeding all over, with splinters sticking out of his hands, he told his boy, "Don't do anything." Dan stood frozen with fear. "I gotta get up," Rags said to himself, and his son watched as he slowly and painfully sat up and then stood. When they got home, his wife dressed her husband's wounds and sent him off to bed. He did not see a doctor and went to work the next day.

The family members tried all sorts of side businesses to make a better life. They opened a nursery, but the flowers and the plants died before they could be sold. They tried a melon stand, but the melons rotted in the Texas heat. Young Dan and his mother made kites but couldn't sell enough to make the enterprise worthwhile. To Rather, though, the effort made much more of an impression than the payoff or lack thereof. You had to *want* to be better; the desire was reward in itself. It has been said that adversity doesn't build character: it exposes it. What Rather witnessed from his parents was character that might seem extraordinary to the lesser among us; what he absorbed were core values that included hard work, determination, and loyalty.

Rather's bouts with rheumatic fever had taken a toll on his psyche as well as on his body. He wrote, "My identity was almost destroyed. I hated my weaknesses, my differences, my inability to keep up with the other boys. My world had collapsed." He spent days and nights brooding about what his life might become as a virtual cripple—all the opportunities missed, all the simple yet exhilarating pleasures of just being young and alive. And then there was the crushing loneliness, the need for simple human contact. Sure, his friends dropped by now and then, but it was like visiting a patient in a hospital: the small talk ended quickly and the awkward silence filled the room.

There were diversions, of course, especially the radio, with the voices of the Kaltenbornes and the Heatters and the Murrows filling the air from faraway places. With the radio, you had to use your mind; you had to imagine the picture instead of just sitting there taking it in.

"We turned on the radio one night, and the Battle of North Africa was in the balance. I'll never forget it," Rather told the Academy. "Gabriel Heatter said, 'The Desert Fox is seven miles from Cairo.' At which point my father picked up the little radio, yanked it out, and smashed it against the wall. My mother quickly shooshed my little brother and sister and me into the back room, mumbling about 'Father's not having a good day.' He was so disgusted and furious. It looked like the Germans were going to prevail. But as it turned out, Rommel never took Cairo."

When Rather finally did return to school full time, some of the sports coaches treated him like damaged merchandise, virtually useless. His gym coach accused him of faking his weaknesses, calling him a "sissy" and a "momma's boy." The same person also coached the baseball team, and after using every trick to keep Rather off the team—like telling him he had applied too late, which was not true—Rather was kept on the bench for every inning of every game right until the last out of the season. The coach told Rather that the glove he was using was "illegal" when, as Rather wrote, "all it was was cheap."

In the bottom of the ninth inning of the last game of a losing season, with two strikes on the batter, the coach told Rather to go out and play right field. "He meant it as a final disgrace," Rather recalled. "But I saw it as a victory. Better to be sent out on the field than to sit on the bench until the end."

Rather's racial views were formed by two realities: the blacks in his neighborhood were no better off than the Rathers were and Rather's parents did not tolerate the denigration of any people. Rather recalls a meeting of the local Democratic club (the Republicans were nonexistent in those parts back then), in which veterans were asked to vote for the hand-picked white slate of delegates to attend the state party's convention. A number of black veterans showed up and when the chairman said, "All those opposed to the nominations, please stand," the blacks stood up and so did Rags.

"Rags," he was told, "you don't understand. You're standing up at the wrong time."

"I understand all right," Rags replied. "These people have a right to be here. And whenever they stand up, I'll be standing with them."

Young Rather was impressed. He also referred to the public whipping his mother had once administered when he had joined with his friends in chanting to a local babysitter: "Daisy is a nigger. . . . Daisy is a nigger!" As Rather's sister, Patricia, recalls the incident, their mother took her son from the backyard to the front yard and beat him soundly, a lesson not only to her son but also to everyone else in the neighborhood.

The plight of blacks and his father's unwillingness to be pushed around by anyone no doubt contributed to Rather's lifelong affinity for underdogs, people who were often at the mercy of others. This played a role in Rather's natural skepticism concerning figures of authority, since his father and coworkers all believed that bosses in general were out of touch and full of baloney. Rags also had what his son felt was a unique sense of what people wanted from others. Being able to do something, of course, came first. But beyond that came shined shoes and an eager, supremely confident attitude. The writer Horton Foote, another notable from Wharton, was a favorite of young Rather because he wrote about the special character of the townsfolk, which not only rang true but also made the small populace a special club that only the members could fully understand. Rather recalled a character in a Foote movie titled *On Valentine's Day* who was "a handsome, proud, dignified young man with surprisingly graceful, fluid movements, dirt poor but endowed with an irrepressible sense of independence—the very picture of my own father!" The film and much of Foote's work paint portraits of ordinary folks enduring extraordinary hardships with a stoic resilience, people who were measured more by the strength of their spirit than by the value of their possessions.

Young Rather was also drawn to stories about brave men who battled against overwhelming odds and who, even in defeat, became symbols of nobility. They included Sam Houston, who in 1860 gave what Rather in his book *I Remember* called "the greatest speech of his life. He stood up for the Union and against secession. It was a lost cause and he knew it. The legislators rebuked him and kicked the father of Texas out of his own house. He got on his horse never to return. Not much later, he died."

Once, on a school tour of the San Jacinto monument, Rather spotted a line that read: "Thermopylae had its messenger of death. The Alamo had none." His teacher explained that in 480 B.C., the Spartans of Greece fought a hopeless but important battle against the Persians and had been wiped out. They had fought for the same reasons the Texans had fought at the Alamo—to buy enough time for a larger confrontation that would result in victory. Rather looked into the story further and found that the vanquished warriors had left behind a message for their brothers who had arrived too late to turn the tide:

> Go tell the Spartans,
> Thou who passest by,
> That here, obedient to their laws,
> We lie.

The impact of those lines was so great on Rather that he had them inscribed on a plaque that was affixed to his office door at CBS years later. When visitors asked about its significance, Rather usually demurred, saying, "It's just something for me."

In *I Remember,* he wrote, "They pointed to something larger than one-self. Something to die for. They reminded me to stay in touch with my core; that ideals did exist that transcend one's basic instincts, standards beyond the normal grubbing of daily existence."

Although Rather insisted that he lacked Tom Sawyer's mischievous predilection for stunts, pranks, and general misbehavior, he did take part in more than a few, for which he generally received the business end of his father's belt. On one occasion, when Rather told a neighbor lady to "Shut up!" he found himself in the tool shed being beaten by his father. Young Rather recalls crying not because it hurt but because his dignity was offended. His father, of course, told him that boys don't cry.

To this day, Rather rejects this notion as old fashioned and resents the fact that on occasions when he has become teary on camera (as on David Letterman's *Late Show* after 9/11), he has been described as "weird" and "Rather strange."

"Standards have changed," Rather insisted. "I refer to the respectability of showing emotion in public, an alleged weakness that some pseudosophisticates have ridiculed in connection with my on camera reporting of the Gulf War, the bombing of our marine barracks in Beirut, the explosion of the *Challenger* and other heartbreaks, fortunately rare. . . . In my value system, the strange ones among us are the few who prefer robots, the would-be highbrows who want us to be zombies frozen in stoicism every time our hearts are hurt. Or worse, those who don't care at all."

Rather's success at selling newspapers on his special corner evolved into greater interest in actually producing a paper or something that could pass for one. While he was still in elementary school, Rather and one of his teachers created a one-page newsletter, which in turn evolved into a kind of neighborhood bulletin board. Lacking typewriters, they hand lettered these sheets about local comings and goings—a personal touch born of necessity. What most appealed to Rather was that as a "reporter," he gleaned knowledge of events before almost anyone else. This made him special and worthwhile.

Rather recalled his father being practically buried under newspapers, stacked high around his favorite chair and not to be moved by anyone. "Those papers had visible power over father," Rather wrote. "They caused his usually well-controlled temper to ferment and explode. A single news item could do it. The rest of the family reacted with a meaningful rolling of the eyes and an unspoken 'Here we go again!'" Rags canceled so many papers so often that he eventually wound up with only the *Christian Science Monitor* and the *St. Louis Post-Dispatch*, both of which arrived a week late. The irony of Rather's father always blaming the messenger for bad news or opinions with which he did not agree was not lost on the future anchorman. "Judging by my mail, quite a few TV viewers today react to the day's news much as my father did half a century ago," he wrote. Rather's father and his uncle John spent hours debating world affairs, such as whether Franklin Roosevelt should run for a third term.

Rather's first encounter with a real-live reporter involved a local tragedy: the drowning of a boy in a nearby bayou. As searchers dredged for the body, someone told Rather that a reporter was on the scene. For the boy, it was like seeing a big-league ballplayer in the flesh. He wrote, "There he stood, a thin man in his early thirties, looking ordinary in ordinary shirtsleeves, quietly writing notes in a notebook. He hardly moved. Here, obviously, was a professional person of competence with access to all that was transpiring, recording an event of significance, which, thanks to his powers, would become known to a great many people."

Rather never got up the nerve to say anything to the man. He felt awe and insignificance at the same time. He had seen what so few are able to see at such a young age—his future.

Because his illness had sidelined young Rather for long periods, he had some catching up to do in matters of the opposite sex. From all indications, he was even more unsure of himself around girls than are most teenage boys. When he was fourteen, he began smoking cigars to make himself appear older, and he spent that summer working with a surveying crew, a job his father had gotten for him through a local entrepreneur. It was miserable work, clearing miles of swampland while fighting insects and snakes of every variety. In the town of Liberty, he roomed with the crew at a hotel that featured "in residence ladies." Rather spied on the action from afar but never joined in.

"In Liberty, I met up with my 'Liberty Bell'," Rather wrote in *I Remember*, "a wonderful, wonderful older woman. She was perhaps nineteen, a waitress, far more beautiful than any of the 'honkey tonk angels' I'd been watching in hazy saloons with my colleagues night after night, week after week. I wish I could report on a roaring romance with my lady from Liberty. But I'd be lying. The most I did was order refills of iced tea just so I could watch her walk and see her smile as she poured. The truth is I can't remember uttering a single complete sentence in her presence. Just 'Yes, ma'am,' and 'No, ma'am.' I didn't say much to the bar girls either. My hormones were willing, but I didn't know what to say or do about that."

B yrl Rather was adamant that her son attend college despite having no money to pay for it. Rather did some research and came up with a small school called Sam Houston State Teachers College, in Huntsville, seventy-five miles northeast of Houston. He deluded himself into believing that he might win a football scholarship and that this would take care of the tuition and living expenses. Before the start of the semester, Rather hitchhiked to Huntsville and sought out the coach. What he found was a broken man who had suffered through fourteen straight losing seasons.

After introducing himself, Rather was told simply that tryouts would begin in March and he was welcome to come out. Rather returned home ecstatic, telling his parents that not only would he have a shot at a scholarship but that he had made up his mind to major in journalism. Rags could not understand how someone could actually make a living reporting the news. He thought that college was for people who wanted to become teachers, engineers, or lawyers.

In any event, the Rathers scraped up enough money to put Dan on a Greyhound bus and barely pay his enrollment fees. After he signed up for courses, Rather met with a journalism professor named Hugh Cunningham.

"What makes you think you can be a journalist?" Cunningham asked him.

"Well, I *know* I can," Rather answered, not the most profound response but the best he could muster at the time.

When he told the professor about his plans to play football, the man laughed at him. "That's crazy. You don't want to play football. You'll get killed."

"It's the only way I can stay in school. This way I can get a scholarship."

Cunningham fixed Rather up with a series of odd jobs, like writing for the *Huntsville Item*, stringing for wire services, calling in sports scores, and writing publicity sheets for the college. Rather's inherent timidity was clearly an obstacle, though—he found it difficult to walk up to strangers and ask them questions. Rather admits that when Cunningham sent him out for interviews, he often invented some excuse as to why he couldn't do it. Yet he did love to tell stories, especially stories about something new, a new invention or some new way of experiencing something old and worn. He also loved words. "I polished them in my mind and adopted some like pets," he recalled. "And I was never at a loss for them. Since early on, I was always pretty glib and insatiably inquisitive."

Of course, there was still the matter of the scholarship and the football tryout. It turned out to be a painful replay of what Rather had endured in high school. The coach took every opportunity to discourage the scrawny kid, deliberately calling plays in which much bigger kids crashed into Rather and sent him flying. But the kid just didn't get the message. One day after practice the coach walked over to Rather, put his arm around the boy, and said, "Son, I watched you out the whole time t'day. And I wanna tell ya sumpun' I hope'll stay with ya the rest of your life. You're little. And you're *yellow*."

Still Rather would not quit. He continued his writing jobs and kept working out with the football team. Before the first game, he was told that he would not get a scholarship but could suit up for the games and the practices. Finally, after the third game, the coach called him in and said, "Son, take my advice. Give it up. It's useless for you."

"And that was it," Rather wrote. "I can remember walking out of his office and into the rain, tears streaming down my face. It was one of the few times in life I can remember crying." Looking back on the episode, he admitted, "I really did believe I could make the team when I went in. But after a while, it became just something I told my parents might happen so they wouldn't worry all the time about my having enough money."

I f he couldn't play the games, at least he could describe them over radio station KSAM. The play-by-play gig became his scholarship and introduction to the world of radio. It was how Walter Cronkite had started his radio career, and Ronald Reagan as well. And Dick Enberg's original color commentator at the University of Indiana sports network was a farm boy named Phil Jones, later to become a White House correspondent.

Rather wrote that his memory became his greatest asset as a play-by-play man. "I possessed a kind of television of the mind. I had no difficulty 'watching' Jarring John Kimbrough on the football field, 'seeing' his slight hesitation . . . and then making up an entire game, play by play, all out of my head."

KSAM was owned by a Baptist preacher, Pastor Lott, and he was so impressed with Rather's ability to invent fantasy games that he had Rather doing virtually all of the sporting events in the region, plus the newscasts. Rather also worked nights, studying while he juggled the music, the commercials, and the newscasts. Rather's break time coincided with the *Gospel Hour,* which allowed him to slip away for food or a rendezvous with an occasional coed. Long-playing records were another welcome relief, like the spiritual ditties churned out by Pastor Lott's brother. They allowed Rather enough time to leave the station, grab some food, and be back before the record ended.

One evening, though, Rather was ordering his food when he received a call from the boss himself. "Have you listened to my radio station lately?" he asked. "No, sir," Rather replied. "Well, you better get back there and fix it, and then you're fired." It seems that the needle had gotten stuck on the words "go to hell" and was repeating the phrase over and over. Later, all was forgiven and Rather was allowed to keep his forty-cents-an-hour job. He graduated from Sam Houston State in three years.

Rather has surprisingly little to say about his enlistment in the U.S. Marine Corps, perhaps because his tenure was so brief. Although the

Korean War was winding down, young men were still coming out of ROTC training and recruitment offices. Rather's military career was cut short, however, when he failed basic training.

The lingering effects of his rheumatic fever made him physically unfit for the corps. Rheumatic fever was on the list of disqualifying prior illnesses. He had already spent a stint in the army reserves in a tank division, but he wanted to go to war and he wanted to be a marine. When the marines let him go, he made a final appeal to a chaplain to put in a fix that might allow him to stay but was told that wasn't possible. Had he been allowed in the corps, many friends believe that he might have made it his career.

Rather ended up working at the *Houston Chronicle* and at the radio station it owned, KTRH, where he met his future wife, a secretary named Jean Goebel. Jean's sister Jo worked at the station, too, and had tipped her sister to keep an eye on this "really attractive, smart, nice guy." Rather asked Jean out the following day. "She was a pretty, lively woman with a smashing smile and gentle eyes. Her energy and vitality attracted her to me. She worked long hours with endless enthusiasm and encouraging words for everyone. There was a don't-give-up quality about her. And she, more than anyone I had ever met, understood my hopes and dreams." Jean Rather also had a practical, realistic view of things that often acted as a balance to her husband's more impulsive and sometimes fearful nature. "It helps," he once wrote, "to have a roommate who has come along in the business and whose head is as clear as Jean's. You *must* have someone who will talk straight with you. I have benefited from Jean's candor and honesty beginning with the time she marched to the closet, pulled down a suitcase, and announced, 'Listen, you're getting big-headed and we are going to take two weeks off and go to Texas.' With the Rathers, you have to know that going to Texas is the cure-all for everything."

They were married in April 1957. A daughter, Robin, arrived in 1958, and a son, Danjack, two years later. Over the years, Rather has always given his wife full credit for having raised their children through their frequent moves and his frequent absences.

"Think of us an Indian family," Jean told the kids. "Your father has to go where the buffalo are." One night, when Danjack was still quite young, he was watching television with a friend when his father walked in. "Who's that?" asked the friend. And Danjack said, "Oh, that's Dan Rather."

The Rathers have always been protective of their children, especially after Rather became a major figure on television. To my knowledge they have never been interviewed about their father. By his account, relayed through friends, his children were both excellent athletes—team stars— and their anchorman father made every effort to attend their sporting events and other important moments in their lives. He does admit to missing Christmas of 1965, which he spent in Vietnam.

By 1961, Rather had pieced together enough broadcasting experience to become news director and anchorman of the CBS affiliate KHOU-TV in Houston. A storm had been percolating across the Yucatan and was heading for the Gulf. The National Weather Service had officially designated it a hurricane and named it Carla. Rather had followed hurricanes since he was a child and he knew much about how they formed, how they gained strength, and how they might move, depending on their track and other conditions. He told his boss that they should send a remote truck to Galveston because they had the best radar system in the area.

When they arrived, Rather was surprised to see the U.S. Weather Bureau's top hurricane expert in the room. This man's presence convinced Rather that his hunch was correct—that the storm would be a big one and was heading their way. It was Rather's boss's idea to show just how huge the storm was by pointing their camera at the radar screen and superimposing the image over a map of the Texas shoreline. For the first time, viewers could actually see the monster, which was now four hundred miles wide and fifty miles across at the eye. An evacuation order was put out for Galveston and the coastal lowlands, affecting some 350,000 people. That evacuation and the warnings that had led up to it sharply minimized the loss of life. Only twelve people died, half of them in the tornadoes spawned by Carla. For its efforts, KHOU was awarded a Sigma Delta Chi citation for distinguished service.

Rather knew that if he had any hope of achieving success in television, he would have to work on smoothing out his Texas accent. His was not of the Gabby Hayes variety, but certain words just gave him away. *Heroin* somehow became her-OYNE. While doing a radio weathercast one night, he spoke of "var'ble winds." An angry woman called and said, "Dammit boy, the word is var-EE-able. Look it up!" The word *miniature*, from Rather's mouth, became "mini'ture."

Despite Rather's verbal shortcomings, CBS News had been so impressed with his Carla reporting that it offered him a job. Amazingly, he turned down the first offer, believing that he was happy and content where he was. But when CBS called again, he came to his senses and accepted it, arriving in New York on February 28, 1962.

R ather was hired by Ernie Leiser, one of the legends who helped to invent television journalism. From the outside, Leiser was a gruff, humorless man who emitted "stay-out-of-my-way" vibes, which we employees always heeded. Away from the newsroom, he was quite charming, even funny, but for some reason felt the need to play the martinet when doing business.

Walter Cronkite had also approved the hiring, admiring the calm with which Rather had hung in there during Carla, "while he was ass-deep in water moccasins." Although Cronkite and Rather revealed totally different personalities, they shared some traits, including their do-anything-for-a story mind-set. When Cronkite was a part-timer for a Houston paper, he was sent to fetch a photo of a man who had just been killed. He went to the deceased's home and found it empty but looked through the window, spotting a photo on the mantel. He broke into the house, stole the photo, and rushed it back to the paper. Unfortunately, he had burgled the wrong house and had taken a photo of the deceased's neighbor. He returned the picture in a plain brown envelope.

Ernie Leiser told Rather that he would spend some time in New York before the network decided what to do with him. "Charles Collingwood was still there," Rather said in an interview with the Academy of Achievement. "Winston Burdett, all the big names. But I didn't know anybody. I wasn't scared but one look around told me I was going to have to work harder than I had ever worked before. Somebody once said, 'It's good to be smart; brilliance is even better. But persistence will trump them all if it comes down to that.'"

On his first day on the job, Rather accompanied a reporter and a crew covering a plane crash outside Kennedy Airport. Rather got to do the radio reports and was off to a good start. Yet weeks went by with no activity until he took a call in the middle of the night to cover the story of some babies who had suffocated in a hospital. By his own account, Rather did a poor job on the story and was unable to correctly pronounce the name of the town where the tragedy had happened: Binghamton.

"I had never heard the name before, and it did not exactly roll off my tongue," Rather said. Ernie Leiser was not amused. "I tell you how confident I am in you, and you *don't even get the name of the town right?*"

Nevertheless, Rather was dispatched to open a new bureau in Dallas, where presumably the names of the surrounding towns would roll off his tongue more easily. Names like Pecos.

Back in 1951 when he was hired by CBS, Phil Scheffler had once stood side by side, sort of, with Edward R. Murrow himself. "The first day on the job, I went to the men's room and walked up to the urinal, and there was Ed Murrow standing at the next one. And he was my hero. He was *every* kid's hero. I was twenty years old and I thought I'd die. I didn't introduce myself at that particular moment. But I thought I'd just collapse because he was there."

Scheffler became a producer for a Friday night half-hour news show called *Eyewitness*. "We would go out and try to do the best story of the week, or one of the best stories. Charles Kuralt was the anchor. Then Cronkite took it over, and then Collingwood followed him. One week there was this story about a guy named Billy Sol Estes, who had scammed everybody down in Texas with phony fertilizer deals. He would move the fertilizer from one tank to another and make guys believe there was fertilizer in the tank."

Scheffler and fellow New York sharpie Bernie Birnbaum were dispatched to Pecos, Texas, where they hooked up with their new correspondent, the young Dan Rather. A garrulous little fellow, Birnbaum could expound at great length on virtually any subject, and the ever-present cigar gave him a Runyonesque persona.

"This was a small town," Scheffler said, laughing, "and Bernie goes out and practically buys the place! He's buying drinks for people, handing out cigars, gladhanding everybody—I mean, we just swept through that place like a hurricane, and I don't think Rather had ever seen how these big shots from New York worked. I mean, we absolutely owned the town within twenty-four hours."

Rather was impressed, but a small problem remained: he didn't have much of a story. A day later, however, they managed to find a rancher named L. B. Johnson.

"He wore a hat, boots, the whole works," said Scheffler, "and he was a great interview. Dan says to him, 'So why did you fall for this scam?' And the guy says, 'Billy Sol, he was *miiiighty* persuasive.' At that moment, I knew we had a story."

As Rather's then boss Les Midgley recalled, "They all arrived late Thursday with the final reels. They had swell stuff, especially the farmers ruefully describing Billy Sol's hard sell. But they still admired his gall. Dan did the narration and then came on live with Collingwood at the close to talk about this Texas con man. 'Pretty good show,' I said to Dan. 'Sure was. I never thought you could do it,' he said, looking a little dazed. He was really astonished to see what our group could film, edit, and put on the air in a few days. It was television like he had never seen it before."

What Scheffler, Birnbaum, and Midgley liked about Rather was his coachability, his willingness to take direction and advice from more seasoned pros. Occasionally, however, Rather ended up the teacher, especially regarding stories in the South.

Reporting on the struggle for civil rights was an extremely dangerous business, especially for reporters from the North. While covering the desegregation of the University of Georgia, CBS's Bob Schakne was hit with rocks and bottles. Someone whacked NBC's Richard Valeriani on his head with an ax handle. And in Mississippi, Dan Rather was struck and knocked down by a National Guardsman's rifle butt. Both Rather and Robert MacNeil were confronted there by men with sawed-off shotguns.

In reporting out of the new Dallas bureau, Rather became an eyewitness and on at least one occasion a participant in some of the most his-
toric civil rights stories of the time. He was there when Alabama governor
George Wallace stood in the schoolhouse door while attempting to pre-
vent the integration of the University of Alabama. Rather was once holed
up in a hotel in Birmingham surrounded by Bull Connor's police for an
interview with Dr. Martin Luther King Jr.

It was a particularly tense period throughout the South, but even
more so for CBS News. Howard K. Smith had just narrated the documentary *Who Speaks for Birmingham?* and the reaction against CBS was so
strong that Bull Connor had threatened legal action. CBS News was
forced to put masking tape over all the logos on its bags, camera gear,
jackets, and the like to have any hope of obtaining press credentials from
Connor and his men.

Rather was teamed with Birnbaum, and he ordered his producer
to stay the hell out of sight. "Dan thought I looked too much like a
New Yorker," Birnbaum said. He also told Birnbaum to "lose that cigar.
. . . people down here don't smoke green cigars . . . they smoke brown
ones!" Rather then laid on his thickest Texas drawl, did his best good old
boy rap, got the credentials, and got the interview with Dr. King.

Bernie Birnbaum was duly impressed. "The interesting thing is that
here was this young Texan—I had worked with Charles Kuralt, too, who
was from North Carolina—and you realized they knew how to talk to the
people down South. They knew how to connect with them."

Rather was also in Jackson, Mississippi, shortly after the assassination of
civil rights leader Medgar Evers. Evers's brother Charles was living in
Chicago at the time. With unconcealed rage, he flew down to Mississippi.

"I told my friends I was going to get me a gun and kill the first white
person who tried to kill me," Evers said to me. "And when I landed at the
airport, there's all these reporters hanging around, and this skinny white
guy keeps coming up to me and trying to talk. I kept telling him to go
away, but he just kept coming back saying things like 'You don't want any
violence—what you gotta do is pick up where your brother left off.' And
I didn't want to hear it. So I get in a car to go to the house and this guy

gets in with me! And he's telling me that he's from Texas and all this, telling me his whole life story. Finally, I said to him, 'What the hell would you know about being a nigger in this country?' And he said, 'Well, I wouldn't know about that. But I do know what it's like to be mistreated.' So, we get to the house, and this guy is just hanging around in the back-yard. He won't go away. So I went out there and we sat and talked all night. This guy really cared about me. And he made more of an impact on me than any white man I've ever known. Yeah, that was Dan Rather. You say hi to him for me, okay?"

The Evers assassination had a strong and lasting impact on Rather, too. When the justice system finally caught up with the killer some three decades later, Rather wrote an essay for the *Nation* about Byron De La Beckwith's conviction and what it meant for the Old and the New South. His conclusion? Not much.

> Look at the white institutions outside the South that still keep ethnic and racial minorities locked away in ghettos. The President of the United States gets a written report every morning on how many Bosnians died last night, but no such briefing on how many people were murdered in Washington. A century after genocidal wars ended on the Western plains, Native Americans are still subjected to con-ditions of hopelessness, poverty and disease. . . . Gays and lesbians are beaten to death in the streets, in part due to an irrational fear of AIDS, but also because hatemongers, from comedians to the worst of the Christian right, send the message that homosexuals have no value in our society. The list goes on and on: Vietnamese-Americans, Arab-Americans, Mexican-Americans, Americans from every corner of the globe are daily subjected to abuses of civil rights, to violence, hatred and inhumanity. Don't try to tell me or any other New Southerner that civil rights was and is a "Southern problem." The Old South shares the worst of its legacy with all Americans.

Medgar Evers was assassinated on June 12, 1963. It was not the last assassination Dan Rather would cover that year.

3

From Big D to D.C.
to the VC

Assassination is the extreme form of censorship.

—George Bernard Shaw

Robert Pierpoint, a native Californian who went to Whittier High School and was taught by a young woman who would become Pat Nixon, had ended up in Sweden after World War II, studying on the GI bill. In 1949, he was contacted by Ed Murrow and asked to become a stringer for CBS News. That was followed by a stint covering the Korean War for CBS radio, and Pierpoint was present at the signing of the truce, an event that later led to a bit part playing himself in the final episode of the TV series *M*A*S*H*.

In 1957, Pierpoint was assigned to the White House, where he covered the Eisenhower and Kennedy administrations. That is what took him to Dallas on November 22, 1963.

He told me, "I had to go everywhere the president went, including that trip. I was at the Texas Trade Mart where all these people were waiting for lunch and the arrival of the president. I sensed something was wrong and ran up to a Secret Service agent and asked, 'Where's the president?' And he said, 'I don't know, I thought he was with you guys.' So I called New York and they told me to get over to Parkland Hospital."

Also at the Trade Mart was Eddie Barker. Barker was a legend in Dallas. As the news director of both KRLD radio and KRLD television, Barker knew everybody worth knowing in town. He had also once been president of the Radio and Television News Directors' Association. That day he was broadcasting live from the Trade Mart.

"The NBC station in Fort Worth had covered the arrival at Love Field and had covered the breakfast that morning. So now it was our turn to cover the lunch at the Trade Mart," Barker told me. "We had our truck downstairs, and they heard the sirens and the whole bit, and one of our guys called and said, 'Hey, they didn't stop! I think they're heading for the airport!' Then we heard they had gone to Parkland Hospital. So I just kept talking on the air."

According to Dan Rather's account in *The Camera Never Blinks*, he was standing near the president's motorcade route when he saw a police car scream by, followed by the president's open-top limousine going at flank speed.

"I had to hotfoot it back to the station," Rather recalled. "I knew the neighborhood and would be there in a matter of minutes."

When he arrived at KRLD, he said, he went straight to the open line to Eddie Barker at the Trade Mart. "Eddie, this is Dan. I think something's happened out there and I think it's bad."

"Yeah," Barker replied, according to Rather. "So do I. We're picking up a lot of funny talk on the radio. The cops are asking each other what the hell is going on."

In Rather's account, he managed to get through on the phone to Parkland Hospital, where a woman on the switchboard put him on with a Catholic priest.

"I'm Dan Rather with CBS News, and I'm trying to confirm whether the president has been shot."

"Yes," the priest answered. "The president has been shot, and he is dead."

"Are you certain of that?"

"Unfortunately, I am."

Meanwhile, Robert Pierpoint had gotten inside Parkland Hospital, and he had been on the radio reporting nonstop. When the priest who administered the last rites walked by, he spoke with Pierpoint but would not say whether the president was dead.

Eddie Barker was still on the air at the Trade Mart when a doctor friend of his walked up to him and whispered, "He's DOA." Barker knew the doctor well and knew he had solid connections at Parkland.

"So I went with it. I'm not sure who else had been picking up our feed, but I know it was heard in New York. They knew my voice. They said, 'Eddie, is that you?' And that's when they first got the word. And all that stuff about Rather being on the phone with me, it's all a crock of poop. When he wrote his book, he called me and we went over it. And he said to me, 'I better warn you, I don't remember it that way.'

Barker maintained that he didn't even remember seeing or speaking to Rather until hours later back at the TV station. "I have no earthly idea where he was," he told me. "He was saying he and I were on the phone, and it's just not true."

Rather said that when he spoke into the telephone and stated, "That's what I hear, he's dead," he thought he was talking to Barker, not to the control room in New York.

"Did you say 'dead'? Are you sure, Dan?" the voice came back.

"Right, dead," Rather said, still believing that he was speaking to Barker.

Moments later, CBS radio, basing its report on Rather, announced that the president was dead. Rather said that he began shouting into the phone that he had not authorized any bulletin.

Accurately or not, Rather was credited with being the first to report the death of the president and, to add even more confusion, was cited in Walter Cronkite's memoirs as having reported it from Parkland Hospital. Rather had never been at Parkland; Bob Pierpoint had. When the mistake was finally pointed out to Cronkite, he insisted at first that he could close his eyes and "see" Rather reporting from Parkland. But when he was shown the actual transcript of what was aired that day, Cronkite ordered the mistake corrected in future editions of his book, making sure that Pierpoint got the credit he deserved.

"I'll tell you one thing I should have broadcast but didn't," Pierpoint said to me. "It was when Mrs. Kennedy came out with the casket. I described her walking slowly with her hand on the casket, but I couldn't bring myself to say she had blood all over her dress and her legs. It was a mistake on my part. I should have said it, but I couldn't."

When Rather finally got an opportunity to call his wife, Jean was concerned about why her husband sounded so detached, given the staggering events still unfolding. As he wrote in *The Camera Never Blinks*, she told him, "This has been one of the better things you've done, and you ought to know that. But it's one thing to hear you on the air with no emotion coming through. I thought I'd hear it from you now, Dan, on the phone. And I don't. It isn't there. And I don't know how to react to that."

"I don't have time for it, Jean," Rather said. "If I let myself go, I won't be able to do what has to be done."

"I know. We'll talk about it another time."

Among the things that had to be done that weekend was the transfer of Lee Harvey Oswald from the basement of the Dallas County Jail. In Washington, a memorial service for the president would be carried live. Television's ability to switch from location to location was not nearly as sophisticated then as it is today. CBS had been set up to switch from the memorial service to a Harry Reasoner piece, then to a Roger Mudd report from Capitol Hill and then to the Oswald transfer, which was scheduled for around 10 A.M. But the memorial was running late, very late, and Nelson Benton, assigned to cover the Oswald move, was screaming to New York that they should come to him now because Oswald could appear at any moment. And just then he did, and just then Jack Ruby lunged from the crowd and took his shot. Anyone watching NBC saw it live. CBS and ABC got caught in the middle of other things. Rather and everyone else at CBS were crushed. It was a devastating lapse. About an hour and a half later, CBS rigged up a projector to run film of the shooting in slow motion, a technique rarely used in television in those days. In a sense, watching the "man in the hat" make his move in slow motion was more dramatic than seeing it live, when the scene was a confusing blur. It was not quite instant replay—that would come later, thanks to Roone Arledge and others—but it was an effective save nevertheless.

Over the weekend, a story began making the rounds about schoolchildren in Dallas who supposedly had applauded when told by a minister that the president had been assassinated. The official response was that the kids had applauded because there would be no school on Monday.

Bernie Birnbaum said he did some checking, though, and found that at least some of the kids were responding to strong anti-Kennedy sentiment among their parents. In fact, the reason for the Kennedy visit in the first place had been to shore up the president's sagging polls in Texas. Decades later, while working on a wrongful conviction case in Dallas for 60 Minutes, I asked an attorney exactly what it had been like back then. "The climate was so bad," he said, "that if I had been a prosecutor at the time, I would have indicted some of our newspaper editorialists and columnists as accessories before the fact in that murder because of some of the hateful things they had written."

Correspondent Hughes Rudd was dispatched to check out the applause story. The minister refused to give an interview, but Rudd managed to piece together a story anyway. Eddie Barker's KRLD staffers watched in horror as producer Birnbaum and film editor Lenny Raff assembled the story, another city-of-hate report—just what Dallas needed. According to Birnbaum, "We said, 'We're just feeding it up to New York so they can look at it. We don't know if they're gonna use it.' But, of course, they did. I was in the KRLD control room and I swear their hair stood straight up as they watched the show."

Moments later, an angry Eddie Barker summoned Dan Rather into his office. "When Dan came out," Birnbaum said, "he came over to me and Lenny and said, 'You and you . . . out. Pack up. We're leaving.' We were being thrown out of the station! So I grabbed all the film—theirs and ours—threw it in a satchel and we left. We go back to the Holiday Inn, and Dan is so emotional that he calls Dr. Stanton to tell them we've been thrown out of our affiliate."

Around CBS News, Frank Stanton loomed almost as large as Paley himself. As the chairman's second in command, Dr. Stanton (his Ph.D. was in statistics) was a man of uncommon grace and common sense. Outwardly, he was a rather bland Midwesterner who had an amazing grasp of numbers and how they could be used to analyze and grow the audience for the fledgling CBS radio network of the 1930s and 1940s. He had been hired to run a research department, which became the forerunner of today's ratings system. His interests also included architecture, modern art, and design. In the early years he rarely saw William Paley and when he did was too afraid to speak to him. Paley was in many ways Stanton's polar opposite: a self-described "half-student, half-playboy" with an insatiable appetite for the finer things in life, especially women. He took money from his father's cigar company and began buying radio stations in the late 1920s, mainly to advertise the cigars. By the mid-1930s, with radio stations popping up all over, the federal government decided to regulate the industry. It was Frank Stanton's brilliant analysis of the nature of the growing radio audience that helped thwart some of the government's more draconian desires to control the powerful new medium. Henceforth, stations had to promise to devote a reasonable amount of airtime to news and public affairs "in the public interest, convenience and necessity." The creation of CBS News was in fact a sop to the government so that stations could continue to reap profits from entertainment programs. According to Sally Bedell Smith's biography of Paley, *In All His Glory*, the decision to send Edward R. Murrow to London to report on the blitz from the rooftops started out as something of a "public relations ploy" to draw listeners away from the larger rival NBC.

Paley boasted with pride about his newspeople when it suited him and complained about them when it didn't. Stanton, however, was a true believer in the value of the news operation, and over the years, he made himself virtually irreplaceable as Paley's deputy and alter ego—or so he and everyone else thought. (The fact was that William Paley did not like sharing credit. When Edward R. Murrow became too big, Paley reined him in and essentially left him with little choice but to resign. And when Stanton defended Walter Cronkite, Dan Rather, Dan Schorr, and the other CBS reporters under fire from the White House during the Watergate turmoil—Paley had supported Nixon—he, too, was forced out at the age of sixty-five on March 30, 1973. It was a bitter parting of a pair that, despite their vastly different personalities, had created what had come to be known as the Tiffany Network.)

When Rather and company were thrown out of KRLD during the JFK assassination coverage, CBS News was on the verge of overtaking NBC as the nation's dominant source of television news. By phoning Frank Stanton, Rather knew he would get action and get it quickly.

"So Stanton tells Dan, 'If they've thrown you out, forget it. We'll find another affiliate,'" Birnbaum recalled. That seemed to settle things for a while until Rather got a call asking him to return to KRLD for a meeting. When he and Birnbaum walked in, they saw a forlorn Eddie Barker sitting at a table with the station's owners, who were none too pleased. The CBS affiliation was worth millions to the station and if that relationship had been jeopardized, they wanted to know why immediately. According to Birnbaum, "The owner says to Rather, 'Who threw you out? Why did you leave?' And Dan looks at Eddie and sees the predicament the guy's in and says, 'Well, nobody asked us to leave.' And the guy says, 'Well, okay, come on back in!' That's how Dan got Eddie off the hook."

With the new administration of Texan Lyndon Baines Johnson, Dan Rather was assigned to the White House and the Washington bureau. "He had done such a good job in Dallas," then bureau chief Bill Small told me, "that when management asked if I wanted him in Washington, I said, 'Oh, yeah.'"

"I liked him immediately," said Small. " He is very personable, very gracious, and very humble. He was never shy about asking people, 'Do you know any good books I should read?' And whenever I told him I thought he was wrong on an issue, he wouldn't get into a big argument about it. He'd think about it and reconsider his views. I don't think he was intimidated by some of the intellects around him. Marvin Kalb liked him a lot. Sevareid adored him."

Management's assumption was that LBJ would show special favors to this young fellow Texan. But Rather, by his own admission, was an outsider in more ways than one. In the first place, he knew virtually nothing about Washington, having visited there only three times in his life. Rather was crushed when LBJ failed to recognize him for a question at one of the president's rare news conferences. He sought out Johnson aide Jack Valenti, whom Rather had known in Houston, and demanded to know why. Valenti explained that LBJ had been searching for Rather among the press corps but, without his glasses, could not see more than ten feet in front of him.

Rather didn't buy it. "As country as I am, I can't swallow that syrup." Rather believed the president was testing the new guy, trying to break him in like a new saddle. LBJ, it seemed, felt that young Rather should be writing more positive stories, and the president made that crystal clear in phone calls to Rather's bosses at CBS. In May 1964, when everything was coming up roses for the LBJ campaign, he called Rather in for a stern lecture. "You did a good job down there in Texas," the president told Rather, according to David Halberstam in *The Powers That Be*, "and then you get up here to the big time and the first thing you've done is fall in with all those Eastern people . . . the *New York Times* and *Time* magazine. So you've come to the big city and fallen for their Eastern ways. Well, you've made the biggest mistake of your life because the best thing you got goin' for you is that you're all Texan, and I'm all Texan. And what you're doing playing an Easterner is phony. And I know it's phony, and you better get it right."

With a wink and a nod, the president and his aides let Rather know that if he did more positive pieces on his fellow Texan, he would be given more access, special treatment, more leaks. The "play ball with us" approach, Rather knew, had been tried by every politician since politics was invented, and Rather admitted that it was tempting. Yet he also knew it was a Faustian pact. "Once a politician takes you into his confidence, it can be hell getting out," Rather wrote. "The only way to fly is to say, 'I'd like you to respect what I do. But I'm not running any popularity contest.' You have make that point early on; if you don't, you never will."

In late October 1964, Nikita Khrushchev was deposed and China exploded a nuclear bomb. LBJ demanded TV time to explain America's position. The Republicans, correctly fearing that Johnson would turn the appearance into a political speech just weeks before the election, also demanded equal time. Sure enough, LBJ's address to the nation was more of a stump speech than a reaction to world affairs, and it fell to Dan Rather to do a recap, or instant analysis. He was given one minute to sum up, and he used it to point out that the Goldwater people were justifiably furious and that it would be interesting to see how the networks would react to their demand for equal time. Johnson was furious, too, but his fury was about Rather's analysis. The president passed his displeasure along to Rather's bosses as only the unprintable Johnson could. CBS president Fred Friendly chastised Rather for having used his one minute to discuss the equal-time imbroglio, calling it " irresponsible."

LBJ called it a lot worse. In the weeks to come he did everything possible to avoid Rather, effectively freezing him out. On the night of Johnson's blowout victory over Goldwater, he chose to speak to CBS's third-string reporter, ignoring Rather completely. As Rather recalled in *The Camera Never Blinks*, "Johnson could say more in a sentence than most politicians could in a filibuster." When Rather and other reporters visited LBJ in a hospital room after the president's vocal cord surgery, Johnson told him, "Son, you stay in Sunday school and keep your nose clean and maybe someday you'll get a pair of pajamas, too." Rather wrote in *The Camera Never Blinks*, "I never got my pajamas. More often what I got was a phone call from the president himself demanding, as only he could, 'Rather, are you trying to fuck me?' And this was even before the war in Vietnam blew out of control and before students were being teargassed in the streets for saying the war was wrong."

It was obvious to the CBS News brass that Rather would be useless covering the Johnson administration. Rather was shocked when Bill

Small suggested that he set up shop in London. Now, Rather's bullshit detector flicked on. "Three things could have happened," he wrote, "and two of them were bad. One, Johnson had applied pressure to get me rotated; two, I had not been very good at what I was doing; or three, CBS had decided my work was done in Washington and God needed me in London. Why London? I mean, World War Two was over." Vietnam, however, was just beginning.

Vice President Ernie Leiser, who had been mainly responsible for hiring Rather, told him flat out that he would never develop into a full-fledged correspondent without overseas experience. CBS had other personnel moves in mind, and its executives would not allow Rather to screw them up by refusing the London assignment. Everyone had to take his or her assigned places, period. In desperation, Rather cut a deal with CBS News president Fred Friendly: he would go to London, but if this thing, this "police action," this Vietnam skirmish began to grow as large as Rather believed it would, that's where he would head next. Friendly agreed. "You have to go to London, but if Vietnam gets as big as you and I think it will, you'll get there one way or another."

According to Rather in *The Camera Never Blinks*, his wife, Jean, said to him, "What is it with you? A move to London is one thing. That's a class move, whatever their motives. Maybe Johnson did ask them to get you on the run. And yes, maybe you haven't done a very good job. But London, that can be a family experience. But *you*, no, you want to go off to some God-forsaken jungle and risk getting your head blown off."

Indeed, other correspondents might well have said, "Why bother with this sideshow of a no-account war when you can eat prime rib and Yorkshire pudding at the Hyde Park?" In fact, there were a few well-paid and well-heeled correspondents who declined a tour in southeast Asia once the war became a national obsession, and, for a time, CBS News would not assign a correspondent to that location who had a family. Still, Rather felt compelled to go. First, though, he had to determine what a Texan was supposed to say, wear, and eat during his stay in London. And for that, his tutor and mentor was the Duke himself, Charles Collingwood.

"Collingwood was the only guy who could impart sophistication to him," Bernie Birnbaum told me. "He could speak French. He was a Rhodes scholar. He was married to an actress, Louise Albritton. He showed Rather how to dress, where to buy his shoes. He took him under his wing, just as he did with Morley Safer." In later years, when Collingwood's career was doomed by alcoholism, Rather and Safer, the oddest of couples, made sure the Duke was treated with dignity. "No one else gave a good goddamn about him except Dan and Morley," Birnbaum said. "He realized he only had two real friends, and those guys carried him right to the end. They were the only two honorable people in this company."

When Vice President Bill Leonard visited London, Rather continued to badger him about going to Vietnam. Leonard, thinking that Rather was crazy for wanting to leave both his young family and the best foreign bureau around, said he would look into it.

Days later, a telex arrived from Fred Friendly: "Provided your wife approves, I'll send you to Vietnam."

Of course, Rather had already discussed the possibility with Jean, assuring her that the hitch would be for only three months and then he would be relieved. But Mrs. Rather wasn't relieved at all. "This war isn't going to be over in three months and if I know you, and I do, I'll be lucky if you come back, period, much less before it's over."

On Rather's plane ride to Vietnam, his seatmate was a young reporter from the local CBS affiliate in Minneapolis, WCCO. The reporter, Phil Jones, told me, "I think we were the first local station to send a reporter and camera there, so we could film Minnesotans fighting for their country." Jones was surprised that this big-time network correspondent was willing to talk for hours with a local news guy. "That hardly ever happened at all," Jones said. When Jones and his cameraman unpacked their bags in Saigon, the cameraman was horrified to discover that he had forgotten to bring the lens adapter without which his lens could not be attached. The pair walked down to the CBS bureau in the hotel, but the bureau chief showed no interest in helping them out. "We figured we were screwed," Jones said. On their way out of the hotel they came across Rather, who asked, "So guys, how's it going?" When Jones explained their problem, Rather said, "Aw, come on with me; we can take care of that."

Rather walked into the bureau chief's office and said, "Look, these guys are from the best and most important affiliate we have. Now just make sure they get everything they need." The clerk miraculously produced the adapter, which he previously had claimed he didn't have.

Rather was determined to get out into the field as quickly as possible. Bernie Birnbaum recalled, "He stepped off the plane and we got him over to the black market where he got his fatigues and everything else he needed, except boots. None of the boots fit. Then he said he wanted to go to Bien Hua because he heard the Christmas truce was falling apart. I said, 'You can't go there at night. It's too dangerous even in the day.' But he went and did the story anyway."

Rather hitched a chopper ride with some marines to a place called Tam Ky, sweeping the rice paddies until the enemy opened fire. "I hit the ground," he wrote, "but I landed on my back and was pinned down for more than an hour. There was heavy fire from mortars, automatic weapons and small arms. I had the strange sensation of lying on a river bank in Texas and daydreaming, except for the noise." When he heard the choppers return, he knew it was time to move. He ran through a hut and found himself face-to-face with a Vietnamese woman, who was holding a rifle aimed right at him. "My first reaction was, well, black pajamas, Viet Cong. This is how the world ends." As he heard the choppers taking off, Rather clasped his hands and placed them in front of his chin, slowly backing out of the hutch the same way he had entered. He jumped aboard the last chopper leaving for the flight back to Da Nang, but en route it had to rescue a marine unit that was on the verge of being wiped out. As the chopper landed, the trapped marines began falling back toward it, laying down suppressing fire all the way. As they struggled to board the chopper along with their wounded, the pilot said, "I don't think we can take all these people."

Rather felt ashamed and embarrassed. After all, he was only a civilian hitching a ride. Finally, everyone got on board, though, and the chopper, struggling mightily to gain altitude, spun and turned for home. "Damned right," Rather heard one of the marines say. "Either everybody goes or nobody goes."

Rather's hitch in Vietnam lasted not three months but about a year. Although he saw more than a fair amount of action and death, one producer believes that Rather's reporting would have had greater impact had he not used an American cameraman who had worked with him in Houston. The shooter, Jerry Adams, was certainly good enough and plenty brave—he had fought in World War Two—but he, like Rather, was learning Vietnam on the job. "Safer was so smart," the producer said. "He had Hac Thuc Can, a Vietnamese crew. They knew what was going on, so it was easier for them to be in the right place at the right time."

Rather's own assessment of his performance was mixed. "I felt I should spend most of my time obtaining the television record of Americans at war. In 1965, I saw the American push as the developing story. I may have been wrong. I did receive some criticism, in and out of CBS, for spending too much time in the field covering combat instead of what to many was a political war. I did some politics. Perhaps not enough. I think the complaint was fair, but I do not apologize for it. For the first time, after all, war was coming into our homes."

Of course, the so-called television war forever changed the way wars would be covered. The lesson the Pentagon drew from the experience was that it could not simply allow the press, especially the television press, to go wherever it wanted to and ask whatever questions it wanted to. Other reporters like Morley Safer, Jack Laurence, and David Halberstam caught hell from both the Johnson and the Nixon administration for their coverage—Safer, in particular. When Johnson found out that Safer was Canadian, he ordered his press secretary Bill Moyers to dig around to see whether Safer had an anti-American bias. Safer has never forgiven Moyers for having gone along with the order. The whole experience made the Pentagon and subsequent administrations realize that they needed to impose de facto censorship on the conflicts to follow.

When Rather returned from Vietnam, Press Secretary Moyers suggested that Rather brief both the president and the national security adviser Walt Rostow on what he had seen and heard. According to Rather, the Rostow session was an exercise in pure fantasy, with Rostow pointing to various locations on a map and describing them as great successes, and Rather, who had just been there, shaking his head in utter disbelief. None of what Rostow was telling him jibed with what Rather had just seen in the field. The session with the president was uneventful as well, despite Rather's suggestion that every now and then, the president fly a contingent of company commanders back to Washington to give him an unvarnished view of what was really happening on the ground.

Rather believed that no one in any branch of the military below the rank of colonel had ever lied to him. "They might be mistaken, but they never tried to bullshit me." The bullshit, he believed, always came from the top. And now that he would be reassigned once again to Washington, he would witness bullshit on a scale that no four-star general could ever imagine. Yet the Washington bureau he would return to was bigger, bolder, and brassier than the one he had left a few years earlier. Here you didn't just walk—you swaggered.

4

Nixon and Gunga Dan

History never looks like history when you are living through it. It always looks confusing and messy and always feels uncomfortable.

— John W. Gardner

From the mid-1960s through the 1970s, the CBS News Washington bureau was home to the finest collection of broadcast journalists ever assembled under one roof. There was Eric Sevareid and Roger Mudd, Marvin and Bernard Kalb, Bob Schieffer, Daniel Schorr, Robert Pierpoint, Robert Schakne, Maraya McLaughlin, Nelson Benton, Lesley Stahl — and Dan Rather.

By the time he returned to the United States, Dan Rather had jumped ahead several spots in this formidable pecking order. Still, he was received with a mixture of puzzlement and amusement by many people at the bureau. Rather felt awkward and self-conscious in this heady and tense environment. He was smart enough to know that internal politics was very much a part of surviving and thriving in this place, and he made sure to stay on bureau chief Bill Small's good side, so much so that he became a sort of teacher's pet, which did not endear him to some of his coworkers. He often simply disappeared for hours at a time without the assignment desk's knowledge, a habit that Bill Small would not have tolerated with any other correspondent. Rather was also smart enough to know how much he didn't know, and he frequently sought out the more erudite of the group, especially Eric Sevareid, and asked them to recommend books that any learned man should read.

According to Rather, Sevareid suggested such weighty tomes as Montaigne's essays, which made some colleagues snicker. The story became part of the Rather folklore and was accepted by everyone except Eric Sevareid.

"Sevareid thought it was the dumbest thing he had ever heard," said Sandy Socolow, later the Washington bureau chief. "He told me directly, 'I have no list like that.' But no one dreamed of going to Sevareid and seeing if the story was correct or not."

Although Rather didn't smoke, except for the occasional cigar, he always carried a cigarette lighter with him and flicked it open the moment any woman on the desk needed a light. The reaction among many people at the bureau was, "Is this guy for real?"

The women at CBS certainly wondered about that. Some of them found Rather's courtly and proper Southern manners a bit much. Here was this handsome young man who knew damn well that he was handsome calling even the secretaries "ma'am," opening doors for them, pulling back their chairs, lighting their cigarettes. They thought it had to be an act. Others found it charming, still others seductive. Fairly or unfairly, at that time Rather was tagged as something of a rake, a character out of a country and western song who had "cheatin' on his mind." But those who knew him best knew that while his mind might wander, it always returned to the business at hand—moving to the top of the hill at CBS News.

One incident that continues to annoy Rather to this day involved an order from William Paley banning the so-called instant analysis of presidential speeches and news conferences, a practice in which a correspondent gives his interpretation of whatever the president has just said. Protest against such analysis had come from the Nixon administration, and Paley, egged on by his friend Eric Sevareid, who was not good at ad-libbing, agreed with their complaint that it was a form of editorializing. The CBS News Washington bureau was outraged, and correspondents led by Roger Mudd and Daniel Schorr began circulating a petition to be sent to Paley, demanding that he rescind the ban. When it became Dan Rather's turn to sign, he demurred, saying that he agreed with "the general principle" but felt it did not accurately reflect his thoughts on the matter. When word came down that CBS News president Richard Salant was very much in favor of the petition, Rather said he'd changed his mind and would sign it. Nothing doing, said Mudd and Schorr; you already had your chance.

"Naturally, I think too much has been made of that," Rather told *Playboy*. "I make mistakes and that was unquestionably one of them. But Mudd and Schorr were not always pulling for me during that period. It happens all the time in the business. It's true that if Salant thought it was a good idea, I should gulp down my reservations and sign it. But at that point, Mr. Mudd and Mr. Schorr rightly figured they had me by the short hairs, and they refused. I am mildly resentful of the fact that this moment has been singled out and concentrated on. It was not my best, but there were moments when Mr. Schorr was not at his best during that period, and I'm damned sure Mr. Mudd was not at his best."

Producer Larry Doyle told me that the superior attitude of some people at the bureau began to change as soon as they realized that Rather wasn't just glad to be in the game—he in fact intended to win it. "Here was a kid who got his reputation covering a hurricane, which the correspondents in Washington just dismissed. To them, that was a *weather* story. And he was from Sam Houston State Teachers College, and there were those who were reluctant to embrace him because he was not their intellectual equal. But then everyone began to see that this guy was a real hardworking, hard-charging, tireless newshound."

Robert Pierpoint found out just how hard-charging Rather was soon after the two were paired at the White House following Pierpoint's coverage of the doomed Goldwater campaign. He said, "When that was over,

I told Fred Friendly [then CBS News president] that I'd like to go back to the White House, and Fred said, 'Fine.' So, when I got back I said to Dan, 'Look, there's going to be two of us here. Why don't you take the domestic stories and I'll take the foreign stories, since I've worked overseas.' And Dan said, 'No, I'll take whatever stories I want.'"

Peter Sturtevant, a young hire on the news desk, watched this mismatch play out with great sympathy for the veteran Pierpoint. "Rather wanted to do *both* the TV and radio, leaving Pierpoint with nothing. And he often did. Poor old Bob really got fucked over. And he's such a sweet guy, too."

For years, Rather and Pierpoint worked side by side in tiny cubicles in the White House without incident or personal animus. Pierpoint accepted the reality that Rather had been anointed the big fish in the big pond and there was nothing Pierpoint could do to change that. To be sure, Pierpoint took mild delight at retelling some of Rather's faux pas and occasional episodes of odd behavior, but he became defensive whenever he heard his former colleague being attacked as a left-wing ideologue. "He was a straight reporter and he did his job. He was much more neutral than I ever was. And I think all this right-wing stuff that he's a liberal is false and unfair. I think they resent the fact that he did his job. They don't want the facts out and they blame the reporters when the facts do come out. I will defend Dan in any forum as not being a liberal Democrat or anything else other than a good reporter."

I told Pierpoint that he was being remarkably gracious about a man who had pushed him aside as White House correspondent and later had kept him off the *Evening News* entirely.

"Well, that's true," he responded. "But I just want to be fair to him. About ten years ago, he wrote me a note apologizing for the way he treated me. It wasn't specific, just an apology. And I accepted it."

Rather's reports did not always hit the target, though. Some missed completely. He was receiving tips from someone in the Washington bureaucracy, and that person was believed to be young Donald Rumsfeld, with whom Rather had begun what would become a long personal and business relationship. Once Tom Brokaw, not realizing his microphone was still on, complained to his producer and was heard on the air saying, "Rummy used to get even with guys in the White House by leaking stuff to Rather that didn't have any basis in fact. Rather was factually wrong a lot of times because he was Rummy's vessel."

Whoever they came from, some of those tips did in fact prove to be wrong, such as when Rather went with a tip that Richard Nixon was about to replace J. Edgar Hoover as FBI chief. "It was October third of 1969," Pierpoint told me. " I remember the date because it was my tenth wedding anniversary. Rather had already reported the tip, but as I was having a dinner party for four or five couples that night, I got a call from the desk saying Bill Small wants me to go to Hoover's house because the president's going there to have dinner with him. I said, 'You tell Bill it's my tenth wedding anniversary and I have guests here and it's not my story anyway. It's Dan Rather's.' Well, they talked to Small and then called back and said, 'Bill says either you go or else.' And so I apologized to my guests and went to sit on the sidewalk outside Hoover's house. Now maybe they couldn't locate Rather, I don't know. But sure enough, the president comes out with John Ehrlichman, and I got a quick interview with Nixon, who denied having any intention of firing Hoover and never did fire Hoover."

Pierpoint also recalled Rather going with a tip that Nixon was about to fire a top U.S. official in Vietnam. That one didn't pan out, either. "I think Dan had an overwhelming drive and ambition, and at times his ambition overcame his journalistic caution. That is a problem we all face, particularly in broadcasting with such rivalry to get on the air. But in Dan's case it got him into trouble at least those couple of times I know of."

In his classic on-the-road book *The Boys on the Bus*, author Timothy Crouse followed the reporters covering the 1972 presidential campaign. The references to Rather are mostly positive, such as, "The print reporters did admire a few TV reporters . . . like Doug Kiker, Cassie Mackin, Dan Rather, Roger Mudd and Dan Schorr. These people were good and they dug for news." But there is also a paragraph about Rather's penchant for "going with his gut": "Rather often adhered to the 'informed sources' or 'the White House announced today' formulas, but he was famous in the trade for the times he by-passed the formulas and winged it on a story. Rather would go with an item even if he didn't have it completely nailed down with verifiable facts. If a rumor sounded solid to him . . . he would let it rip. The other White House reporters hated Rather for this. They knew exactly why he got away with it: being as handsome as a cowboy, Rather was a star at CBS News, and that gave him the clout he needed."

Yet Crouse also praised two extraordinarily long segments on Watergate that had aired on *CBS Evening News*, prominently reported by Walter Cronkite, Dan Rather, Dan Schorr, and others. (These reports displeased Chairman Paley; he complained that they were too long and lacked balance. What he failed to mention to his new executives was that CBS had been getting major heat from Nixon enforcer Chuck Colson, with thinly veiled threats about payback if the Watergate reports continued.)

Rather, along with senior bureau men Ed Fouhy and John Armstrong, and bureau chief Bill Small, pushed CBS News to stay on the Watergate story. It was not an easy sell. In the first place, Watergate was not much of a television story. There were no pictures to shoot except the exterior of the building and the inside of the Democratic National Committee office. And few of those involved, from the small fish to the biggest players, would go on camera for an interview. As Ben Bradlee famously screamed at his *Washington Post* editors, "When the hell is somebody gonna go on the record on this damned story!"

With Dan Rather at the White House and other top guns like Daniel Schorr, Roger Mudd, Lesley Stahl, and Connie Chung hacking away at pieces of the conspiracy, CBS News made Watergate much more of a national story than it would have been. CBS continued to produce special reports, usually anchored by Rather and coproduced by Bernie Birnbaum, that would guide the viewer step by step through the increasingly complex developments, often featuring surprisingly candid interviews with players who had a huge stake in the outcome. There was a remarkable exchange between Rather and Senator Barry Goldwater, the man who would ultimately tell Richard Nixon that resignation was his only option:

RATHER: What can the president do vis-à-vis Watergate? What needs to be done most, right now?

GOLDWATER: Most, he has to convince the American people that he's telling the truth. Now, I don't know how he's going to do this. I don't buy the idea that he has to have a press conference. I don't see any advantage to his making a national television statement again; he's done that once and released a rather lengthy document that maybe half the people believed.

RATHER: Senator, should President Nixon resign?

GOLDWATER: No, I don't think he should. And I don't think he should be impeached. Now I might not take that position if it can be proven that he's lying. Now, if it gets down to the fact that he's guilty, and I don't think he is, I would say resignation would be the cheapest, easiest, and quickest way. Put Agnew in and get going!

On the day after the so-called Saturday Night Massacre, when President Nixon fired the three top government officials investigating the Watergate affair, Rather opened the special broadcast with: "This man is no longer attorney general of the United States. This man is no longer deputy attorney general of the United States. And this man—the special prosecutor in the Watergate Affair—has been fired under orders issued by the president of the United States."

CBS's crackerjack Washington bureau became particularly adept at reminding viewers of the misleading information being churned out by the White House and it seized upon every opportunity to separate the known facts from the official spin. One broadcast, based entirely on the first batch of audiotapes the White House was forced to release, detailed point-by-point differences between the Nixon aides' public statements and what they had said behind closed doors:

H. R. HALDEMAN [White House chief of staff]: I totally disagree with the conclusion that the president was aware of any type of cover-up. And certainly Mr. Dean did not advise him of it at the September fifteenth meeting.

NIXON [from the tapes of that meeting]: Oh, well, this is a can of worms. As you know, a lot of this stuff that went on — and people who worked this way are awfully embarrassed. But the way you [John Dean] have handled all this seems to have been very skillful, putting your fingers in the leaks that have sprung up here and there.

Perhaps Rather pushed the story more than most TV journalists did; he worked the phones and pounded the pavement for whatever scraps he could come up with and usually had to settle for standups in front of the White House and still photos of the people involved. It wasn't so much that he and CBS were breaking stories as Woodward and Bernstein were, but the network was giving the ongoing saga the kind of national attention that the *Washington Post* simply could not. Rather was smart enough to cultivate sources outside the White House, so whenever the Nixon aides cross-examined one of their own about leaks, they often found that the leak had come from somewhere outside the administration.

Correspondent Phil Jones went to Rather with a potentially dangerous and explosive story. Jones had solid confirmation from inside the Watergate grand jury that when the prosecutor had asked for a show of hands among jurors who thought that Richard Nixon himself should be indicted, all the jurors raised their hands. "In fact," Jones said, "my source told me some people raised *both* their hands." Not only would broadcasting this story be a violation of grand jury secrecy, it would likely result in subpoenas and tampering charges. Jones asked Rather if he would go with the story. "Yes, I would," Rather replied. Jones recounted the same information to Roger Mudd and asked his opinion. "No, I would not," said Mudd. "And you shouldn't have been talking to that grand juror in the first place. The grand jury is a very sacred thing and there but for the grace of God go all of us." The story never ran, but it is an interesting contrast between the cautious Mudd and the persistent, aggressive, lock-load-and-fire Dan Rather.

Correspondent Richard Wagner, who was based in Los Angeles at the time, recalled his first meeting with Rather, who was in town to shadow

Nixon as the beleaguered president tried to find some peace in San Clemente. "I went up to Dan and introduced myself," Wagner said to me, "and then I asked him to tell me what he made of Richard Nixon." According to Wagner, Rather stood ramrod straight, frowned, and began by saying, "Richard Nixon: the bottom line . . ." and then proceeded to recite a dizzying array of facts, anecdotes, personal impressions, dates, names, places, word-for-word exchanges—a warehouse of knowledge about the president. Wagner was amazed. "It was almost like a script, almost as though he had written it and committed it to memory."

Rather's persistence made him an enemy to the Nixon administration and set the stage for that defining moment in Houston when Rather and Nixon had their "Are you running for something?" exchange. There was fallout, to be sure, but it made Rather a star. Thanks mainly to Watergate, Rather had become, with the exception of Walter Cronkite, the public face of CBS News. He was on the air more than any other CBS correspondent, he was by far the most controversial reporter, and to many he was one of the few TV news people willing to challenge every statement churned out by the White House. His critics called it "showboating," but his admirers saw in him the man he had so much admired.

"He had a more dramatic persona than the others," recalled Bob Pierpoint. "And when he did the Watergate stuff, it was his mannerism and his delivery that, in a sense, made him almost a second Edward R. Murrow."

"He stood up to the Nixon White House," said writer John Mosedale. "He made their enemies list. He incurred their wrath at the time when political Washington was talking about the genius of Richard Nixon. He was the one who stood up and asked the hard questions. Nobody asks hard questions now." TV critic Tom Shales added, "In answering back Nixon, he was sort of defending all of broadcast journalism. He just seemed to stand for something."

It was the first crystal-clear manifestation of a key element of Rather's character—a fierce, unshakable refusal to be pushed around or dictated to by authority, especially government authority. Don't quit, and if you're knocked down, get up quickly. Had he asked tough questions of fellow

Texan Lyndon Johnson during LBJ's presidency? Yes. Yet for all of Johnson's expletive-deleted bluster, Rather did not consider him a bully as Murrow had considered McCarthy a bully. The Johnson White House was not peopled by sinister *capos*. The McNamaras, Bundys, and Rostows were misguided perhaps, but the Ehrlichmans, Haldemans, Mitchells, and Colsons were a different breed entirely. This was blood sport to them and the winner would be the last man standing. Rather's exposure to the corrupt inner sanctum that Nixon had constructed was for him a sign of things to come.

"They had chosen to transform the White House into an embattled fortress," Rather wrote in *The Palace Guard*, "sealing it off from what they regarded as an alien city around them, a city infested with hostile groups seeking to bring harm to them and to their president. Yet because so much of their poison was bottled up within those walls, it was inevitable that it should spread inward and that they themselves should become the ultimate victims."

Rather's part of the coverage, making the enemies list and all, was a source of pride for him but also of grave concern. His daughter came home from school one day and told her father that kids at school wondered why he "hated the president." In trying to explain the situation in a different context, Rather made a remark that would be a harbinger: "The White House is not just another beat. Any mistake on a story is apt to be a big one, pressure of no mean proportion in itself. You don't live with someone who is under that lid and not be aware; it comes through by osmosis. The pressure placed on me was felt by my family." The Rathers received several death threats in the mail every week as well as the occasional threatening phone call. A woman on a plane accosted Rather and as she returned to her seat said, "Somewhere, you are going to get yours. If I have to arrange it, I will."

Rather was at least as concerned for his family as he was about the story. This was not a TV melodrama—the characters involved were all too real. "I tried to fight against the tendency to become paranoid," he wrote. "There was a time when I thought we had leaned over too far not to be careful, to convince ourselves that we couldn't live in fear. Jean and

I did so during the civil rights story in the South, again when I went to Vietnam and once more during the worst of Watergate. We had to recognize that the world is a tough neighborhood. If we forgot that, we were in peril. We wouldn't and didn't live in a fortress with burglar alarms and floodlights and triple locks. But we didn't want to be foolish either."

In the conclusion to his book *The Palace Guard*, Rather waved a red flag about the public's reaction to crises that with just a change of a few words and places could apply today: "In the course of the past decade the American people have gone through three national traumas: Vietnam, Watergate, and now, a deep and complicated economic crisis. In all these cases there were early warning signs of the ordeals to come. But we as a nation chose not to recognize them. At a time when we should have been vigilant, we, as a people, were apathetic. Much later, when the truths finally asserted themselves, most of us came around to acknowledging we should have been paying closer attention all along."

When Nixon finally did give up, Rather bent over backward to avoid being accused of gloating, going so far as to describe one of Nixon's final speeches as "having brought a touch of majesty" to the moment. That brought a look of utter disgust to the face of Roger Mudd, who pointed out bluntly that Nixon had still not admitted to much of anything and had not brought himself to apologize to the American people for having put them through a nightmare.

At this point, Rather's stature had grown so large that it would have been something of a demotion to have left him at the White House to cover the Ford administration. Instead, Rather was asked to return to New York to be chief correspondent of *CBS Reports*, the once-proud but now decidedly low-priority documentary unit that at one time had been run by Murrow and Friendly. Again, Rather's innate fears kicked in: was he being promoted or was CBS bending to White House pressure to get him out of Washington and away from the new administration? The mail to CBS News president Dick Salant came pouring in. From Glens Falls, New York: "We got to trust him, and his apparent reward from CBS was to send him into oblivion. You've made him another Watergate casualty."

From a priest in Terre Haute, Indiana: "Your actions indicate that CBS News is bending to outside pressure. . . . That would cause to me question the integrity of the CBS News department, and I can assure you that I would no longer remain a viewer."

Salant and his aides continued to insist that Rather's new assignment was a reward, not a punishment, but between viewer discontent and Rather's own paranoia, his stay at CBS Reports was brief. It did, however, include a commendable body of work, including a rare (at that time) sit-down with Fidel Castro in Cuba. Among the more interesting exchanges between the cigar lover from Houston and the cigar lover from Havana was Castro's contention that Richard Nixon, not John F. Kennedy, was the real villain of the 1961 Bay of Pigs invasion led by U.S.-trained Cuban exiles, even though Nixon was not even in office at the time.

> RATHER [voiceover]: The Cuban premier now says that Richard Nixon not only supported the invasion at the Bay of Pigs but wanted to use United States armed forces in it to ensure its success.
>
> CASTRO: Nixon proposed to Eisenhower that U.S. Armed Forces be used against us, and defended it. And when, in the middle of the Bay of Pigs crisis, Kennedy consulted Nixon, Nixon again proposed that the armed forces of the United States be used. This was Nixon's advice. Kennedy did not take it. It should not be forgotten that Kennedy had taken a courageous stand in those days. When everyone was blaming each other, he said success has many fathers but defeat is an orphan. And he assumed responsibility for all that had happened. Of course, this was undoubtedly a courageous stand on his part.

When asked what he made of Watergate and the president's resignation, Castro replied that the scandal was serious enough to warrant resignation and that Nixon had been wise to step down to spare the United States the embarrassment of an impeachment trial.

Rather's documentaries also included a prize-winning series that reexamined the assassinations of John F. Kennedy, Robert Kennedy, and

Dr. Martin Luther King Jr. and the near fatal attack on Alabama governor George Wallace. Rather told his boss, Les Midgley, that whenever he spoke on college campuses, the questions most frequently asked were about the assassinations. To buttress his case for the series, Rather and his colleagues came up with two hugely important pieces of evidence: access to the original Zapruder film, whose ownership the Zapruder family had regained from Time, Inc., and the autopsy X-rays and photographs of the late president that had been embargoed in the National Archives for five years on orders of Robert Kennedy.

For a fee, Bernie Birnbaum got the Zapruder family to agree to allow CBS to send the original film to the finest, most sophisticated film laboratory in the United States. CBS also hired one of the nation's top pathologists, Dr. James Weston of New Mexico, to examine the autopsy results. After painstaking analysis of the film, the Itek Corporation of Boston concluded that the head movements of the president were consistent only with shots fired from the rear, and Dr. Weston said that his examination of the X-ray photographs indicated the same thing. Asked by Rather whether he was willing to stake his professional reputation on that conclusion, Dr. Weston replied, "Absolutely. Yes."

While the conspiracy theorists may have been disappointed, the viewers and the critics were not. The Kennedy portion of the Assassins series received a George Foster Peabody Award and it is considered the highlight of Rather's brief stay at *CBS Reports*.

With Cronkite still firmly ensconced in the anchor chair, there was only one fitting venue left for Rather—the fast-rising *60 Minutes*, which in the mid-1970s featured Mike Wallace and Morley Safer. Rather's debut on Sunday, December 7, 1975, was also the start of the broadcast's fateful and lucrative switch from 6 P.M., where it was often shortened by pro football runovers, to 7 P.M. Whether the ratings soared because of the time switch or because of the addition of Rather or both is still debated. What is not debated is the fact that the broadcast would hit number one overall by the end of the decade.

This was Rather's meat—longer pieces; more time for depth and nuance; some of the best producers and editors in the business; the manic guidance of Don Hewitt and his deputies, particularly senior producer Palmer Williams, who had been one of "Murrow's boys"; and the opportunity to go just about anywhere in the world at a moment's notice. Money, ratings, and major airtime—no reporter worth a damn could have asked for anything more.

Rather's *60 Minutes* reports included tough investigative pieces on the insecticide Keypone, fraudulent practices in the meatpacking industry, and the dangerous habits of big-rig truckers. Rather's reports also featured a story about efforts to mainstream emotionally troubled children into public schools in Michigan. Producer Scheffler and associate producer Brooke Townsend found a mother who had struggled successfully to get her emotionally impaired son into a public school.

"We had to work very hard to get her to talk about her son," Townsend recalled. "But she did. And when we asked the boy if we could follow him to school, he was ecstatic. So, we followed him in his little yellow school bus and hung around in school with him a bit, and it was great. He thought he was a hero, a big star."

Shortly after the report aired, however, Townsend called the boy's mother to see how she and her son had liked it. "She told me he had run away from home. He'd had no idea he was emotionally impaired. He just thought he was a special kid. He was gone for two days and now he won't go to school because his friends know he's emotionally impaired. So I went to Dan's office and I told him that although it was a terrific piece, we had ended up ruining this family. He asked for the boy's phone number, which I gave him, and then he closed his office door. He was on the phone for a long time. And then he came out and just put on his coat and went home. I called the mother back, and she was so grateful Dan had called. Her boy was in seventh heaven. He was going back to school and felt like a hero again. To this day, I have no idea what Dan said to him."

Correspondent Richard Wagner recalled a similar incident regarding Rather's kindness when Wagner discovered that his minivan had been broken into and burgled while he and Rather were on location in South Africa. "I said to Dan, 'Goddammit, they stole my Paul Stuart bush jacket! That's my foreign correspondent's uniform!' Dan turned to Tom Bettag, his executive producer, and said, 'Hey, where did you pack my bush jacket?' Tom had to rummage through Dan's luggage until he found Dan's Paul Stuart bush jacket, which he handed over to me. It fit pretty good, too."

When Rather learned that an editor in the radio department was suffering from cancer and had to travel almost every day from his home on Long Island to a hospital in New York, Rather put a car and a driver at the man's disposal for every day he had to make the trip. And on assignment in Afghanistan, Rather and his producer—coincidentally, Mary Mapes—came across a twenty-one-year-old translator named Wahid, whose dream was to study in the United States. They arranged for a scholarship for him at Southern Methodist University, Mapes put him up in an apartment above her garage, and in three years Wahid received his master's degree in civil engineering. Rather is said to have spent tens of thousands of dollars on Wahid, but he has never spoken about it.

Rather has a complex makeup. In a way, his somewhat conflicting personality recalls that of Frank Sinatra. On his good days Sinatra was capable of great generosity. But he was also capable of acting like a thug, once dumping an entire plate of spaghetti on his cook's head because he found the pasta a little too al dente.

While Rather was never accused of such boorish behavior, he could turn ice cold and threatening when he felt he had been betrayed or otherwise let down. He once had a producer fly all the way across the country for a personal hour-and-a-half browbeating because the producer's story had been fed to New York a few minutes late, causing the lineup to change. "I felt so furious," the producer said, "that if this guy had fired me, I would have kicked him in the nuts."

Rather's first trip to then Soviet-occupied Afghanistan in 1980 became by far his most memorable effort for 60 Minutes. In Rather's account, he and Don Hewitt decided not to tell management where he was going, out of fear the project would be shot down. First, it would cost a lot of money. Second, there was every reason to believe that Rather and his party would not be allowed beyond the Pakistani border, let alone be permitted to find and film an actual Soviet military base. And third, Rather had just a signed the contract that would make him Walter Cronkite's successor, and it was unlikely that management would agree to allow the heir apparent to take on such a dangerous assignment.

Producer Andy Lack was already in Pakistan. He told Rather that if he was going to come, he must come right away because there would soon be a break in the brutally cold Afghan winter and the Soviets would be increasing their presence. On a story as iffy and treacherous as this, the key player in the group is the cameraman. Unless he or she is willing to take prudent risks, put up with the agony of having to carry heavy gear over long distances, and be ready to shoot at a moment's notice, one might as well just stay home. In Mike Edwards, they had the right man at the right time for the right job.

Edwards and his soundman Peter O'Connor were sent along with a second crew that would serve as a backup and a relay for communication with New York. As the group assembled in Peshawar, producer Lack made it clear to Rather that the so-called freedom fighters, the muja-hedeen, were broken up into tribes that did not trust one another. With-out the assistance of at least one of the tribal leaders, entry across the border would be impossible. They finally found one whom, in Rather's words, "we distrusted the least," and he turned them over to a twenty-year-old named Mirwaz who would be their guide.

The group used various means of transport to get past the checkpoints in Pakistan's outer regions. As Rather wrote in *The Camera Never Blinks Twice*, "Some of the locals suspected we might be Russians. They stopped us, crowded us, and pushed and shoved us. Knives and guns were brandished—theirs, not ours. Mirwaz was the only one among us who had a gun. He and our passports and buying a round of tea eased the sit-uation and we moved on. We looked at one another and rolled our eyes. Nobody had said this was going to be easy."

They could have been turned around at any point but managed to bluff and cajole their way until the next-to-last checkpoint. It seems that the local leader would not meet with the group until the end of a long and drawn-out televised cricket match. "This could take days," Lack moaned. Finally, the match ended and the group was given papers that would supposedly get its members through the final roadblock. There they found a man for whom intimidation was his pleasure.

"After the niceties and after studying us," Rather wrote, "he spoke directly and to the point. The rough translation was: 'You lie, you die.'" That was followed by a lengthy interrogation in which Rather swore to God and Allah that the group members were who they said they were, and they were there to observe and report, not to spy or fight. With a wave of the man's hand, the group was cleared and finally entered Afghanistan. "We were told to pare down to only what was absolutely essential," Mike Edwards recalled. "We were given blankets that we could wear as shawls. You could also use them for camouflage when the helicopters came down low. We covered ourselves and lay in balls, which looked like rocks from the air. We just hoped they didn't have heat-seeking equipment, which apparently they didn't. The helicopters came very close to us, and that was scary."

The Afghans made a discovery about Edwards that truly shocked them. "They were horrified to find out I had blue eyes. The only people they had ever come across who had blue eyes were Russians. So they gave me a kind of makeup to make my eyes look as dark as they possibly could."

The group, now joined by about fourteen fighters, walked for days and days. They slept for short periods in safe houses, where Rather, Lack, and the crew could not bring themselves to eat the food that the local women cooked. They ate bread but only the insides, not the crust, since they had no idea where the hands that had touched the crust had been. They had brought along water purification tablets plus a flask of Kentucky bourbon that Rather often kept with him. The rest of their clothing had been left behind at one of the earlier checkpoints when they had been told to take only the essentials. Now, as they reached a mountain some ten thousand feet high, they were told they must pare down yet again.

Lack and the female interpreter who had accompanied them had to stay behind. If a battle started, there wouldn't be much for a producer to do, and even less for an interpreter to interpret. Soundman Peter O'Connor was also told to stay behind because Rather knew how to use the tiny audio recorders Edwards had brought with him.

Now it was just Rather, Edwards, Mirwaz, and the fourteen or so mujahedeen who would have to scale the mountain to get to the Soviets on the other side.

"We got to the top of the mountain about a half an hour before dusk, and we peeked over this ridge at the valley below and saw a bridge over a stream," Edwards told me. "Two tanks were parked there, obviously guarding the bridge, and there were some more vehicles farther away, but we couldn't make them out. The mujahedeen spread out all along the ridge, and I took that to mean they were going to attack once it became dark.

I set up my tripod and began filming, as Dan began giving a running commentary into the tape recorder. We had traveled so light that my little camera could only hold two-hundred-foot rolls of film, which is less than five minutes per roll. We had only brought ten cans with us, so, at best, we only had fifty minutes worth of film."

At some point, flares went up and the Soviets began firing rifles and machine guns. "The Afghans with us opened up with automatic weapons," Rather wrote in *The Camera Never Blinks Twice*. "Another flare and then another. The whole area, the ridge where we were, the tanks and their support below, was bathed in an eerie light. The Afghans fired one of their anti-tank rockets. Then another. Silence. Followed by a tremendous explosion near us. Artillery shell. Then another blast near us. Mortar."

Based on sound, it is impossible to guess where a mortar round will land and the explosions were now getting closer to their position on the ridge. "So we came off the ridge," Edwards said, "and were just lying close to the ground with no cover at all. Dan was as cool as ever. Obviously, he had been in Vietnam and knew what every sound represented. He just kept giving his commentary into the recorder."

Finally, the mujahedeen ordered a retreat, but getting all the way down that mountain in the dark proved far more difficult than their trip up in the daylight had been. "We stumbled and crashed down that mountain," Edwards said, "falling all the time, hitting rocks, but you had to just keep running."

As they reached the bottom, they found that they had to cross an open field of rice paddies before the Soviets came around the mountain and cut them off. They heard the rumbling of vehicles heading in their direction and began the slippery race through the paddies with only the silhouettes of their fleeing partners to guide them. At one point, Rather slipped and took a particularly nasty fall against a dike, injuring his testicles in the process. "I was doubled over in pain," Rather wrote, "and I thought I might faint. Mirwaz picked me up and said, 'Must keep running, must keep running.'"

Edwards came close to giving up as well. "I always thought I could keep running indefinitely if my life depended on it. But I couldn't. I had to stop and pause for breath. We kept running for what seemed like forever until we got to this stone house where it was safe."

When Edwards and Rather later rejoined O'Connor, Lack, and the interpreter, they learned that the most feared rebel leader of all, a legend named Younas Khalis, was fighting a little north of where Rather and Edwards had just been and had consented to an interview. That would mean yet another trek back down the dirt roads over the rice paddies and mountains, a prospect that seemed surreal to the exhausted team.

Rather felt that this was what he was living for. "This is why you paid the price all those years, standing in the rain with a microphone in your hand, covering dull city hall meetings; this is why you sold radio time, 'a dollar a holler,' to stay on the staff in Huntsville," he wrote in *The Camera Never Blinks Twice*. "This is why you took all that bull from newspaper city editors, nightshift wire-service supervisors, station managers, and sales directors. This is why you left a young wife home with your babies when you knew what a wrench it was. It was all to get to a place like this, at a moment such as this."

In debating the matter, Rather asked Andy Lack if he had ever read Cornelius Ryan's *A Bridge Too Far*. Lack admitted that he hadn't. It is the true story of one of the dumbest, most inept battle plans ever hatched by a military leader, Bernard Law Montgomery, the pride of the British Army. His plan, rammed down General Eisenhower's throat by Winston Churchill, was designed to seize the bridges in Holland, one by one, and cross over into the Ruhr, the industrial heart of Germany, thus bringing the war to an early end. The problem was that if the Allied forces failed to capture and hold a single bridge, particularly the final bridge in Arn-heim, the entire plan would collapse. It did, at the cost of eight thousand Allied dead.

"So?" Lack asked.

"Nothing," Rather replied. "Except the thought nags at me that *this*, this whole idea, just may be a bridge too far."

"If that means the better part of wisdom and valor is to take a pass, I say amen to that," Lack responded.

So they took a vote on it. The plan was voted down four to one. "It made little sense," Mike Edwards told me. "We just didn't have enough film left. Had we known we were going to get in, we would have brought more. But we had our story, and that was enough."

After the broadcast aired, Rather was no doubt surprised to read that Tom Shales of the *Post* dismissed the report as something of a stunt. Under a headline that read "Gunga Dan," a nickname that would forever after be linked to Rather, Shales wrote, "As usual, *60 Minutes* was effec-tively personalizing an otherwise abstract, distant story. But the report also smacked of showy one-upmanship and theatricality. Perhaps Barbara Walters is right now wondering how she'll look in a mufti or having a designer disguise prepared. Geraldo Rivera may be trying on caftans at this very moment."

Twenty-five years later, Shales has a more sober assessment. "I was probably too critical," he told me. "And I never gave him the name Gunga Dan; that was given to him by a headline writer named Reed Beddoe. I got asked about it so much that Reed finally said, 'It's quite all right. I bequeath it to you.' It's just too bad that the most quoted thing I ever said, I didn't say."

The Rather report would be one of the few times the American audi-ence got to see and hear from these Afghan fighters who would force the Soviet military from their land. Having had a taste in Vietnam of how massive firepower could fail when opposed by men who had a much bet-ter reason to fight than did their invaders, Rather knew that American intelligence was wrong, that in time, the Afghans would win and win decisively. What he didn't foresee was that these same fearless guerrillas, or at least many of them, would morph into a group known as the Taliban and morph yet again into another group known as Al Qaeda. The mujahedeen hated godless Westerners only slightly less than they hated the Russians. But for eight days, strange as it may seem today, it had been in their interest to keep the man soon to become America's most famous journalist from getting his head blown off.

5

Life without Walter

"Now what do we do?"
— Senator-Elect Bill McKay, *The Candidate*

Of anchoring, Dan Rather once told *Playboy* magazine, "It's one of those jobs where the harder you try, sometimes the worse you are. That runs counter to everything I've ever been taught. Always before, I had said to myself, 'You aren't doing the best you can; you simply have to try harder.' Now, with anchoring, it turns out the harder you try, the harder you are seen to be trying and the more uncomfortable that makes people."

That, in a concise quote, captures the fear that many people at CBS had about the possibility of Dan Rather one day becoming the anchorman of the *CBS Evening News*. Sure, he was a fearless and tireless reporter. But why would one put such a restless, intense, uptight presence in the anchor chair each night as the calming, reassuring voice of the nation's preeminent television news broadcast—while the Most Trusted Man in America, Walter Cronkite, was leaving?

By the early 1980s, the issue of Walter Cronkite's successor had been the subject of industry gossip for more than a decade, and it was a particularly touchy subject within CBS News. As early as 1973, then president Dick Salant was attending a company-wide management meeting and was asked point blank who would take over for Cronkite. Salant, who knew his own retirement date was six years away, simply pointed out that it would be someone else's problem. But then the questioner said, "Come on, Dick. What if Walter was hit by a truck?" Salant replied, "I'd sue the trucking company." The questioner wouldn't stop, though. Finally, Salant said, "Ed Asner," at which point another executive reminded Salant that this meeting was "all in the family" and whatever he said would not be repeated. Left with little choice, Salant said, "Roger Mudd."

Sure enough, that was the headline in the next day's *Variety*, and Salant believed that Rather never forgave him for it. It was an off-the-cuff answer to a hypothetical question, yet it triggered the usual controversy. Salant noted with some sarcasm that many of the same affiliates that were calling for Rather's head during the Watergate period later considered him their guy following his success on *60 Minutes* and later on the *Evening News*.

Salant had been right about one thing: the choice ended up being someone else's problem, and that someone turned out to be Vice President Bill Leonard. Contrary to all that has been written and said on the subject, Dan Rather was not Leonard's first choice. In fact, he was the third choice.

Moreover, Walter Cronkite was not "pushed out" to make room for a successor. Cronkite had tried to retire at least once before, in 1978. Executive producer Sandy Socolow, Cronkite's closest professional friend and confidant, remembered it well. "Walter wanted to retire years before because he was afraid that Bill Small was ruining CBS News." By then the executive vice president, Small was a brilliant newsman, but he had, as my late father used to say, "all the warmth of a five-watt bulb."

"Remember," Socolow told me, "Bill Small was the guy who bragged that he had ripped out the coffee machines at the CBS bureaus and saved like $70,000. So Walter felt as if he were standing on a pile of sand. He was very anxious to retire as number one, and he was afraid that if he hung around, that might not happen. So he went to Dick Salant and told him he wanted to retire." Salant, whose retirement date was already set, implored Cronkite to stay at least one more year. He did not want Cronkite leaving the anchor chair on his watch. "So, for whatever reason," Socolow recalled, "Walter backed off."

Bill Small, who was next in line to succeed Salant, said to me, "When I was there, I had a verbal agreement with Rather and Mudd that when Walter finally stepped down, we would have a dual anchor, with Rather in New York and Mudd in Washington. Mudd didn't want to leave Washington. And both of them were amicable about it."

Mudd strongly denied having ever made an agreement, verbal or written, to coanchor with Rather. But the issue became moot when, to almost everyone's surprise, Small was passed over and Bill Leonard was named interim president. That was effectively the end of Small's career at CBS, and he left shortly thereafter. It was understood that Leonard, who was nearing retirement age, would be a caretaker president until the company could find a younger man for the job.

On Leonard's second day in office, he had a visitor: Walter Cronkite. For the next year and beyond, Cronkite picked up where he had left off with Salant, hounding Leonard about giving up the nightly anchor duties for a much lighter load. Leonard continued a holding pattern, keeping Cronkite at bay while figuring out what to do. There was certainly no rush for the network to cash in its meal ticket. Much to Cronkite's credit, he corrected the misperception that he had been pushed out in his 1996 memoir, A Reporter's Life.

But the decision could not be put off forever. Leonard canvassed his inner circle of executives, some of whom voted for Roger Mudd and some for Dan Rather, whose contract would be coming up for renewal soon. "I must confess," said Socolow, "that I preferred Dan because with Mudd, it would have been chaos for non-news reasons. There were many things Roger refused to do. For example, when CBS celebrated the fiftieth anniversary of the network, its executives invited all the CBS stars from entertainment and news out to Hollywood. Roger wouldn't participate.

The anchorman is the public face of the network, and you have to do a lot of stuff that Cronkite willingly did—you had to work the rooms, glad-hand the affiliates—and Roger Mudd wouldn't do it. He wouldn't even do promos. So, with Roger, you could see yourself getting into a situation where every day would be a wrestling match about some non-news problem."

Although Mudd was peerless as a political reporter—he could get any committee chairman on the phone with one call and he was on a first-name basis with the leadership of both parties—at a certain level he believed that the universe existed inside the Washington beltway. He had little interest in foreign stories and he had an inexplicable disdain for any stories involving space, perhaps because Cronkite was such an enthusiastic booster of the U.S. space program.

Contrary to what Bill Leonard wrote in his book *In the Storm of the Eye*, his first choice was the dual anchorship of Roger Mudd and Charles Kuralt. "I'm telling you," said Sandy Socolow, "I'm willing to go to jail if I'm lying. His first choice was Mudd and Kuralt. And Mudd loved the idea. He was a great admirer of Kuralt. As for Kuralt," Socolow continued, laughing, "we now know he had a lot of other things on his mind besides having the dream job of all time."

In fact, Kuralt had a secret extended family out in Montana. After his death in 1997, court papers revealed that he had kept a mistress there for some twenty-nine years. He had supported her, put both her son and her daughter through college, and over the years had given her roughly half a million dollars, plus a cabin, land, and even a home in Ireland.

At the time that Leonard proffered the idea of pairing up with Mudd, Kuralt couldn't turn it down fast enough. He told Leonard he already had the best job in the world, his "On the Road" series, and he did not want to be tied to an anchor desk in New York or anyplace else.

Leonard then went to Plan B: another dual anchor, only this time with Mudd and Dan Rather. When Rather quickly agreed, Vice President Bud Benjamin was dispatched to have lunch with Mudd and get him to sign on. Benjamin didn't have to wait long—he didn't even have to wait for the food to arrive.

"I wouldn't do it," Mudd said quickly.

Benjamin asked, "Is that your final answer?"

"Yup," Mudd replied.

So now it was time for Plan C: a solo anchor, either Mudd or Rather.

Rather's agent, Richard Leibner, was urging his client not to sign a new contract until Leibner could test the waters at the other networks. In an interview in *Playboy* magazine in 1984, Rather described what Leibner told him: "He said 'There are people out there who are willing to pay you more money than you ever dreamed possible, and they'll let you write your own ticket. You describe what you want to do journalistically over the next five or six years, they'll write that into the contract.'"

The main person out there was Roone Arledge of ABC. He met with Rather at an Italian restaurant for what became a three-hour getting-to-know-you lunch. Arledge said he was so smitten with Rather that he was ready to write out a deal on the tablecloth giving him anything he wanted. The only problem was that Rather still had a year to go on his contract and he had no desire to order Leibner to find a loophole, a skill at which the agent was a master.

"Roone," Rather said, "I don't know whether to look at my watch or bark at the moon, I'm so tempted. But I'm from Texas. And in Texas a deal's a deal." Roone remembered thinking, Why couldn't he have been from Jersey? The two met from time to time in the months that followed, and reports of their huddles soon found their way into the gossip columns, no doubt planted there by Leibner.

Leonard confronted Rather about the stories, wanting to know why CBS wasn't being given the right to negotiate. Rather denied that he was negotiating with ABC, which technically he wasn't. But Leonard knew he had to get a move on and negotiations between CBS and Leibner began shortly thereafter.

Leibner wanted to keep Arledge in the game, if for no other reason than to scare CBS into offering much more than it wanted to. Arledge pulled out all the stops for Rather: anchoring or coanchoring *World News Tonight*, his own magazine show, his own handpicked producers, a seat and a vote at every meeting of the ABC News power structure, and most of all $2 million a year, which was twice what CBS had initially put on the table. Arledge even threw a lavish dinner party for Rather and Jean that was attended by all the ABC News brass. Arledge sensed that Leibner was urging Rather to take the ABC offer, and from the hug Arledge got from Jean Rather before leaving the party, he believed that she was on his side as well.

Rather and Jean had discussed his plans once before. When Rather was covering the civil rights story, a CBS executive offered Rather an anchor job on the *Morning News* at twice his salary. When Dan asked Jean what she thought, she replied, "You told me that when you went to work for CBS this was a career decision. This was a chance to do what you wanted to do with your life. Be a reporter. Now, you're talking about going to New York, for double the money, to read the news. Either this move is wrong, or else you are not what you said you wanted to be. Which is it?"

That exchange, of course, was long ago and far away, and the stakes in this game were infinitely higher. There was no question that Rather would end up anchoring a network evening news program somewhere.

Arledge, a master manipulator, had yet another card to play: Roger Mudd. Roone knew that Mudd was boiling mad about rumors that Rather would be offered the job Mudd felt was rightly his. And Arledge figured that his best tactic would be convincing Mudd to threaten to quit CBS if he didn't get the Cronkite chair; this might scuttle the Rather-CBS plan. He took Mudd to lunch. When Arledge asked Mudd whether he was interested in ABC if Rather won the CBS job, Mudd replied that he could never work for an organization that employed Geraldo Rivera and then he proceeded to harshly critique ABC News. Besides, Mudd added, he had no doubt that the Cronkite job would soon be his.

Producer Jim Houtrides, who worked for both Mudd and then Rather on the *Weekend News*, said, "I honestly believe that if Roger hadn't decided to give up the Saturday show because he didn't feel like coming to New York, Dan would have never gotten that job. I really believe that. Because Rather would have been blocked. It also didn't help Roger that he refused an assignment in Vietnam." In addition, Mudd had refused to attend the Paley-organized extravaganza in Los Angeles celebrating the network's fiftieth anniversary. "I'm a journalist," Mudd said, "not a celebrity."

Richard Threlkeld, who would soon leave for more money at ABC, believed that Mudd was overly confident at the very least. "There was a sense that Dan was more of a hardworking, rock-'em, sock-'em sort of guy. And Dan did an enormous sales job. He'd gotten to know virtually every station manager and owner in the country who were CBS affiliates and he had a number of them write to Paley and the others. Roger just assumed that the job would come to him because he was Roger, and he was avuncular like Cronkite. Roger just didn't work as hard as Dan." Mudd believed that politicking was for politicians, not for journalists. Lobbying, glad-handing, and doing lunch were demeaning. Besides, he felt that his years of service, especially as Cronkite's main substitute, had eliminated the need to sell himself or his abilities.

Variety TV critic Verne Gay saw it the same way. "I can't say what Roger would have ultimately done. But he wouldn't go to Vietnam. The last quarter of the century, these guys had to go on the road and do what they had to do and become symbols of their news divisions. It wasn't good enough to just sit in an anchor chair in Washington and then head home to Chevy Chase or wherever. Dan had itchy feet. He got up and he went."

By this time, Bill Leonard had concluded that either Mudd or Rather would most likely quit if the anchor chair was given to the other, and that losing Roger Mudd would be less serious than losing Dan Rather. Cronkite himself did not believe it was appropriate for him to weigh in on the issue. To him, this was purely a management decision. But he did admit to a colleague over lunch that he had once told management, "If you pick Mudd, there'll never be any foreign news on the air. Look what happens every time I take a vacation and Roger sits in. There's no foreign news in the show." But Cronkite said that this was the only comment he ever made about it.

While Cronkite and Mudd's relationship was cordial and professional, the chemistry between Mudd and Rather was strained, to say the least.

Correspondent Morton Dean recalled a preconvention meeting among the floor correspondents, a sit-around bull session that usually amounted to nothing since each reporter knew what his assignment was. "It was Dan and Roger, Mike Wallace, Harry Reasoner, and me," Dean recalled, "and Dan was leaning back in his chair with his chin tilted toward the ceiling and his hands in front of his face. He was just sort of clapping as he blew into his hands so that they made a popping sound. Roger elbowed me, pointed to Rather, tilted his head back, and began mimicking him. I mean, Dan just drove Roger nuts! And I always thought Roger wanted to be Dan Rather. He wanted to have the cachet Dan had, but he just didn't know how to do it."

Dean also recalled another preconvention tradition—lunch with chairman William Paley. There was usually a long table at which Mr. Paley sat at the head. Everyone, including Cronkite, Sevareid, and the rest of the elite team, could sit where they wanted. "So Dan plopped himself down to Paley's right. And way down at the other end of the table, staring directly at Paley, was Mudd." The group had recently completed a pilot for a proposed one-hour nightly newscast, and everyone was curious about Paley's reaction. Cronkite said that the hour could be redone with fresher news if Paley thought it would improve the pilot. "Then Dan popped in and said something about how important it was to be first among the networks in going to the hour. As Dan spoke, I looked over at Mudd and I thought he was going to go up in fucking smoke! He just couldn't bear Dan being so close to Paley and talking right after Walter. Then Paley said, 'I've always believed it is better to be the best than be the first.' And then he said, 'You know what we need? A Sunday morning news show, patterned after the Sunday Times Week in Review.' And I remember walking out of the meeting with Mike Wallace, and Mike said, 'Jesus! Can you fucking believe that? Paley's losing it! A Sunday morning news show?'"

Leonard decided on Rather. He had instructions to offer him $1 million, plus being sole anchor. Leonard knew from his sources, however, that the money pot would have to be more than just sweetened. Ultimately, he met with Leibner and laid out an astonishing proposal that would pay Rather $22 million over ten years and give him the sole anchor spot on the *Evening News*, plus the managing editor title that had been granted to Walter Cronkite years earlier. The latter might not have seemed like a big deal — it was really more of an honorary title — and during the Cronkite years it wasn't a big deal.

"Walter wanted the managing editor title because he didn't trust Don Hewitt's news judgment," recalled Sandy Socolow. "At that time, in the sixties, Hewitt was the boss of the *Evening News*, and Walter wanted to have veto power over Don. The managing editor title puts him over the executive producer if there are disputes about the lineup or choice of stories. But the veto power was never really used with Walter. Through all of his executive producers, including me, I can't think of a single occasion in which we were at loggerheads and Walter had to put his foot down and say, 'We're gonna do it my way.'"

Of course, with a different anchorman, an anchorman who might feel less secure than Cronkite, that power could be a paralyzing force. As longtime *Evening News* writer John Mosedale told me, "With Walter, you had a man who knew exactly what he wanted to do. The question 'What should we do?' was not part of his vocabulary. That wasn't always the case with Dan."

Now it was time to sell the deal to CBS president John Backe, who was the latest in a string of presidents hired and later fired by Chairman William Paley. Backe came out of CBS's publishing division and had something less than deep respect for television. Joining Leonard would be Gene Jankowski, the head of the CBS Broadcast Group and a man of boundless optimism. Of Jankowski, it once was said, "He could find something nice to say about a mushroom cloud." According to Leonard's account, Paley and Backe seemed annoyed at being called to an unscheduled meeting, not knowing that Leibner wanted an answer from CBS by 6 P.M. that evening.

Jankowski opened with a "We've-got-great-news" flourish. "We've kept Dan Rather!" Backe seemed underwhelmed; Paley seemed annoyed. "Why would anybody even think about leaving CBS News?" the chairman wondered.

"Money," Jankowski replied.

"Money?" Paley said. "We've got money. What's all this about?"

Jankowski then ran down the whole story of the ABC overtures and the long negotiations with Richard Leibner.

"What made us decide on Dan Rather?" Backe snapped. "I don't even trust Dan Rather. There's something about him."

Jankowski explained that Rather had become a very hot property over the past few years, arguably the hottest property in television news.

Paley then spoke up. "Gene, I thought you told me we could probably keep Rather if we paid him $1 million. Well, goddamm it, that's what you said."

Gently, Jankowski explained that they could hold Rather but that it would cost a good deal more. "What the hell does that mean?" Backe thundered. "What's a good deal more?"

When Jankowski revealed the numbers, Backe appeared to have a meltdown. "You made that deal?" he asked.

"Well, it's a handshake deal."

"Well, un-shake it! That's the most obscene, indecent, irresponsible thing I ever heard of. You have vastly exceeded your authority! Furthermore, and I'll say it again, you put Dan Rather up there, and people will see the same things I do, that he's just too happy to please, trying to be too much to too many people—not his own man!"

Jankowski pointed out that since Rather had joined *60 Minutes*, the ratings had gone up sharply.

"But what about the time he talked back to Nixon?" Backe shot back. "What that means is that if he's your anchorman, half the people in this country will hate him forever." While this was going on, Paley said nothing, but Jankowski gently slipped a piece of paper in front of the chairman. On the paper, it said, "1 pt = $5 million." In other words, a gain of a single rating point on the *Evening News* meant a profit to CBS of $5 million.

"Is this true, Gene?" the chairman asked.

"It is, Mr. Chairman."

Leonard said, "Gentlemen, we have a meeting with Rather's agent in one hour. And I need to tell him if we have a deal."

"I'm still dead set against it," said Backe. "We'd be making a terrible mistake."

Finally, Paley spoke very slowly. "It's been my experience in life that some of the cheapest things turn out to be the most expensive, and some of the most expensive things turn out in the long run to be the cheapest."

And with that, Daniel Irvin Rather became only the third anchorman in the history of the *CBS Evening News*. The deal was formalized on February 18, 1980.

Cronkite and Leonard had loosely agreed that the changeover would take place in November 1981, but they soon realized that Walter would be on vacation for most of the summer and into the early fall. It made little sense for him to come back for just a month or so and then leave. So they agreed on a new date: March 9.

On the evening of January 11, 1981, Dan Rather called a meeting of the entire editorial staff of the *Evening News*. What made this unusual was that (1) Rather was still two months away from succeeding Cronkite, (2) it was a Sunday night, and (3) the meeting would take place at Rather's apartment on Manhattan's East Side near Central Park. It was also the night of the AFC Championship football game between the Oakland Raiders and the San Diego Chargers. This had special meaning for me because there were big bucks involved. In an office pool organized by outgoing president Leonard, I had prize money riding on the Chargers.

The night of the meeting I left my place early so that I could at least watch the first half of the game at a bar around the corner from Rather's apartment. The half ended with the Chargers ahead but only by a few points. The rest was a nail-biter I didn't get to see.

Rather lived in a typical high-rise with a typically tiny elevator, seemingly built for dwarfs. Some twenty-five to thirty of us had to go up four at a time, like miners being hauled out of a pit. It was a cold night, and I was hoping the Rathers were serving brandy. Rather's wife, Jean, met us at the door and on the table were cookies and milk. Cookies and milk. No Chargers and no Raiders and no brandy. We sat on the couches and on all available chairs; some of us sat on the floor. Rather began with some innocent remarks about how we needed to retain the quality of the *Evening News* while moving it forward. He said, "Walter and I might wear the same suit jacket size, but that doesn't mean it will fit the same way." Fair enough, I thought. Next, he announced some personnel changes that we already knew about. Then his mood changed. It was almost as if some button had been pressed in his head; he became darker and somewhat threatening. Jean sat behind him on a stool with a smile frozen on her face.

One producer remembered Rather looking slowly around the room like a panning camera, staring at each of us in turn. "He said, 'Not everyone in this room voted for me [as if any of us had a vote in the first place] and if I find you out and you betray me, you're out!' It was very threatening. 'You're either with me or against me.' It was very Nixonian."

I remember that. I also remember him saying, "And if I go down, you're all going down with me."

"I was mystified," producer Richard Cohen told me, "totally mystified. Because there was no context that made any sense. I mean, we were there with open pores. We wanted to take in a new regime. We wanted to be on Dan's team. He was young and charismatic, and this moment revealed a great deal about what made him tick, how his mind works, how dark he can be. It revealed his paranoia. He saw us as Walter's people poised to sabotage him. He was obsessed with Cronkite and he couldn't figure out how he was supposed to be or how he was supposed to do it."

This was our first up-close-and-personal view of our new leader, and it was a study in contrasts: first the warm welcome, then the cold blast of reality.

One of his personal assistants told me, "He was the consummate player. He reminded me of the politicians of the fourteenth century. He knew where he wanted to go and was very Machiavellian about it. He was happy to manipulate other people's careers to whatever end he needed. He always had a game plan."

On the elevator ride down, I looked at another producer next to me and said, "This is not going to be easy." He simply stared at the floor and nodded.

The fact is that few of us cared who management picked to succeed Cronkite. Our jobs and responsibilities would remain the same. We would have to take our daily assignments and come up with stories of our own. We would have to use all of our skills to produce the best broadcast we could even if Groucho Marx were in the anchor chair.

It seemed that the pressure was getting to Rather. Perhaps the realization that within two months he would be replacing the Most Trusted Man in America had triggered this uncomfortable evening. Even Rather's own agent claimed that he had tried to talk Rather out of the deal. "There are rocks under the water," Leibner told him. "The first guy in after Cronkite gets his head blown off."

Given Rather's DNA, though, along with the challenge of pulling it off and the ghostly lure of his hero, Ed Murrow, his decision became obvious. Sure, the $22 million over ten years didn't hurt, but there is no doubt that Arledge would have topped that price had he been given the chance. The crown would soon be Rather's, but that night we could all see that it would not rest easily on his head.

I returned to the bar in time to see my Chargers fall to the Raiders.

B ill Leonard had done little in the way of transition planning. One camp believed that it was time to change everything—the set, the opening, the graphics, the entire look and feel of the broadcast. A second believed that any drastic changes, however cosmetic, would be too jarring to an audience used to seeing Walter in the chair in front of a burnt orange wall and this camp advised Leonard to do nothing except sit Dan in the chair and let him do the news. Aside from painting the walls a cool blue, that's pretty much all Leonard did. Getting Dan to sit in the chair was another matter. Rather wasn't sure whether he should sit down and do the news or stand up and do the news.

"He was being told too many things by too many people," writer John Mosedale told me. "I noticed early on in television that everyone has an opinion. I know he was being told to stand up and sit down, as if that would make some kind of difference. They had announced there were going to be all these big changes, but when the time came, nobody knew what changes to make." Rather compromised by sitting on a telephone book, which made his posture appear odd on the air.

"It's fair to say there was no shortage of advice," Rather recalled in *Playboy*. "Some of the criticism I got was genuine and was honestly believed by those who made it. Some was calculated by our competitors to throw me off stride. Fair enough. If I'd been in their shoes, I might have done the same thing. But I was never frightened and I didn't spend much time trying to sort it out. In the end, Cronkite and Sevareid gave me the best counsel. They told me, 'There's a limit to what you can do. Mostly, it takes time.'"

"I'll never forget the day he took over the anchor chair," correspondent Richard Wagner told me. "We bumped into each other in the cafeteria, and I said, 'Congratulations and best of luck' and all that. And he said, 'Richard, remember one thing: I want stories with victims.' Victims? So that's what I went out and did. A two-part piece on sweatshop laborers in the Bronx who were hanging over their sewing machines for eighteen hours a day. He said he wanted victims."

There was understandable tension during the first week Dan went on. As fate would have it, some technical glitches occurred in the first few broadcasts: the wrong slide came up, the audio dropped out momentarily from a piece, the technical director punched up the wrong camera — the kinds of mistakes that happen in live television. They always seem to come in bunches. You can go an entire month with nothing but clean broadcasts, and then for the next few days, it's glitch city.

Rather said nothing to the staff, but he was rumored to have complained to management that someone or some group was trying to sabotage him. "I remember the snafus," news editor Lee Townsend told me. "But Dan didn't talk to me about them. He was always very polite. He never threw copy back at you for a rewrite the way Walter did. Even when he got mad at you, he was polite. With Walter, I remember one night when we had a guy filling in whose writing Walter didn't like. And at one point during the commercial, Walter stood up and said, 'I demand a writer!' Dan bent over backward to make people on the staff feel they were doing a good job. I remember a case when a young desk assistant had to take copy over to the teleprompter. And on this one night, Dan rewrote something while we were on the air. The kid took the new page to the prompter, but the wrong page came up. And it threw Dan, naturally. This kid looked like he was just going to go out and kill himself. But at the end of the show, Dan told everyone to stay. And he said, 'I just want you all to know that this was not this young man's fault. It was mine.'"

While he was cordial to his staff, more than a few people noticed eccentricities that made them uneasy. Not only were the World's Greatest Books displayed on his office shelf, but a large open Bible was prominently propped on a lectern. It was the secret job of one of his assistants to turn the pages every few days so that it would appear to visitors that Rather had actually been reading it. And while his reputation as a tireless reporter in the field was well known, as an anchor his reputation was somewhat different.

"This was not what you would call a hard worker," said one of his several assistants. "He'd show up around two in the afternoon, go schmoozing all over the building, disappear for an hour or two, and come back in time for the news. Which I suppose is fine. It's fine unless you're also saying I'm this freakin' hard worker and I'm a really truthful guy and you can trust me. If you can't recognize the truth in yourself, how are you going to recognize it in the rest of the world?"

On the rare occasions when a print reporter was allowed to spend a day hanging around with Rather and the *Evening News*, the staff saw a different Rather, the managing editor, someone who showed up early for the morning conference call, who debated the lineup with the executive producer, who called bureaus near and far to quiz them on the day's events, and who even answered a ringing telephone. "News . . . Rather here," to which the startled caller usually responded, "*Who?*"

Although his supporters counseled patience while Rather struggled to find his groove, others were already writing him off. While walking down a hallway one afternoon, Rather passed an office and overheard an executive telling someone, "Rather's bombing. It's only a matter of time."

A producer with whom I shared an office seriously suggested that he and I go to management and insist that either Rather be replaced or we would leave when our contracts were up. I told him as politely as I could that I thought his idea was insane.

Rather was struggling, indeed, trying to find a hook, a style, something to set him apart, a schtick, a *persona*. "He was always looking for something and that betrayed a true insecurity in the guy," TV critic Verne Gay told me. "Walter's style came naturally to him. But with Dan you always got the feeling that he was the anchorman playing the anchorman, that it was never entirely sincere."

If showmanship was what Rather felt he needed, it would soon arrive in the form of a woolly bear of a man who made Rather believe he could make all his problems simply disappear. The transformation would be magical indeed.

6

Seduced and Abandoned

The price one pays for pursuing any calling is an intimate
knowledge of its ugly side.

       —James Baldwin, *Nobody Knows My Name*

With Bill Leonard halfway out the retirement door and most of
the remaining executives considered Cronkite loyalists, Dan
Rather was feeling somewhat adrift by the spring of 1981.
The ratings were fluctuating, predictably, as viewers began to sample the
NBC and ABC newscasts. At one point, *CBS Evening News* actually fin-
ished in third place for the week. The broadcast was still Walter
Cronkite's broadcast; the only difference was that now it was anchored by
Dan Rather.

As if the transition weren't difficult enough, the broadcast suffered the
loss of correspondents, producers, and directors to ABC News, where
Roone Arledge had been given a seemingly blank check to raid CBS even
if it meant overpaying for talent. Arledge may have lost out with Dan
Rather, but he thought he could beat CBS another way—by hiring
Rather's staff, grabbing everyone of note that NBC couldn't grab first.

Within a short span, CBS had lost Marvin and Bernard Kalb, Richard Threlkeld, Roger Mudd, and star producer Rick Kaplan, among several significant others. There had been an institutional reluctance on the part of CBS to become involved in bidding wars in the haughty belief that anyone who would want to leave the House of Murrow for something as trivial as money wasn't a true CBSer. But as the raids continued, management finally came its senses and began matching Roone's offers just to keep the people it had.

With the death of longtime anchor Frank Reynolds, Arledge dumped the unwatchable three-headed anchor newscast that he had stubbornly kept on since his arrival as ABC News president, and he chose Peter Jennings as his one and only anchor. Arledge also brought his unique, gifted production eye to the broadcast, making it seem more like the exciting future than the stodgy past.

Rather heard the talk in the hallways about how he was bombing, how the team wasn't pulling together, how the Mudd loyalists were snickering up their sleeves. There was nobody around to help, and the ship was taking on water.

The gossip columns determined that the field for the next CBS News president had been narrowed to two candidates: Van Gordon Sauter, then the network censor, and Edward Joyce, a veteran manager of CBS-owned local stations. Sauter had been a newspaper reporter in Detroit and Chicago, a radio reporter and a news director, a TV news director and a station manager, the Paris bureau chief for CBS News, and president of CBS Sports, despite his lifelong loathing of sports of any kind. Ed Joyce had been a widely respected radio reporter and executive and by happenstance became CBS News's lead reporter the night Ted Kennedy's car went off the bridge in Chappaquiddick. He had also been news director and general manager of CBS stations in New York, Chicago, and Los Angeles.

Joyce, a man of considerable intellect and cutting wit, was considered a topflight newsman and administrator who ran a very tight ship. At WCBS-TV in New York he was known as the Squire for his wardrobe befitting a country baron. He surrounded himself with a team of mostly lesser lights whose specialty was instilling fear in the staff as a motivational tool. The pressures of being number one in the nation's number-one television market created enough tension in the newsroom without the incessant criticisms from Joyce's posse. But the station remained at or near the top of the 6 P.M. and 11 P.M. ratings throughout Joyce's tenure, so, while his management style may have belied his cultured, sophisticated personality, it did get results.

On the other hand, Sauter had come to know Rather somewhat from his days of running CBS-owned stations. He had even bought a home in Connecticut near the Rathers. They spent time discussing why the *Evening News* seemed stuck in the 1960s, why it still felt like Cronkite's show without Cronkite. Sauter convinced Rather that this problem was the result of institutional failure and a rigid bias against change, and not due to whether Dan stood up, sat down, spoke more slowly or more quickly, or didn't smile enough when he signed off.

"Van wanted the job," Rather told Peter Boyer in *Who Killed CBS?* "He said so. It was Van at his best. He said I'd be good for you and for CBS, too." Sauter also made sure that he had the ear of Rather's agent, Richard Leibner.

Joyce, meanwhile, was considered the favorite of CBS Broadcast Group president Gene Jankowski and his deputy Tom Leahy. Although Joyce had spent years at network radio, he was an outsider to network TV. But Jankowski and Leahy were thought to believe that Joyce was just the kind of new blood CBS needed to control that unruly mob in the News Division.

Rather knew the decision had been pared down to the two men. "I was the general manager in New York," Joyce told me, " and I got a visit from Rather. And he said, 'I just want you to know I would support you as president of CBS News. I have to tell you Van would be my first choice, but I would support you.'" Joyce began laughing. "He was covering all the bases! It was vintage Rather. It was the same guy who called me and said, 'Ed, I need your guidance. I've been offered the anchor chair at ABC by Roone Arledge, but if they would give me the anchor chair here, I'd rather stay.' Now I wasn't born yesterday. He wanted me to do exactly what I wound up doing: calling Jankowski and saying, 'Do you really want to lose Rather?'"

Rather was at his political best in angling for Sauter, and Sauter, a political animal to the core, played his cards with equal expertise. Sauter wanted to move up in the company—all the way up. Rather wanted to remake all of CBS News, not just the *Evening News*, in his image. It was a marriage of convenience.

Management knew that picking Joyce alone would set off a revolt among the rank-and-file; after all, he was a guy from "local" and not one of them. Sauter had at least worked the network TV side. What appeared to be a compromise was reached: Sauter would get the presidency with Joyce as executive vice president. Sauter didn't see it quite that way. "They said the job was mine. But they knew Ed Joyce was a very effective executive, very well liked for his skills and the way he conducted himself. He was witty and well read and a guy I liked. But they knew that sending him in there alone would set off a shit storm. So, they decided that Sauter and Joyce would be more effective than Sauter alone."

The pair had practically nothing in common. Sauter looked like the proprietor of a centuries-old pub on a New England wharf, with his over-sized wool sweater, faded jeans, docker shoes, small, black-framed glasses that gave him an owlish look, and a grand, full-flowing beard. He was the anti-suit, and the press ate up the image that Sauter played to the hilt. He was also known to knock back a few with staffers after hours, something Ed Joyce would never do.

Sauter had a free-spending reputation as a manager, while Joyce was known for strict financial controls, accountability, and attention to detail. But they both agreed that the old guard, the Cronkite, Leonard, and Salant loyalists, had to go and that a new guard composed of those totally devoted to Rather and the *Evening News* had to take their place. Sauter had a myriad changes planned but he knew that to execute them, it would not be enough to simply convince Rather—he had to seduce him, make him feel that he was the center of the universe and believe that his needs and wants were the top priority at CBS News, regardless of whose toes might be stepped on and whose feathers ruffled.

"Then Van did that interview with *Esquire* in which he said, 'I intend to be married to Dan Rather,'" Joyce recalled. "Well, my jaw just dropped." So did jaws throughout CBS News. What Sauter meant was that he intended to give Rather more than cosmetic changes or words of encouragement. He intended to give him more power than any anchorman, including Walter Cronkite, had ever been given, power that went well beyond the *Evening News*. Dan Rather was about to *become* CBS News.

As part of his effort to remain married to Dan Rather, Sauter allowed the anchorman to take part in even the most minor decisions, regardless of whether they had anything to do with the *Evening News*. Rather had become more than just managing editor—"I gave him the title," Bill Leonard once lamented, "and I've regretted it ever since"—he had become a de facto member of upper management. With the exception of *60 Minutes*, which no one screwed around with, every new idea or personnel change, no matter how trivial, had to at least be passed through Rather.

"Dan was really the guy running *News*," said Bud Lamoreaux, who was executive producer of *Sunday Morning*. "Our show would have suffered more if we didn't have a pretty good working relationship with some people in the front office. Because Dan wanted everything for the *Evening News* and people like [executive producer] Howard Stringer allowed it to happen. Sauter, too."

Rather expected every correspondent's primary loyalty to be to the *Evening News*. One had to be ready to serve his show at a moment's notice, regardless of what other assignments might be pending for other broadcasts or what might be happening in one's personal life.

Correspondent Richard Wagner didn't fully grasp this unwritten rule until years after he had left CBS. "I was the resident South African CBS News correspondent and Nelson Mandela was about to be released. So in came Dan Rather and Bob Simon to do the main coverage. Hey, that was okay. I know what 'big footing' is about and I didn't mind it. But one day while waiting for something to happen, Dan and I were just sitting by ourselves and he said, 'Richard, what do want to do with your life? I mean, do you want to do this forever?'" Wagner had spent the previous two decades covering some of the worst hot spots in the world: Northern Ireland, El Salvador, Nicaragua, and two tours of Vietnam. He said, "You know, Dan, I've been to some amazing places and met some amazing people. And I've always wanted to be a creative writer. So I thought I might try turning some of my experiences into entertaining novels."

Rather didn't respond. But a few weeks after the anchorman left South Africa, Wagner received a stunning phone call from CBS News vice president Joe Peyronnin in New York. "He told me they're closing the South African bureau and they wanted me out of there tomorrow. I said tomorrow? Are you *kidding*? I've got a wife and dogs and a house. It'll take at least a few weeks." Peyronnin then told him that he was being sent back to New York but would not work on television—ever. In a state of shock, Wagner said, "Look, I've got two years on my contract. If you want to buy me out, if you don't want me, then just pay me." No, said Peyronnin. They would not buy him out. They wanted him back in New York but for radio only, mostly overnight radio. Wagner never appeared on television again and was never told why. "I guess telling Dan that I really wanted to be a novelist was a horrible mistake," Wagner said. "I sure didn't realize it at the time."

Walter Cronkite had also had plenty of power in his day, but he seldom used it. He rarely communicated with producers, writers, and correspondents about his likes and dislikes—which most veterans knew anyway—and he had no interest at all in micromanaging. Rather, on the other hand, once summoned a newly hired low-level correspondent who had given up his leased apartment and moved to New York to tell him that he might not get the job after all because Rather was displeased that he had not been informed of the hiring at the time.

"I remember Ernie Leiser complaining to me that he couldn't hire a copy boy in Chicago without Rather's approval," Sandy Socolow told me. "That was not the atmosphere under Cronkite. Cronkite didn't give a shit about anything but the *Evening News*. Rather effectively was running the News Division. I mean, Sauter wouldn't do a goddamn thing without Rather's okay."

Rather sat in on every weekly personnel meeting at which management discussed hiring or firing an associate producer, changing a bureau chief, moving an assistant director—rarely any issue that involved the *Evening News*. Rather wanted to know everything that was going on within the division. The weekly meetings became longer and longer as people around the table discussed, mainly for Rather's benefit, employees he rarely even knew. But if Rather did know the individual and he considered him or her to be one of "his guys," the debate would end there. Otherwise, the move in question would be tabled or discarded completely.

Although Rather said very little publicly about the changes occurring almost daily within CBS News, it was clear to his friends that he enjoyed having his own personal president, Sauter, a man who would sacrifice just about anything (except himself) to make Rather feel that he was steering the ship. The two became social friends, as did their wives, and they often spent weekends together. Rather compared Sauter to a surgeon while referring to the departed Bill Leonard as a hospital administrator.

When asked about the criticism that he needed to please and be loved by everyone, Rather told *Playboy*, "No. Which may be one reason why I'm not liked by everyone. I guess it's true that in my desire to get along I sometimes wonder how far I can go without risking compromising my principles. I do want to get along, to be liked by my bosses, by my colleagues. I think F. Scott Fitzgerald called it the American disease."

Thanks to the Sauter-Rather nexus, the anchorman's popularity among many of his peers was dropping rapidly. Cronkite loyalists were either being forced into retirement or given meaningless responsibilities, and correspondents perceived to be yesterday regardless of their age simply could not get on the *Evening News*. Bob Pierpoint, with whom Rather had had some skirmishes while in Washington, found himself on the B list.

Young reporters like Rita Flynn ended up there, too. Flynn had worked hard on a State Department story only to see the key elements of it folded into a report by a senior correspondent. Her mistake was complaining about it, and the complaint had gotten back to Rather. Joyce told her not to worry, that in six months it would all blow over and that in the meantime she could work for the *Morning News*. But six months later, Flynn emerged totally deflated from a meeting with Rather. "It was terrible," she told Joyce. "He's still angry. He called me arrogant. He'll never forget. I can't take this anymore. Would you please let me out of my contract?" Joyce obliged, and Flynn left for a job at the United Nations.

At the time, Pierpoint was the lead correspondent at the State Department and Flynn was number two. Now, neither of them could appear on the *Evening News*. A similar fate befell Martha Teichner, who was then in the London bureau. "Rather asked Martha what kind of stories she liked to cover," Joyce told me, "and she said, 'Well, the *Sunday Morning* kind of stories.' Boom! That was it for her. She wasn't going on the *Evening News*. I flew to London and talked to Martha and she said, 'I just want to show how good I am. But I never get assigned to cover wars.' So I came back and asked [Vice President] John Lane about it and he said, 'Well, maybe I'm old fashioned, but I don't think women should be assigned to cover combat.' Well, bingo. I sent Martha into combat and she did great."

When a suicide bomber crashed his truck into the U.S. Marine barracks in Beirut, killing more than 160, Morton Dean began preparing for his Sunday *Evening News* broadcast only to find out that Dan Rather had shown up and would be doing the show himself. "Well, that's just fucking obnoxious, that's what this is," Dean complained to executive John Lane. Years later, Dean told me that he'd had it out with Rather at a very unpleasant meeting. After Dean left, he bumped into John Lane, who said, "So how did it go with Rather?' And I said, 'You know, I don't really know Dan Rather.' Lane, who had known Dan forever, said, 'I haven't known Dan Rather for many, many years.'"

I reminded Sauter that Lane had once told him and Joyce, "Rather thinks you guys are the answer to all his problems. But you haven't seen his dark side, and I pray to God that you never will." Sauter scoffed at the quote, saying, "I don't know what a dark side is. Yes, he was ambitious, but I don't see that as dark. Does Don Hewitt have a dark side? Don Hewitt is one of the most ambitious, Machiavellian, manipulative people on the face of the earth! Do I think he has a dark side? No. He is what he is, a powerful person who wants to keep what he has and get more. Dan is an individual who came from a very simple background and he had to over-come a lot of impediments just to get traction at the base of the hill. He was incredibly ambitious, but that's not a pejorative. He was a superb journalist, but he was also Machiavellian. He was a politician, a very Machiavellian politician. A lot of other people in that business certainly were, too."

While Sauter viewed Rather's politically ambitious nature as a plus, others saw it as a continuing deception and believed that the self-effacing, courteous, just-thankful-to-be-here young Texan was really a master manipulator who, at his core, cared mainly about not only buttressing his power but widening it as much as he could regardless of the conse-quences. A staffer who had worked closely with Rather said, "The guy that Dan portrayed was a humble, generous, concerned patriarch who believed in God and the Bible and had a monogamous relationship and whose family was everything. His real life didn't reflect that at all. He certainly wasn't the person he was trying to project to the public."

The changes Sauter had in mind concerned not only who appeared on the *Evening News*, but what appeared. "The kind of thing we're look-ing for," Sauter told *Esquire*, "is something that evokes an emotional response. When I go back there to the fishbowl, I tell them goddammit, we need to touch people! They've got to feel a relationship with us. A lot of stories have an inherent drama, but others have to be done in a way that will bring out an emotional response."

Sure enough, touchy-feely features began creeping into the nightly lineup, especially stories in which someone wept on camera. The big hard-news stories were still covered the old-fashioned way, and on those, CBS usually bested its competitors. But "moment" pieces always got a gold star from Sauter and raspberries from veterans like Cronkite, who was a regular critic. "It's all sob sister stuff now," complained Cronkite. "Too many soft features. They're trying to lighten up the news, make it brighter. Perhaps they feel they can't cover everything and therefore don't even try."

What shocked nearly everyone at CBS News was that Rather, whom Tom Brokaw once sarcastically referred to as "Mr. Hard News" after Rather had obliquely referred to NBC as "News Light," was not only buying into

Sauter's "moments" directive but actually encouraging it. "It was really appalling to a lot of us," said a staffer who watched the format change. "It was really manipulative; we were really manipulating the news. Dan was, at best, very complex and, in my opinion, a really deceitful guy who worked very well with the idea of presenting news as though it was some sort of product with a wrapping on it rather than having a truthful social function. Dan had a lot of greatness in him, and it was very interesting to be around that greatness. But he was also a very duplicitous human being."

Washington news was sharply curtailed, much to the consternation of the bureau. Senate and House committee hearings almost never appeared unless there was some shouting match among the legislators. Foreign news took a hit as well unless it involved Americans in trouble in some faraway place.

Twenty years later, Sauter made no apologies. "They say I took the news soft?" he asked me. "Well, it kept winning awards as the best news show year after year. They can't have it both ways; they can't accept the awards and then say I took the news soft. Every year the *Washington Journalism Review* would vote Rather the best anchorman. My concern with moments, very simply, was that if you're going to do a story that has those attributes—and God knows we did a lot of them—you should tell that story in an evocative way. I mean, we're in the business of telling stories, and a lot of our people didn't understand storytelling."

As for the ratings, it was hard to argue with Sauter's formula. At one point in the mid-1980s, the CBS *Evening News* ran off a string of more than two hundred consecutive weeks as number one, and it stayed number one, with a few dips, for much of the decade. Sauter and Joyce followed Arledge's lead and brought a snappier new look to the *Evening News*, touching off a rather childish spat between ABC and CBS. "They've copied our whole format," whined an ABC executive, "and now they're doing more razzle-dazzle than we are." A CBS executive responded, "We did take some of what Roone did, but we refined it."

From all indications, Rather was quite pleased with the new format, especially since the *Evening News* was back on top. In an *Esquire* interview, Rather said, "Van wants stories that reach out and touch people. Every broadcast needs moments. When someone watches something and feels it and smells it and knows it, that's a moment. If a broadcast does not have at least two or three of those moments, it does not have it."

A typical example one afternoon was a lineup debate about which story would lead the broadcast: the Falklands War, the slaughter of Palestinian refugees in Beirut, or the birth of the Princess of Wales's baby. "We fought about it in the lineup meeting," Rather said, "but I decided we had to go with the royal baby on the back-fence principle. You imagine two neighbor ladies leaning over a back fence at the end of the day and you figure out which one of your stories they'd most want to know about. Well, you have to say today it's going to be what happened with the princess—did she have her baby?"

This was not the CBS News of Murrow, Salant, Collingwood, and Cronkite. On the subject of Cronkite, the unwritten rule was that the grand old man was simply not allowed to appear. Rather remarked in a 1984 *Playboy* interview that "He certainly has not been shunted aside, to the best I can judge. I think Walter is still in the process of figuring out how much time he wants to spend sailing, how much time at his place in Martha's Vineyard, and how much doing reporting. But this much is clear: Walter is welcome on the *Evening News* any time he has the time or the inclination to be here." The evidence, however, simply doesn't support this claim. The fact is that Dan Rather didn't want Walter Cronkite on the air and neither did Sauter. The page had been turned, they believed, the new chapter was being written, and there was no need to resurrect the past. The story they floated around was that Cronkite had been asked to participate from time to time but said he had been too busy with speaking engagements or other commitments. "The idea that Walter said he was too busy to participate is bullshit," Sandy Socolow snapped. "That's ex–post facto history to cover someone's ass."

The what-do-we-do-with-Walter problem became a thorn in the sides of Sauter and Joyce. For the 1982 midterm elections, the first national elections that Cronkite would not be anchoring in more than twenty-five years, it was decided to place him in CBS News's Washington bureau along with some pundits. The plan was for Rather, at election headquarters in New York, to occasionally throw it to Walter for some deep political chatter. What happened instead was that during the few times Rather switched to Cronkite, he cut Cronkite off to report some winners and losers. Cronkite, sitting in a room of distinguished guests with only a monitor to watch, was angry and humiliated.

For the 1984 conventions, Rather agreed to allow Cronkite to share a commentator's role with Bill Moyers, who in his on-again, off-again relationship with CBS News was at the time on again. The two were given a reasonable amount of airtime, but as far as Rather was concerned, that would be the end of it. For the 1984 elections, there would be no Walter Cronkite.

Joyce said that he attempted to convince Rather otherwise. "Walter could do a smaller version of what he did at the conventions," Joyce recalled in his book *Prime Times, Bad Times.* "There was something good about the sight of the two generations working together."

Rather was not buying it. "I think I gave a lot to Walter at the conventions," he said. "I brought him right into the anchor booth with me under the heading 'It's all right to test my good nature; just don't start abusing it.' Walter has had a lot of election nights. This one is Dan Rather's."

Joyce said to me, "What did Dan want? Just total control. That's all. And, after my time there, he solidified that control more and more."

Joyce recalled a bizarre event in October 1985 when Palestinian terrorists took over the cruise ship *Achille Lauro* with five hundred passengers on board. One of the tourists, sixty-nine-year-old Leon Klinghoffer, an American in a wheelchair, was murdered and his body dumped overboard. During CBS's coverage, Joyce received a phone call from CIA director William Casey, who had learned that CBS was intercepting radio messages between the terrorists and "an Arab state." CBS *was* monitoring the transmissions. But Casey warned that if the network reported this, it would cut any link U.S. intelligence had with the terrorists and whom they were working with and it could further threaten the lives of the passengers. Joyce said that he called Washington bureau chief Jack Smith and Pentagon correspondent David Martin and told them he could not justify reporting the information they had under the circumstances. Both men agreed, but Smith added, "Dan is determined to put it on."

Joyce said, "I went steaming down to the studio, it was just twenty minutes to air, and I said, 'Dan, this cannot go on the air, and it will not go on the air.' He threw a temper tantrum that was not to be believed. 'You cannot allow the government to dictate to us what we're going to do!' he shouted at me. I said, 'Dan, we'll talk about that tomorrow. But it is not going on the air.' And it did not." Joyce probably worked around Rather more than any CBS News president had, which no doubt accounted for his relatively short stay in the post. He told me, "When it was apparent that Dan and I were coming to the end of our string, Dan said to Bill Moyers, 'Don't you think the anchorman of the CBS Evening News could also be president of CBS news?' Bill said, 'No. We all need someone who can say no to us.' Bill told me, 'That did not get through to Dan at all.'"

The Dan as Diva atmosphere continued long after Sauter and Joyce had left.

"Howard Stringer was president after Sauter and Joyce," Sandy Socolow recalled, "and Gorbachev had taken over in the Soviet Union. At the time, the guy was considered the biggest threat to the United States. And Walter, who, of course, had been retired for a number of years, got a call from the Soviet legation in Washington, or maybe from their man at the UN. It seemed they'd had discussions in Moscow and decided that Gorbachev should explain himself to the American people so that they could get to know him. And they were offering Walter Cronkite an interview on CBS News. From the Soviets' point of view, CBS was still the preeminent news organization in the United States. And Walter—Jesus! This was the scoop of the year! So Walter called Stringer and said, 'Hey, I got Gorbachev! We can do an hour! We can excerpt it! We can do whatever!' So Stringer said, 'I'll get back to you.' And he called Cronkite back and said, 'Walter, I just can't do it.' The subtext was 'Rather won't let me.' So the Soviets turned to Brokaw and NBC and it was a tremendous scoop. And Dan Rather, Walter Cronkite, and Howard Stringer stayed at home and watched."

Rather had solidified his control. What remained unsettled in the post-Cronkite era was the shaky, ever-changing management of CBS at the very top, and a very shaky economy that led to falling advertising rates. This was compounded by an error made by the CBS sales department that resulted in a shortfall of some $100 million in projected earnings. In 1983, Gene Jankowski, on orders from CBS chairman Thomas Wyman, hired by the semiretired chairman emeritus William Paley with no broadcasting experience whatsoever, demanded a $12 million cut in the News Division's budget along with the elimination of sixty full-time jobs. The division had already taken a $7 million cut the previous spring. The *Washington Post* reported that Sauter and Joyce threatened to resign over the cuts, but in interviews with me neither man recalled ever threatening to resign over anything.

Somehow, Jankowski was convinced to drop his demands, settling instead for a request that Sauter and Joyce "do the best you can" to reduce costs. It would be the last time that corporate would back down on a budget cut. Rather, who attended the meeting, told Jankowski, "Know this: CBS News was with Gene Jankowski yesterday. CBS News is with Gene Jankowski today. And CBS News will be with Gene Jankowski tomorrow."

It was a nice sentiment but not quite original. Shortly before Ed Murrow's broadcast on Senator Joseph McCarthy, William Paley is said to have called Murrow and told him, "Ed, I was with you yesterday, I'm with you today, and I'll be with you tomorrow."

As for personnel, more than a few of the old guard, the so-called Cronkite loyalists, continued to be eliminated or exiled, including Ed Fouhy and later John Lane, whom Rather's agent Richard Leibner had accused of working to undermine his client. Sandy Socolow, who had been given the London bureau chief's job and was running a solid operation, also became a target. Joyce was hearing stories that Socolow had been badmouthing Rather and the *Evening News* and those stories were getting back to Dan.

"I flew over to London," Joyce recalled, "and I said, 'Sandy, you've got to stop this.' And he said, 'I'm not doing it!' But Howard Stringer had many Brit friends in the bureau and they'd call him and tell him what was going on."

"They were accusing me of being a government in exile," Socolow fumed. "And it was all bullshit. I think those guys made up those stories about me badmouthing them. They made up a lot of things. I think, for their own purposes, they needed another enemy. So they decided I would be the enemy."

In September 1983, Sauter was promoted to the newly created title of executive vice president, news and television stations, which gave him oversight of not only the News Division but of the programming of all five stations then owned by CBS. For Rather, this was a mixed blessing. On the plus side, his guy Sauter would still be overseeing the News Division but this time at the corporate level where he would have more power. On the downside, Rather would have to accept Ed Joyce as the new CBS News president and he would lose Howard Stringer as his executive producer because Joyce wanted Stringer as his new deputy.

The management changes turned out to be a disaster for everyone concerned. The News Division was angry because another layer of management had been placed between it and the top corporate management. Sauter quickly became disillusioned with being a corporate suit and actually mused to Ed Joyce about a comeback. The situation was bad for Joyce because everyone knew that although he was the nominal president, Sauter was still over him. And most important, Dan Rather was unhappy. He and Sauter truly had become married, spending much of their free time together trout fishing, a skill that Rather had taught Sauter. Joyce was perceived as aloof and remote, lacking the backslapping bluster of Van Gordon Sauter.

Once again, the complaints from Rather about not getting the best correspondents began making their way from the *Evening News* to Joyce's office. Joyce told me, "Rather came to me and said, 'You took Meredith Vieira away from us and put her on *West 57* [a snazzy new magazine show produced by Andy Lack]. So I went back and checked. Meredith had not appeared on the *Evening News* in six months! He would start an argument and then come around and say, 'You know, Ed, I'm hearing all this chatter about a quarrel between you and me and I know it's not true. How did all this get started?' And I'd say, 'Dan, I'm so glad to hear that.' I remember telling Lane Vernardos [who succeeded Stringer as executive producer] that Dan often said to me, 'No hard feelings, right?' Lane said, 'How come he never says that to us?'"

While watching a performance of *The Best Little Whorehouse in Texas*, Joyce suddenly laughed loudly during one of the songs, much to the embarrassment of his wife. "One line from a song particularly amused me," Joyce wrote in his book, *Prime Times, Bad Times*. "The line went 'I'm a poor boy come to greatness, so it follows I cannot tell a lie . . . oooo . . . I love to dance the little sidestep—now they see me, now they don't.' That was Dan Rather's song!"

Joyce's mortal sin was protesting the wildly out-of-control salary increases paid to a relative handful of CBS News stars, a situation that Joyce believed was seriously undermining the ability of CBS News to do its job. He said, "In order to pay these salaries, we were having to cut bureaus all over the world. Today's there's no real Moscow bureau. In Asia, you've got one guy based in Tokyo covering all of that. Domestic bureaus were closed. I remember presenting a chart—Jankowski and Wyman were there—showing them that if this trend continued, what the disastrous fallout would be. And they said, 'Don't let that happen.' But then they added, 'But don't lose this guy and don't lose that guy.'"

When Rather was asked in an interview why he didn't offer to take a pay cut so that more correspondents, crews, and the like could be hired, he replied, "Yeah, there's a logic to that. But I don't think it's ever going to happen. Look, it's like saying 'Let's not go to the moon. Let's take that money that we were going to use for that and let's build hospitals.' I'm a space buff, as you know, and I like the idea of going to the moon. But if someone could guarantee that the money used for the moon shot would go into hospitals for the poor, I'd say, 'Fine.' Now the next time around, and I hope God smiles and I'm lucky enough to have a next time, next time you bring me a contract that says instead of giving me a raise they'll raise the following ten correspondents' pay by X number of dollars, I'll buy into that in an instant."

In the spring of 1985, Ted Turner made a hostile bid to take over CBS. Turner's bold move came on the heels of a call to conservatives by Senator Jesse Helms to buy up CBS stock and "become Dan Rather's boss," after which Rather came to see Joyce and offered to give up the anchor chair if it would make everyone's life easier. Joyce laughed at the memory. "Yeah, right. And if I had said, 'Dan, I think that's a really good idea? This is the same Rather who had come to me and said, 'You're not my first choice but I can live with you.'"

No one on Wall Street took Helms's threat seriously, but Turner was another matter. The price would be huge, but with enough junk bonds, the Mouth of the South just might pull it off. CBS responded with a complicated poison pill plan to buy back 21 percent of its stock at the cost of more than $1 billion. A restructuring that would result in some $300 million in savings by mid-1986, under a plan approved by Chairman Thomas Wyman, would reduce about a third of that debt. The financially weakened company was badly in need of capital and of sharply reduced budgets. Contractual commitments to both talent and union personnel meant that savings could come only through firings and lots of them. Even as Laurence Tisch was busy buying up CBS stock, the hierarchy of CBS News was drawing up plans for the largest round of layoffs in the division's history.

At a meeting at CBS's headquarters, Jankowski outlined a liberal early-retirement plan that would add an additional ten years of service for employees over the age of fifty-five and thus significantly improve the payout. Still, the rumors about draconian cuts were already making the rounds at CBS when Sauter's wife threw a fiftieth birthday party for her husband at their home in Connecticut.

The invited guests were the Joyces, the Rathers, the Brokaws, and the Stringers. The Rathers arrived last, with Dan brushing by Brokaw and mumbling, 'Hi, Tom,' without even looking at him. When he finally realized that Joyce was standing there with his hand extended, Rather, according to Joyce, not only shook his hand but gave him a kiss on the cheek.

Apparently, it was the same kiss Michael Corleone gave his brother on New Year's Eve in Havana. Joyce learned that after he and his wife had left, Rather and Sauter began discussing how to remove Joyce from the presidency and bring Van back.

"Yeah, it hurt," Joyce told me. "I mean, it was not written in the stars that I had to stay. But the way it was done — it was backstabbing, plain and simple."

"Oh, that's bullshit," Sauter said. "First of all, I think I had too much wine at that party to get involved in that kind of thing. Dan was never part of those conversations. Dan's a very smart man. He would never say, for instance, 'Van, we really want you back here and we want Ed out.' He's too smart for that. What he would do is send Leibner over to have lunch. And we would begin by discussing some associate producer in Miami or somebody at NBC who wanted to come to CBS. And then in the middle of the conversation, he would say, 'You know, Dan really misses you. Dan was so much more comfortable with you than with Ed. You know, Dan's the last guy to complain, but he's really unhappy.' That's how that would work. The fact is there were a lot of people who were unhappy with Ed Joyce, who didn't like the way he was running the place, who just didn't like him period."

When I relayed that remark to Morley Safer of 60 Minutes, he threw back his head and roared. "Didn't like him! Yeah, guess why they didn't like him? Because Sauter made him his hatchet man! He made Ed do all his dirty work!"

The dirty work included the announcement on September 19, 1985, of the elimination of 125 jobs in the News Division, a 10 percent reduction in the workforce. A month later, Don Hewitt, whose 60 Minutes staff had barely been touched, approached Jankowski with an outlandish grandstand play. Hewitt claimed that he had put together a consortium that included Dan Rather, Mike Wallace, Morley Safer, Diane Sawyer, and unnamed but deep-pocketed associates who had enough money to buy CBS News, if CBS was willing to sell. Jankowski told Hewitt that CBS News was not for sale, but the publicity from the stunt sent a message to corporate that the natives, especially the star natives, were upset with the people running the News Division.

Although Hewitt swore that getting rid of Joyce was not his intention, that was the net effect. In early December, Joyce was fired, offered a temporary no-show job, and replaced by Van Gordon Sauter. Although many people at CBS saw Rather's fingerprints all over this coup, Rather told the *New York Times*, "That is absolutely, unequivocally untrue. If any of this is being raised as an assault on him or that I have some responsibility in that, my response is absolutely no, it's not true."

Then Laurence Tisch slam-dunked Thomas Wyman and took control of CBS. The day after he took over, Tisch fired Sauter and replaced him with Howard Stringer.

What reason was Sauter given for his firing? "None," he told me. "I had supported Wyman because he had a real grasp of the issues facing the industry. He saw the changes coming in the new communications environment. He understood the concept that you couldn't run a network news division unless you had a cable outlet to lay off your costs. Tisch didn't understand any of it."

Others saw Rather's hand at work once again. He and Sauter had had an enormous shouting match over Sauter's decision to abandon the always-last *Morning News* and turn it over to the Entertainment Division. Publicly, both men said they agreed to disagree.

Now CBS, the creation of William S. Paley, was firmly in the control of Laurence Tisch. There was dancing in the aisles at CBS News. Ding dong, the witches were dead. Don Hewitt was shamelessly effusive in his praise of the new chairman. Now here, he told everyone who would listen, is a man we can do business with.

It was a foolish and naive game the CBS newsies played with Tisch. They were, after all, reporters. Weren't they aware of Tisch's reputation for slash-and-burn cost cutting? Had they all bought into Tisch's honeymoon vows to be "a friend to news"? He said he wouldn't cut the news budget and he did. He said he wouldn't sell the Magazine Division and he did. He said he wouldn't sell CBS Records and he did. Rather felt personally betrayed, but he decided to proceed with caution.

"Larry Tisch looks to me like a good man to ride the river with," Rather told the *Chicago Tribune*. "I like the look in his eye and the warmth of his handshake and what he says about news. My job is to get off the truck every morning and go to work. I don't go looking for the boss, but if he wants to talk to me he knows where to find me."

When Tisch demanded a $50 million cut in the news budget, Stringer, Rather, and others came up with a $36 million plan that was mostly smoke and mirrors. Part of the scheme consisted of throwing the editors of all the broadcasts into a common pool to save overtime costs; the plan was so impractical and unworkable that it was quietly abandoned not long after it began. Yet everyone seemed so ecstatic to be rid of Wyman, Joyce, and Sauter that they failed to see the greater threat just around the corner. The underlying problems remained. There was still a sizable debt to be paid down, and the sound of oncoming trains was getting louder: ABC and NBC were moving up and gaining momentum and CNN had become something more than an industry joke. But it would be all right, they thought then. They still had 60 Minutes — and they still had Dan Rather in the anchor chair.

At this point, the Evening News was on top and climbing. The Rather-Sauter-Joyce trio had disrupted a lot of lives and had helped to end the careers of more than a few people. It had forced an entrenched bureaucracy to change, some would say for the better, others for the worse.

But for the first time in just about anyone's memory, the man at the center of the whirlwind seemed at ease, even at times content. "Hey, man," Rather told an interviewer, "this is fine, ain't it?"

Edward R. Murrow, groundbreaking broadcast journalist and hero to the young Dan Rather, in London in 1941.

CBS founder William Paley, at left, and CBS president Frank Stanton on the set of the Kennedy-Nixon debates in September 1960.

Rather at the beginning of his career as a reporter at KTRH radio in Houston around 1955. He also worked for the *Houston Chronicle*, the newspaper that owned the station.

Producer Bernie Birnbaum, at left, with Rather in Dallas for the Kennedy assassination report.

Rather questioning President Richard Nixon at Nixon's first White House news conference on January 27, 1969.

Lieutenant George W. Bush
of the Texas Air National
Guard in 1971.

Rather in Afghan garb for his *60 Minutes*
report on the Soviet invasion of Afghanistan
in 1979. Some called him Gunga Dan.

FEBRUARY 2, 1980 $1.25

Dan Rather

THE
$8,000,000
MAN
TV'S NEWS EXPLOSION

Rather on the cover of *Time* magazine on February 2, 1980. Rather's contract was actually
$22 million over ten years, a record then but low compared to anchor salaries now.

Roone Arledge, who offered Rather a virtual blank check to defect to ABC News in 1980. Rather declined, but Arledge eventually drove ABC News to number one anyway.

The command center of *CBS Evening News*, known as the fishbowl, in the early 1980s. From left to right, senior producers Mark Harrington and David Bucksbaum, executive producer Sandy Socolow, Dan Rather, news editor Lee Townsend, and writer Sandy Polster.

I'm on the right, Rather's at the left, around 1981.

CBS News national correspondent and weekend news anchorman Roger Mudd in May 1982. On the day Rather was announced as the successor to Walter Cronkite, Mudd left the CBS News Washington bureau and never returned. He's shown here anchoring at NBC News.

The three CBS News anchormen—from left, Walter Cronkite, Douglas Edwards, and Dan Rather—joined by executive producer Sandy Socolow, at the right.

Rather in the CBS News anchor chair in 1988.

Mike Wallace celebrating his seventieth birthday in 1989. He finally announced his retirement as *60 Minutes* correspondent in spring 2006.

60 Minutes' longtime correspondent Morley Safer.

Dan Rather and Connie Chung as coanchors in 1993. When the experiment failed, Chung accused Rather of having undermined her, a charge he denied.

CBS CEO Laurence Tisch, whose deep and frequent budget cuts contributed to the decline of CBS News in the early 1990s.

Rather with Fidel Castro in Cuba in 1996.

CBS News president Andrew Heyward and Rather at a news conference in 2001. Rather says he asked Heyward personally to oversee the controversial Memogate report in 2004, but an independent investigation concluded Heyward largely delegated responsibility to subordinates.

Dan Rather and his wife, Jean, attending a movie premiere in 2000. The fellow Texans have been married since 1957.

Typical of the political cartoons post-Memogate, this one appeared in the *Detroit Daily News* and the *Investors Business Daily* as well as on numerous blogs.

Dan Rather and U.S. defense secretary Donald Rumsfeld in Baghdad in September 2003. Rumsfeld was said to have leaked stories to Rather in the 1970s. The two men have been friends for more than thirty years.

Producer Larry Doyle and Dan Rather in Baghdad in 2003. Rather scored exclusive interviews with Saddam Hussein both before the Gulf War in 1991 and before the U.S.-led invasion in 2003.

On January 3, 2006, CBS Corp. begins trading on the New York Stock Exchange as a separate company split off from its parent company, Viacom. From left: Paula Redstone, CBS CEO Les Moonves, Viacom and CBS chairman Sumner Redstone, NYSE CEO John Thain, and Viacom president and CEO Tom Freston.

Tom Brokaw and Dan Rather at the 57th Annual Emmy Awards in September 2005. The image of Peter Jennings, who had recently died of cancer, is on the screen. The three men were honored for their decades of work as anchormen and reporters for the three major TV networks.

7

What Is the Frequency?

I'm really a timid person. I was beaten up by Quakers.

—Woody Allen

T he question of who was really running CBS News became especially important whenever Dan Rather took to the field. Typically, when a producer and a correspondent are on the road, the producer represents management even if the correspondent happens to be a star earning ten times what the producer makes. If the two cannot agree on a particular issue or plan of action, the appropriate next step is a phone call to a bureau chief or an executive producer who will hear both arguments and make the decision.

Dan Rather wasn't just a star; he was not only the *Evening News* anchor and managing editor but thanks to Van Gordon Sauter he had become a member of management as well. This would prove to be a difficult and dangerous mixture, especially given Rather's personality. While he was known to be cool under fire, his temper could flare at any moment, especially when he felt challenged by authority of any stripe. To use his cowboy phrase, he did not "back up or back down" and was "impossible to herd."

On September 11, 1987, *CBS Evening News* was originating from Miami, as were the other networks, to cover the visit of Pope John Paul II. It had already been a tough year for Rather and CBS News. That spring the new administration of Laurence Tisch announced the layoff of 215 News Division employees, the largest cutback in the division's history. Obviously, news personnel felt betrayed; their white knight had turned out to be Blackbeard the Pirate. CBS News president Howard Stringer was particularly upset by a quote in the *New York Times* in which Tisch said, "I never said to Howard, 'We have to cut the budget at the news division.'" So did Stringer simply awake one morning and decide to do it himself? Elsewhere in the *Times*, an op-ed column appeared titled "From Murrow to Mediocrity?" in which the author wrote that the cutbacks "mean a product that may inevitably fall short of the quality and vision it once possessed. . . . the news division could be profitable, but anyone who says it *must* make money is misguided and irresponsible."

The column carried Dan Rather's byline, but everyone at CBS knew it had been written by producer Richard Cohen. He and Rather believed that it would have more impact if it carried Rather's name. To add even more corporate grief, CBS news writers were on strike, and Rather briefly joined the picket line. "I want people to know I care," Rather told reporters. "I care about every person who works at CBS News." But some people within CBS saw the column as another grandstand move by Rather. "'From Murrow to Mediocrity' made me puke," said Don Hewitt. "That's a scale, right? Murrow to mediocrity? Put Dan Rather on that scale."

An editorial in the *Arkansas Democrat* referred to Rather's ghost-written piece as "self-serving, breast beating, whining. Nowhere in his column did Rather point out that he makes more in a year than Ed Murrow made in a lifetime of service to CBS. Nowhere does Rather admit that, according to *Newsweek* magazine, the TV news divisions are guilty of such costly practices as flying an anchorman's favorite shoeshine man from coast to coast to comfort the news reader during an assignment."

Walter Cronkite was so angry, he threatened to resign from the CBS board of directors. Instead he had Tisch convene a board meeting at which for more than two hours Cronkite vented about the cuts. "My God," he said, "you can go by any fire station in town and see these guys playing checkers and say, 'Why do I have to pay ten guys to play checkers?' But when a fire comes, you'll wish you had thirty out there, not ten. This is journalism. It's not a production line. It doesn't work that way."

The ratings made matters worse. By the summer of 1987, *CBS Evening News* had dropped to third place, due in part to aggressive counterprogramming with game shows and other entertainment fare against the network news broadcasts. There was a 6:30 feed of the broadcast, which some stations picked up, but in New York, the number-one market, the *Evening News* was still seen at 7 P.M. Many ABC stations had already made the switch to 6:30, which meant that Rather was now competing against shows such as *Wheel of Fortune*. In Cleveland, CBS station WJW had been doing just fine with its local news followed by Rather's network news at 7 P.M. Then ABC station WEWS, which had been a ratings loser, bought *Wheel* and put it on following the ABC network news and directly against Rather. The result was dramatic. "Now Rather's getting his clock cleaned," said a station executive. "We're really getting our brains beat out." Of course, *Wheel* did help at those CBS affiliates that had bought it, but the example served only to underscore that no matter how diligently and aggressively network news shows produce their product, they are often at the mercy of factors beyond their control. CBS's only hope at the time was that the A. C. Nielsen company, which supplies the television ratings, was about to switch to a new system called "people meters," a system whose sampling of viewers was expected to strongly favor CBS's older viewing audience, which it eventually did.

In August, at the urging of his bosses, Rather agreed to significantly alter his on-camera delivery, slowing it down and making it less intense. The *Washington Post*'s Tom Shales wrote that Rather appeared to be on Valium. The experiment lasted only a week.

Said Rather, "I keep hearing that we should be laid-back, homogenized, 'yuppie-fied' because that's the fashion of the '80s. I'm not sure I know what that means. I don't know how to do that well, and I'm not sure

I want to." Across the board, CBS was a mess. Its morning show, which the outgoing president Van Gordon Sauter had turned over to the Entertainment Division, was still running a distant third. Moreover, the CBS owned-and-operated stations in all the major markets, which serve as a lead-in to the *Evening News*, were also lagging behind their competition.

Rumors began to circulate that Diane Sawyer, then at *60 Minutes*, would either replace Rather or be asked to coanchor. Responding to this, Rather said, "I'll do whatever is best for the broadcast."

So no one was in a particularly good mood in Miami that September afternoon as the *Evening News* prepared to go head to head with NBC and ABC on the papal visit. A scheduled mass by the pontiff had been canceled because of thunderstorms in the area.

Back in New York, Don Decesare, then vice president for news coverage, began to feel uneasy when the clock showed 6:20 EDT. The first feed of the broadcast to many stations was just ten minutes away. CBS was still showing a U.S. Open tennis match, a live semifinal with American Lori McNeil against the great Steffi Graf.

"I don't know much about tennis," Decesare told me, "but someone poked his head in my office and said, 'This thing looks like it may run long.'" Decesare warned the fishbowl of the possible runover and then called CBS Sports and got its executives to agree to get off the air and throw it to CBS News as soon as the match point was made.

Down at CBS affiliate WTVJ in Miami, in a makeshift control room with just a monitor showing the small set that had been constructed for Rather, director Richie Mutschler was beginning to sweat as well. "It was about 6:22, or 6:23, and one of the suits, I don't remember who, said, 'I think we might have a problem here.'"

In New York, Decesare could now see the line monitor, the feed from Miami. Rather was sitting in his chair, and he was not a happy camper. Decesare said, "So I called down to Miami and asked the bureau chief, John Harris, 'Who do you have down there other than Dan?' And he said, 'I've got Richard Roth in the bureau.' I said, 'Do not let him out of the building.'"

Back to Miami and Richie Mutschler. "It's like 6:27 and I look at the preview monitor and there's no Dan! I tell New York, 'Don't come to me! *Do not come to me! I do not have an anchor!*'"

In New York, Decesare asked Harris, "Where the hell did Dan go?" He was told that Rather had walked down the hall to call News Division president Howard Stringer. "So now," Decesare told me, "now I *want* the tennis to run over. I said to Harris, 'Get Roth into makeup and put him in that chair.' So they put Richard in the chair, looking ridiculously uncomfortable, and I don't know what he was thinking."

Roth, for his part, has no recollection of being put into makeup and then into the anchor chair. "What I remember is they asked Bernie Goldberg to do it, and he said, 'Not while Dan Rather's in the building.' And then they asked me to do it, and I said, 'Not while Bernie Goldberg's in the building.'"

In any event, the show was to begin with a four-minute wrap-up of the pope's day, and there was also a two-minute commercial block ready to end the first section. In other words, even if no one was in the anchor chair, someone could have ordered the first piece to roll—this is called a "cold open"—and then gone to commercial. That would have bought six minutes to get the anchor or someone with a pulse into the anchor chair.

Mutschler said, "I couldn't have rolled anything if I had wanted to. We had taped everything and they assembled it in New York. I'm the remote; I really couldn't do anything." Producer Lucy Spiegel had put together the taped opening of the broadcast and had fed it to New York at about 6:27. She went next door to get a soda out of the refrigerator, then looked up at the clock on the wall. "It said about 6:29 or something, but that clock had been running a little fast all day. I reached into the refrigerator to get a Coke and I heard a voice behind me say, 'As long as you're in there, Lucy, could you get me one, too?' And I turned around and it was Dan! I said, 'Jeez,' and I glanced at the clock. I thought either they were running a long taped piece or everything was running late because of tennis. So I handed him the Coke and we just stood there, chitchatting! And then Bettag came in."

Tom Bettag was not only the broadcast's executive producer but one of Rather's closest friends and allies. "Dan had his jacket off, slung over his shoulder," Spiegel continued. "He put his foot up on something and was just sipping the Coke while I heard Bettag pleading with him. I walked out of the room and down to the studio/control room. And it was just bedlam. Absolute bedlam. Bernie Goldberg had his little kid Brian in there, and Richie Mutschler was screaming, 'Don't fucking come to me, New York! I don't have anyone to put in the fucking chair!' And the little kid said, 'I can sit in the chair.' And Richie screamed, 'Get this fucking kid out of here!' Of course, the kid burst into tears."

In New York, Decesare said that he told the fishbowl (the command center of CBS Evening News), "'I don't know where Dan is, but you can go on the air with Roth.' And they looked at me like I was a jerk. So instead we went to black. In other words, they purposely went dark. The network had options to go on the air and they didn't."

The match ended at 6:32 and as promised, CBS Sports threw the air over to CBS News. What followed on stations across the country was more than six minutes of dead air, an unprecedented event in television history. Within seconds, the phones at CBS in New York were ringing off the hook from angry station managers. "The only time I remember that happening," Decesare told me, "was when we chose not to lead the Evening News with the death of Elvis." No wonder—Roger Mudd was anchoring that night.

Rather's account in The Camera Never Blinks Twice differs from those of his colleagues. "We were in Miami," Rather wrote, "on the verge of breaking through and winning the week in the ratings with an important story, and the network was going to let tennis take precedence over the pope's coming to America?" Rather insisted that he'd made it clear that if the match ran over by even a minute, CBS Sports should not get out immediately but it should fill in until CBS News had a chance to regroup and figure out what to do. Rather said that he and Bettag were on the phone to Howard Stringer when Bettag heard Mutschler tell him, "The network is in black."

"You mean, they're in commercial," Bettag said.

"No, the tennis is over. The network is in black."

"They may have made some phone call at some point," Spiegel told me, "but they sure weren't on the phone when they were standing right in front of me talking. I could see faces pressed up against the window of the bureau—people were wondering what the hell was going on."

Six minutes later, Rather was back in the anchor chair. Monumental damage had been done. CBS searched around for something to tell the press. Rather was told not to say anything, an order he bristled at but obeyed. Sure enough, the bulk of the blame was placed squarely on him, and Rather resented it.

"Maybe I deserved it," he wrote. "But I certainly didn't deserve all that I was getting. My silence hadn't helped. I was in trouble now, deep trouble, and hurting. Nothing hurt more than the constant reminders that some people I had trusted were talking and were saying a lot of damaging things, untrue things on a 'don't use my name' basis." Fortunately for Rather and everyone else involved, Larry Tisch didn't think it was much of a big deal. He issued a statement to the effect that "mistakes were made and we shouldn't let them happen again."

What is curious about Rather's account is that on the one hand, he attributed the disaster to an honest confusion about who was supposed to take the air and when. But then he remarked, "I fault myself for failing to make the point that there was a matter of principle involved. . . . Within the company, there was a growing argument that Sports should take precedence over News. I don't think, and never will think, that this should be the case." So did he leave the set because there was confusion, or did he leave the set to make a point to his superiors?

John Harris, the Miami bureau chief at the time, vividly recalled what happened after the fiasco. "After the second show went off at 7:30, Rather and Bettag were on the phone for quite some time. And around 8:30, Bettag came into my office. He had his shoulder bag and was heading for the airport. He said, 'Well, we really stood up to Sports.' His and Dan's position, apparently, was that if Sports ran over by just a minute, News would not do a shorter show, which was contrary to the agreement we had with Sports. Then he said, 'And if anybody asks, tell them we're proud of what we've done—that we stood up to the Sports Division.' Well, I was appalled, just looking at WTVJ having to put up a slide after so much black and knowing that maybe a hundred other stations had to do the same thing. But Bettag was boasting about what they had done."

Harris told me that over the weekend, Bettag's story changed again. "On the Monday morning conference call, Bettag cooked up another story. He now blamed everything on WTVJ, claiming they had cut off their signal because they didn't realize that Sports had gone off, which was a completely preposterous story. Then he asked me to endorse it, and I declined as politely as I could, saying, 'Yeah, whatever you say, Tom.'"

In any case, Walter Cronkite publicly opined that Rather should be fired. "There's no excuse for it," Cronkite said during an interview with the student newspaper the *Daily Texan*. "The rationale that he was standing up for a principle in journalism, that you don't let anything impinge upon the time that news is allotted on the network, doesn't hold any water whatsoever."

Responding in the *Washington Post*, Rather allowed his frustration with Cronkite's periodic criticism to show for the first time, sounding like a son who could not gain his father's approval. "Walter's a great journalist, a justified living legend, and naturally I'd always like to do things of which he approves. It turns out that no matter how hard I try, it just isn't possible. I like him. I hope he likes me."

On the *Tonight Show*, Johnny Carson joked that the six minutes were "CBS's highest ratings of the year. The network has just signed the black screen for thirteen weeks!"

The *Times of London*, in a dispatch from Los Angeles, asked the question, "Is Dan Rather, bishop of the nation's news business, losing his marbles?" The article went on to recount recent bizarre incidents and speculated that "Mr. Rather has been going a little dotty."

In Hong Kong, Larry Doyle was amazed to find the story on the front page of the *South China Morning Post*. "'My God,' I said. 'It's reached that proportion way out here?'"

Most CBS staffers who were not present in Miami could not understand what had happened, why it had happened, and why it had gone on for so long. They knew Rather was intense and competitive in the extreme, but this was inexplicable. "Tom Bettag should have never allowed that," Phil Jones said to me. "Bettag runs around, and I like Tom, but he runs around scot-free. And now he's a legend and he's Ted Koppel's guy. Give me a break!" Jones then rattled off the names of previous executive producers who were in fact legends in their time. "Tom's good and he's smart, but he's weak in some of these areas. He and his people were intimidated by Dan. None of Bettag's predecessors would have allowed it."

Producer Harry Moses told me about another incident in which Rather, out in the field, would not back up or back down. Moses and Rather were in a French village trying to film a scene in an apartment where some nefarious deed had been done. Rather and Moses tried to enter the apartment, but the tenant adamantly refused to let them. So they decided that the next best thing was to have Rather walk down the block, describing the events leading up to the incident, and at the moment he got to the punch line, the camera would tilt up, aim at the window, and zoom in. Fine enough, except that every time they tried this maneuver and the camera tilted up, the tenant was standing in the window with his thumbs in his ears, wiggling his fingers and sticking out his tongue. After three or four takes, the sun cooperated by casting a shadow across the window. The mocking clown was still there, but now he couldn't be seen. Satisfied that they had finally gotten their shot, the crew began packing up when the tenant, a skinny little man with a long white beard, came racing out of the building with a policeman in tow, screaming that his privacy rights had been violated. All of this was in French, of course, but Moses had hired a teenage girl as an interpreter and she was now trying to make some sense of this bizarre scene.

"So Dan got on his high horse and said to the girl, 'I want you to translate what I am about to say.' And, of course, the girl was quaking in her boots. Dan said, 'Tell this man who I am.' And he proceeded to recite his resume, which, of course, was having no impact at all. Then he said, 'Tell him I am a personal friend of the American ambassador to France. And

if he doesn't want him to hear about this, he better back off right now!'
Well, the next thing you know, we were arrested! We were taken to a
police station and thrown in a cell—me, the camera crew, and Dan.
Behind bars with Dan Rather! Of course, that lasted for about a minute
and a half. They let us go and told us to never come back."

As Moses thought about his other travels with Dan, he added, "There
was always at least one moment when he got on his high horse. It happens whenever he feels threatened or challenged."

Robert Pierpoint remembered another episode involving Rather on
the road. This one was less benign. It had happened during the Nixon
administration when the president was taking what was laughingly
referred to as his "dictators tour." The first stop was Yugoslavia and talks
with Tito, then on to Spain for talks with Franco.

"We were in Belgrade," Pierpoint told me. "And we were to pack our
bags at five in the morning and leave for Madrid. So I took my bags down
and got on the bus and [producer] Lane Vernardos came up to me and
said, 'Where's Rather?' I said, 'I don't know, maybe he's on the other
bus.'" No, he wasn't on the bus, and when the two press planes took off
for Madrid, he was a no-show once again. Rather was scheduled to do a
scene-setter for the *Morning News* in Madrid, but instead Pierpoint,
totally unprepared, was thrown on the air, where he managed to vamp for
several minutes. Rather's whereabouts were unknown for three days. He
finally showed up in England, where the planes had landed to refuel for
the trip back to Washington.

"He had a black eye and a bruised face. He said that when he missed
the flights—this is his story—he went out to the airfield and boarded a
British cargo plane and hid in the men's room. After he came out, the
pilots were very upset that he was aboard. They said, 'We're going to land
at the next airfield and put you off.' And they did. And he said he was
jailed and beaten by the Yugoslavs. As he told it, they would not let him
contact the American ambassador for at least twenty-four hours."

"He just has this ability to inflame people or at least get their
attention," writer Tom Shales told me. "And it drove Tom Brokaw crazy.
I remember that when the 'Kenneth, what is the frequency?' thing

happened, a guy from NBC called me and said Brokaw was livid. 'What is it with this guy?' he supposedly said. 'How come he's always in the headlines?' Brokaw was a little bit jealous of that."

The Kenneth thing was the assault on Dan Rather in Manhattan one night in the late summer of 1986. "We all surmised it was the work of a jealous husband," Ed Joyce said to me—an opinion shared by many at CBS. It was common knowledge among CBS staffers that Rather was very popular with women, and he was certainly not alone among TV news stars.

Rather was walking along Park Avenue at about 10:30 P.M. when he was set upon and pummeled, while repeatedly being asked, "Kenneth, what is the frequency?" Rather managed to make it into a building lobby where the doorman and the superintendent came to his aid. Rather was treated at Lenox Hill Hospital for blows to the jaw and the left side of his back. He told police that he had no idea who the attackers were and doubted that they knew who he was. *Spy* magazine published a story that repeated the rumor that the attack was "engineered by a man angry because he thought Rather was having an affair with his wife."

None other than Laurence Tisch came forward to squelch the ugly rumors, saying that people were just jealous of Rather's wholesomeness. "He and his wife are happily married," Tisch told the *Washington Post*. "Everything is wonderful with them. People can't stand that idea. There's not one phony thing about Dan. Anytime you're that straight, people can't believe it. They start making things up."

Perhaps the many people who doubted Rather's story felt a twinge of guilt when in 1994 police arrested a man who had just shot and killed an NBC technician outside Rockefeller Center. The killer, William Tager, said he shot the technician, who was wearing an NBC logo on his jacket, because he believed the networks were beaming painful signals into his brain. When Tager's picture appeared in the *New York Daily News*, Rather called the police and said that Tager was the man who had assaulted him on Park Avenue almost a decade earlier. A forensic psychologist, Dr. Park Dietz, examined Tager and found him to be a paranoid schizophrenic and criminally insane. Dr. Dietz also concluded, after three years of treatment, that there was no question in his mind that Tager was the one who had assaulted Rather back in the summer of 1986.

The only problem was that many news reports of the original assault, as well as the police report, have Rather describing two men. Rather's account was supported by the building superintendent who had come to his aid. After Tager's arrest, Rather said that he might have been confused and that there might have been only one assailant. But author Paul Limbert Allman, writing in *Harper's* magazine, interviewed the family of the superintendent, Robert Sestak, now deceased, and they vividly recall Sestak describing two men.

If Tager was the only assailant and he believed that the networks were tormenting him with broadcast beams, it seems odd to me that it took him eight years to strike again. And if he had an accomplice, is it possible there were two paranoid schizophrenics, working in tandem, who believed that the networks were trying to destroy them?

As for the "Kenneth, what is the frequency?" business, Allman found a very curious coincidence in the work of short-story writer Donald Barthelme. Barthelme was from Houston, Rather's hometown, and once worked for the *Houston Post*. A running character in his stories, published long before the assault on Rather, is a man named Kenneth. In one of the stories a character is asked, "What is the frequency?" In another story, Barthelme describes an imperious newspaper editor, whom he calls "editor-king" and "editor-imperator." His name is Mr. Lather.

In October 2004, Allman turned his musings on the strange case into an off-Broadway play in which the character Dan Rather searches vainly for his assailants. In response to a mildly favorable review in the *New York Times*, the Manhattan district attorney, Robert Morganthau, wrote a letter to the editors stating flatly that William Tager was the lone assailant and that only he could have known nonpublished details of the incident. Why the district attorney of Manhattan would write such a letter in response to a minor work of drama is puzzling. Puzzling also is how a positive ID of the assailant could have been made 11 years after the incident and after both the victim and an eyewitness had described two attackers.

The evidence is clear that for whatever reason, Rather somehow brings out the worst in some people. Why him and not Brokaw or Jennings? This question prompted *TV Guide* to run a strange piece in which psychiatrists and psychologists were invited to comment on the "Why is it always Dan?" issue. One Dave Turkat, a so-called media psychologist from Atlanta, suggested that Rather suffered from "a failed ghost-buster syndrome. He's still living with the ghost of Walter Cronkite. Walter is sacred. He's more than a father figure. He's a legend. How can anybody live up to that?"

Dr. Joyce Brothers praised Rather precisely because his emotions seemed genuine. When he reported the death of an American soldier in a terrorist attack, "You could see Rather's eyes glistening, near to tears, and you felt warmer and better about him because of that." Justin Frank, a Washington psychiatrist, said that Rather, in his role as anchor, "was confined as in a stable. So it's not surprising he occasionally gives the barn door a kick." Of course, with Rather the barn door had a tendency to kick back.

The black eyes he had received in Manhattan and Belgrade would gradually fade away. The black eye that he had given the network in Miami would be rubbed raw by his critics for the rest of his career . . . and one of them included a man who hoped to become president of the United States.

8

Live Fire

Everybody was up to something, especially, of course, those
who were up to nothing.

— Sir Noel Coward

It was no secret that Dan Rather wanted to be thought of as the next
Murrow, as someone who, in a phrase Rather wore out over the
years, "spoke truth to power." But, as the Miami debacle proved, his
repeated attempts to convince any and all that he was as tough, as princi-
pled, and as passionate about journalism as his hero Murrow often back-
fired. Too often, he overplayed his hand, leaving the News Division in a
damage-control mode.

This scenario played out again in the run-up to the 1988 presidential
election. Among the networks, the routine prior to the primary season
was a series of profiles of the various candidates of both parties, usually
two-and-half- or three-minute pieces showing the hopefuls on the stump
and answering questions about taxes, crime, and the like. This was the
plan again for the 1988 campaign, but the mood this time was different.
The year 1984 had been a boring blowout in which Walter Mondale

never stood a serious chance against Ronald Reagan. But now, Reagan's vice president, George Herbert Walker Bush, would be running and he would do so amid a scandal known as Iran-Contra.

In the mid-1980s, producer Richard Cohen had been put in charge of political coverage for the *Evening News*. Cohen had joined the *CBS Evening News* staff in 1979, having worked with Bill Moyers on public television and at ABC News before it became a serious player. Richard was tall and handsome and outrageously funny. Once when he and I were stuck in the longest traffic jam I had ever witnessed, en route to the launch of the space shuttle, Richard suddenly turned to me and said, "Would you like to dance?" In Beirut during the worst of its civil war, he often strode into the rooftop restaurant of the Intercontinental Hotel and asked the maître d' for a table "with a view of the shelling, please." He created a fictional "sound bite room" where a producer could go to have an actor record the sound bite he needed to make his piece better. In a college prank, he had once stolen an actual electric chair, which he was forced to return.

Eventually, he became Dan Rather's personal producer, especially on political stories. Putting him in charge of election coverage seemed logical to some people, but others wondered if he was really up to the task, not because he lacked the talent, the intellect, or the energy, but because he was known as something of a scatterbrain, someone so filled with ideas that he would have trouble focusing on details. He was, in a word, disorganized. After things seemed to go well enough during the uneventful campaign of 1984, the arrangement seemed to be working, though. Cohen worked closely with Rather for years, apparently without incident. Still, he would not describe his relationship with Rather as close.

"Dan shared almost nothing about himself," Cohen told me. "He asked me questions about myself and my personal life, but there were very clear lines with Dan, things you didn't ask him. I don't know anything about his politics. I suspect he's sort of a liberal on some issues, but Dan doesn't reveal anything. He sits there with cards in his hand, but he never plays them."

As Cohen, Rather, and the rest of the political team planned their coverage for 1988, the country was preparing a reluctant good-bye to Ronald Reagan, the economy was dipping into a recession, and Iran-Contra was threatening not just the Reagan legacy but the candidacy of the man who hoped to succeed him. Throughout the congressional hearings on the affair, in which the United States had secretly sold weapons to Iran in return for U.S. hostages and money that was then illegally channeled to the so-called Contra rebels, anticommunists fighting the freely elected Sandinista government of Nicaragua, Vice President Bush maintained that he had been "out of the loop" while all the skullduggery was going on. A growing mountain of evidence, uncovered by the press and leaks from the office of the special prosecutor engaged to investigate the affair, told a much different story—that Bush had been in on the plan from the very beginning and that he had in fact been a key player.

The usual candidate profiles would be done, but when the subject turned to Bush, there was a new twist. The vice president's top media man, Roger Ailes, insisted to CBS that any interview with the candidate be conducted live. This was problematic for two reasons: first, it gave the person being interviewed a great advantage in being able to stonewall questions and change the subject. Since he would not be edited later, as is the custom, he could effectively control the interview. Second, it had not been a concession afforded to any of the other candidates being profiled, and they could justifiably protest.

"It was a joint decision among me, Rather, and [executive producer] Tom Bettag," Cohen told me. "It took a long time to convince Rather, but I said, 'We know who Bush is, we know his résumé, and we know all the unanswered questions about Iran-Contra. Let's give them live and let's do it on Iran-Contra.' I thought, why not go for it and remove their last excuse to not address the issues? So Dan finally agreed, and he agreed to do it himself."

"I honestly believed at the time that George Bush would be anxious to answer the questions," Rather wrote in *The Camera Never Blinks Twice*, "as fully and as often as it took to get them over with, set aside, and, if possible, out of the way of his campaign. I was wrong about that and much else. I thought I knew George Bush pretty well. I'd certainly known him for a long time. Our relationship had always been mutually respectful. But now, unbeknownst to me—unplanned and unwanted by me—that relationship was about to change."

The live interview, which ended up running nine minutes on the *Evening News*, almost half the broadcast, was, for Rather, either a milestone or a millstone, depending on one's point of view. The interview was preceded by a well-produced and well-written explanation of the Iran-Contra affair and the specific allegations that had surfaced about Bush's role in it. When the piece ended, there was Dan, sitting in his anchor chair, looking straight at the vice president on a television monitor.

Bush was trailing Bob Dole in the polls and he had been on the cover of *Time* magazine just weeks before with the word WIMP? emblazoned across the bottom. Ailes believed that it was time for the vice president's de-wimping. Indeed, it was reported that just before the interview began, Bush was heard to say, "If he throws Iran-Contra at me, I'm going to throw Miami at him."

"I was in the control room," Cohen recalled. "They had moles inside CBS and we had moles in the Bush camp. Dan was increasingly agitated. At one point, I walked out there and he said, 'They're gonna throw Miami at me.' And I didn't know what to say. The trouble is, if it hadn't gone where it went, Bush couldn't have thrown Miami at him."

The contest began with Rather getting directly to the point, asking Bush why he hadn't yet fired an aide who was involved in running arms to the Contras. Bush responded by defending the aide and saying that the issue had already been looked into. He then added, "And so I find this to be a rehash and a little bit, if you'll excuse me, a misrepresentation on the part of CBS who said you're doing political profiles on all the candidates and then you come up with something that has been extensively looked into."

Rather replied, "Mr. Vice President, what we agreed to or didn't agree to, I think you'll agree for the moment, can be dealt with in another way. Let's talk about the record—"

From there, it was like an eighteen-wheeler just cresting a large hill and then picking up speed on the way down. Bush had obviously been coached to stay loose and relaxed, to let Rather work up a head of steam, to keep cutting him off and throwing questions back at him. Within a few minutes, the exchange sounded like *Crossfire*, *The McLaughlin Group*, and every other cable show that featured grownups behaving badly.

BUSH: I am hiding something. You know what I'm hiding? What I told the president and that's the only thing. Now, if you have a question—

RATHER: Please, please—

BUSH: Go ahead.

RATHER: I have one. Now, you've said that if you'd known this was an arms-for-hostages swap, you would have opposed it—

BUSH: (interrupting) Exactly.

RATHER: (continuing) You also said you did not know—

BUSH: (interrupting) May I answer that?

RATHER: Yes, it was a statement and it was—

BUSH: . . . and created this program—

RATHER: (interrupting) Let me ask the question.

BUSH: (continuing) . . . has stated publicly that he did not think it was arms for hostages. It was only later, and do you know why I went along with it, Dan?

RATHER: (interrupting) That wasn't the question, Mr. Vice President.

And so on. It was David Mamet without the f-words. It turned out that Roger Ailes, who never left anything to chance, was standing off camera near the vice president holding cue card notes, just waiting for the moment to unleash that big right hook. That moment came a few minutes later.

RATHER: I don't want to be argumentative, Mr. Vice President—

BUSH: You do, Dan. This is not a great night because I want to talk about why I want to be president, why those forty-one percent of the people are supporting me—

RATHER: (interrupting) Mr. Vice President—

BUSH: And I don't think it's fair to judge a whole career, it's not fair to judge my whole career by a rehash. How would you like it if I judged your career by those seven minutes when you walked off the set in New York? Would you like that? I have respect for you, but I don't have respect for what you're doing here tonight.

Rather froze for a second. Then he said, "Mr. Vice President, I think you'll agree that your qualifications for president—what kind of government you'd have and what kind of people you'd have around you—[are] much more important than what you just referred to."

Okay. Rather hadn't walked off the set in New York; it was Miami. And it wasn't seven minutes; it was more like six. Maybe Bush couldn't read Ailes's idiot cards.

The two men continued to raise their voices, trying to be heard over the other in what was now an out-of-control situation. At one point, Rather was practically shouting, "You've made us hypocrites in the eyes of the world," referring to the long-standing U.S. policy of never negotiating with hostage takers.

As the clock approached nine minutes in, Rather was given a frantic "Get off" in his ear from the control room. But Rather heard it right in the middle of asking Bush another question: "Are you willing to go to a news conference before the Iowa caucuses and answer questions from all comers?"

Bush replied, "I've been to eighty-six news conferences since March—"

Then Rather said, "I take it the answer is no. Thank you very much for being with us. We'll be back with more news in a moment."

The cutoff had been brusque, but that was not Rather's fault. The exchange had gone on for so long, it threatened to bump the rest of the news and become a single-event show. As Bush was unhooking his microphone, which was still on in the control room, he was heard to say, "The bastard didn't lay a glove on me." He was also heard to say that Rather was "more of a pussy than Lesley Stahl."

The affair was a classic example of how television can so easily convey emotion without content having a chance of getting through. As has often been said, most people who listened to the first Nixon-Kennedy debate on the radio believed that Nixon had gotten the better of the young senator. But on television, Kennedy's tanned, youthful appearance contrasted so sharply with Nixon's five o'clock shadow that little in the way of content registered with the viewers. There is little debate that Rather, Bettag, and Cohen, veterans all, should have known better. Iran-Contra was a fairly complicated issue in the first place; despite the well-explained scene setter that preceded the interview, it still required a certain amount of concentration from the viewer in terms of who had allegedly said what to whom. And given the time constraints of an evening news program, was it realistic to assume that the litany of names, dates, and allegations could be crammed into the allotted time period in a manner that made any sense at all?

Moreover, the Bush people knew that Rather's natural aggressiveness, normally a strength, could be turned against him and made a weakness simply by their candidate's bobbing and weaving enough to make him frustrated. They knew they could push Rather's buttons, making him tense and angry. In a sense, Bush and Ailes had pulled a rope-a-dope, allowing Rather to flail away without getting a clean shot in. The fact that Bush did not answer the questions was lost in the postmortem, in which Rather was described as at best rude and at worst out of control.

"I made some mistakes that night," Rather wrote in *The Camera Never Blinks Twice*, "but this is no mea culpa. My biggest mistake was not anticipating the pitfalls and that the interview might provoke such a powerful national reaction. I'm not naive; some of it I know was orchestrated by the Bush campaign. But long after they gave the wheel a spin, the ball kept bouncing."

In Rather's account, he left the anchor chair after the broadcast and made his way up the stairs to his office. On the way, he passed a woman who was his senior assistant. Rather asked, "So, what did you think?" The assistant took a deep breath and replied, "I think you're an interesting person who does interesting interviews." As he reached the top of the stairs, he saw Donna Dees, who was then the press representative for the *Evening News*. Rather asked her, "Are we in trouble here?" Dees burst into tears and uttered just one word: "Apologize."

Rather wrote, "I turned cold steel right there. I made sure my eyes locked right on to hers. 'Wait a minute,' I said. 'I haven't done anything to apologize for.'" Minutes later, Rather said, he walked into the fishbowl where senior producer Bill Crawford, a wise old hand, was waiting for him. Crawford extended his hand and said, "Good interview. Really tough. And now you start to pay the price." Rather wasn't sure what that meant, but he noticed all the phone lines were lit up.

A hired consultant for CBS News came over to Rather and said, "You have got to get busy with the spin. These phone calls are coming from sophisticated phone banks, from party operatives well organized in advance to make exactly this kind of telephone call to newspapers and radio stations night or day. And that will impact tomorrow's press coverage." Today, that response would be generated by millions of computer bloggers, many linked or connected to the same political propaganda bank.

For his part, Rather claimed to be mystified by all the to-do about the exchange. "These kinds of interviews happen every day on the campaign trail, but viewers don't see them. I understand it makes some viewers uncomfortable when they do, but it's part of the process."

Many CBS affiliates, however, did not see it that way. A major market station manager who declined to be quoted by name told *Electronic Media*, "I don't see any upside to this at all. I think a negative impact and negative image has been made and people aren't going to forget it. There should be more involvement by CBS management, and someone should exercise more control over Mr. Rather."

From his perch among the pantheon of still-living legends, the long-retired Eric Sevareid weighed in as well. "I'd never seen brother Dan lose his cool before," he told an audience at the Museum of Broadcasting. "I'm sorry it happened. I don't think a hard-news show should become controversial. Neutrality should be preserved."

Sure enough, much of the coverage adopted the "ambush-turned-sour" theme—that Rather and CBS News had tried to surprise Bush with the Iran-Contra questions but that Bush and Ailes had deftly turned the tables. The Bush campaign produced a letter, sent in early January, from Richard Cohen, requesting an interview with the vice president, "as part of our early coverage of 1988 campaign." No mention of Iran-Contra. On his copy of the letter, Bush wrote, "I feel comfortable with Rather. Make sure this guy gets a reply soon."

The notion of an attempted ambush, however, was absurd. CBS had been running promos all week, even during 60 *Minutes*, about how the live interview would be about Iran-Contra. And even though Bush ended up finishing third in the Iowa caucuses (behind Bob Dole and Pat Robertson), he had gotten his de-wimping. He had taken on the rough, tough Dan Rather and won on style points if not on content.

Rather didn't see it as a prizefight at all. "This was an effort to deal with substance and news—real news as opposed to just the appearance of news," Rather told reporters who had gathered around his apartment. "I would gently and respectfully submit that critics and others who write about television can't have it both ways. When we don't do substantive pieces dealing with issues, they criticize us for having no depth. When we do, it's 'Oh, shame on them.'"

Howard Rosenburg, TV critic for the *Los Angeles Times*, had an appropriately cynical take on the episode. "Bush was shocked? Flabbergasted? Stunned? He didn't expect Rather to extensively and forcefully pursue the issue most on the minds of the media these days when it comes to Bush's candidacy? Bush is that dense? If he is, then heaven help us if he's elected president. . . . No, it was CBS News that was dense, for allowing itself to be set up by agreeing to a live interview."

Time magazine, describing the exchange as "a defining moment," said, "Their contretemps was not just a conflict between two men, but between two institutions, two symbols: the Vice President and the anchorman, the loyal emissary of the Reagan establishment taking on the embodiment of the East Coast liberal press."

Like the Nixon exchange in Houston in the early 1970s, Rather was again being portrayed as having a political agenda. But to many of his coworkers, that was both simplistic and inaccurate. "He has no politics," said more than one person. Yes, he knew the players, and he knew the issues, but making a splash, making the sparks fly—getting the goods on someone in power was his real goal.

The following evening, Rather led with a story about the Bush exchange and then said, "Now a personal word, if I may, about last night's interview. First, no, CBS did not mislead the vice president about the subject of the interview. Secondly, I, of course, respect the office of the vice presidency, the institution, and the vice president. . . . The intention of even persistent questions in a spirited interview is to do an honest, honorable job. The fact that more attention is sometimes given to the heat than to the light is regrettable, but it goes with the territory."

Richard Cohen found nothing to feel good about. To him, the gambit had been a fiasco. His next mistake was in saying that to a reporter for the *Des Moines Register*.

"Look, I think Dan made mistakes," he told the reporter. "I think his posture was probably too aggressive, but that's not the issue. I'd be the first to say we made a tactical error in agreeing to go live, because you can't control a live situation. We took a very heavy hit. I think it was very damaging to us, to Dan, to our credibility. I feel responsible for that and it's enormously frustrating. We did not set out to 'get Bush.' We set out to nail Bush on an issue."

Rather did not want to read this. It was one thing for Cohen to express his feelings on the matter to his colleagues, but quite another for Rather to see them in public print. Cohen had made the same mistake Bernie Goldberg would make years later when he wrote an op-ed piece for the *Wall Street Journal* hammering an *Evening News* story for having a liberal bias: he had criticized CBS News in public, and in Cohen's case, he had criticized Rather as well. The anchorman was furious and as soon as he arrived in Iowa, he summoned Cohen.

"By this time, I had been close to Dan for eight or nine years," Richard told me. "I knew him pretty well but I had never seen him like this. He didn't ask questions. We didn't sit down. He just stood ramrod straight. I wanted to talk it through with him, and as I was looking at him, I saw the light go out in his eyes. I swear to God, I saw the light go out in his eyes. He was cold and clipped and he started criticizing various things I had done. And he said he never spoke about them publicly. 'You shouldn't have done this,' and 'You shouldn't have done that' — to me it was totally ambiguous. He was quietly, coldly, implicitly threatening me. He never said 'therefore . . . ' It was all implied."

Cohen returned to the newsroom and was told that he had been barred from the *Evening News* Iowa set. He was made to sit in the newsroom for hours with nothing to do and no one who would talk to him. "I felt like I should be wearing a dunce cap," he said to me. Finally, he told an executive that he was going back to his hotel to pack his things. Following the caucuses, he was supposed to leave with the others on a Lear jet for New Hampshire to cover the primary. But as he packed, Cohen wasn't sure that he was still invited, and he was even less sure that he wanted to go even if he were. The executive called and said, "We've decided that you'll be allowed to go to New Hampshire," Cohen recalled, "Like it was some big concession. And I said, 'Look, I'm not sure I want to work for this organization anymore.' And that was it. I was just a dead man walking."

The immediate fallout of the interview consisted of anti-Rather columns in the media and complaints from CBS affiliates that Rather had been unprofessional. The last thing Rather needed to hear at that time was criticism from his own producer.

Even as the public opinion polls began to swing on the Rather/Bush episode, with more and more people supporting Rather's attempt to make Bush answer the Iran-Contra questions — in one postinterview poll, 72 percent of the respondents said they believed that Bush knew more about Iran-Contra than he was letting on — Cohen knew it was too little too late for him. He left CBS in March 1988 after refusing several other assignments.

CBS News president Howard Stringer, alluding to earlier articles Cohen had written, including an op-ed piece that encouraged journalists to boycott South Africa rather than be dictated to by the apartheid regime, said, "We want to allow freedom of expression, but we have a greater purpose. It's not self-expression of our own egos, but getting on the air with the best political reporting we can do."

Cohen replied, "If we spent more time demonstrating concern over issues and less time on the Kafkaesque internal politics of CBS, we'd be a much better place for it. They want it both ways. They want us to protect the public trust until push comes to shove. And the minute there's dissent, the minute the public face is not perfectly made up, they go into their corporate mode. They can't have it both ways. Journalists of all people know that the world is not always pretty."

Things got even uglier. Cohen was told that Rather "called two reporters and told them off the record that I was emotionally unstable, that I was having a midlife crisis, and that I couldn't deal with my wife's success," he told the *Washington Post*. Cohen is married to Meredith Vieira, then a rising star of the CBS News magazine *West 57th*. "At first I didn't want to be dragged into it," Vieira told Howard Kurtz of the *Post*. "But then it crossed the line, saying that somehow I was destroying my husband. My marriage is far more important to me. I'm not going to sit here and listen to that." When Vieira spread the word that she might quit if the anonymous public attacks on her husband didn't stop, they did—pronto.

"I really loved calling myself a journalist," Cohen told me recently. "I always did. I always have. It's something that has so much importance to me on so many levels, so I don't regret that. But in the postbroadcasting phase of my life, especially now that I've written books and articles for magazines and stuff, I realize I could have done something with writing. We used to call the *New York Times* the newspaper of record and we liked to think of ourselves at CBS as the broadcast of record. If I had to choose between the two now, I wouldn't choose the broadcast of record. I just don't think network news is serious news anymore."

The facts about President Bush and Iran-Contra finally did get out. The *Final Report of the Independent Counsel for Iran-Contra Matters*, headed by Lawrence E. Walsh, was published in August 1993, eight years after the Iran-Contra scandal broke. In chapter 28 of the report, the authors point out that among the final acts of outgoing president George Bush in December 1992 was the pardoning of defense secretary Caspar Weinberger before he even got to trial, in addition to pardons for national security adviser Robert McFarland, former assistant secretary of state Elliott Abrams, former CIA Central American Task Force chief Alan Fiers, former CIA deputy director Clair George, and former CIA counter-terrorism chief Duane Clarridge. "The Weinberger pardon," Walsh wrote, "marked the first time a president ever pardoned someone in whose trial he might have been called as a witness, because the president was knowledgeable of factual events underlying the case." The report laments the fact that because Bush had been elected president from 1988 to 1992, he could not be questioned repeatedly.

After years of foot dragging and stonewalling by Bush's attorneys, the independent counsel finally got access to Bush's complete personal diary in December 1992. Walsh also pointed out that Bush's public statements during the 1988 campaign that "the president and I cooperated fully with the various investigations, turned over thousands of documents, and directed our staffs to do the same" were simply not true. In fact, time and again, the prosecution had complained that material that the court had ordered to be turned over had never arrived, and what had arrived was often incomplete.

In short, the report concluded that Bush had had numerous meetings with the large cast of characters involved in Iran-Contra, including Oliver North, and could not by any stretch of the imagination claim that he had been "out the loop." In fact, if there was a hero to come out of the scenario laid out by Walsh, it was Secretary of State George Shultz, who refused to get on board with the illegal scheme. Shultz had actually threatened to quit unless National Security Adviser Admiral John Poindexter was fired.

A s the 1980s moved into the 1990s, Rather and CBS seemed to be making a comeback. The network's on-the-spot coverage of the massacre at Tiananmen Square in the spring of 1989 garnered such praise and ratings that *TV Guide* in a piece about that year's "what's in and what's out" declared that "Dan Rather bashing" was now out again.

The euphoria would be short lived. CBS News was back on top, but as the final decade of the twentieth century began, it was the last time that would happen on Dan Rather's watch.

9

Surviving

You can't teach an old dogma new tricks.

— Dorothy Parker

I f the event had occurred in Los Angeles, a passerby might have mistaken it for the Academy Awards or at least the Emmys. Limousines lined the block, and photographers and cameramen elbowed one another for position. The guests walked past the herd but did not smile. Richard Nixon, Abba Eban, Alan Alda, Swifty Lazar, Barbara Walters, Arthur Schlesinger, and Oscar de la Renta all walked by. . . . Mike Wallace, Morley Safer, and Ed Bradley arrived together. . . . Dan Rather arrived alone.

It was November 12, 1990, at the huge Temple Emanu-El in Manhattan and many of the world's rich, famous, and powerful had come to pay their respects to the legendary William Paley, who had died at the age of eighty-nine. The speakers gushed in their praise for the grand old man of broadcasting. Much of that praise was deserved, but not all of it. At about the same time, Sally Bedell Smith's huge and extensively researched biography of Paley was arriving in bookstores, and, like any thorough, fair, and talented reporter, Bedell Smith revealed truths about Paley that were not spoken of at the memorial: that he had a nasty, dark side largely hidden from the media; that although he was considered a champion of the press in general and CBS News in particular, he willingly went along with the blacklisting of alleged communists in the early 1950s and had effectively taken Ed Murrow off the air.

While it was true that a part of the broadcasting industry had died with Paley, it was not quite true that a part of CBS News had died with him. That organization had been slowly bleeding to death for years.

After the Iraqi invasion of Kuwait and the buildup to the Gulf War, President Bush seemed to renew his old feud with Dan Rather, with the White House accusing Rather of describing Iraqis as "brave souls." Rather not only denied ever using that phrase, he fired back from the Gulf: "I deeply resent any question or innuendo about my patriotism or my intentions to do a right journalistic job out here. I take it seriously and I take offense." As the massive buildup of troops, armor, and matériel moved into Saudi Arabia, Rather responded to an accusation that the press was stirring up war fever back home. "If war fever is being stirred up, it is being stirred up by the top leadership of the United States of America. No member of the press ordered the greatest expeditionary force of modern times out here. Let's have it clearly understood where this came from and who's responsible for it."

On the night of August 29, 1990, Dan Rather caught a break he'd been working on for what seemed like forever: a one-on-one with Saddam Hussein. "I said to myself that I've spent my life preparing for this. Now step in there and do it." During the ninety-minute exchange, Hussein declared that Kuwait was part of Iraq and that Iraq would not negotiate with the United Nations or anyone else until U.S. troops were removed from Saudi Arabia. Even before his Hussein scoop, Rather filed twenty-two stories in less than two weeks from Amman, Baghdad, Saudi Arabia, and wherever else he could find news.

Asked about Rather's coup, an ABC News official snapped, "So what?" One NBC News executive, widely believed to be that network's resident wiseguy, Steve Friedman, dismissed Rather's efforts, saying, "The only action Dan Rather has seen is a fight between housekeeping and room service in his hotel."

That remark got Rather's attention. "Steve Friedman said that. We know it. He knows it. He speaks for Tom Brokaw. I respect Tom Brokaw tremendously, but this I don't respect—even less so because they didn't have the guts to put their names on it. I guess when you're getting the hell beaten out of you, you do desperate things."

That wasn't all that got his attention. According to *Time* magazine, when Rather heard that a high-ranking U.S. diplomat had called him a "friend of Saddam Hussein," Rather exploded. "That's fucking outrageous!" he shouted. "I'm going to call him on that. In fact, I'm going to call [Secretary of State] Baker on that!" Even after he cooled off some, Rather was still mumbling about what he called "the back shooters. I was in Vietnam; they weren't. I had my career and my whole professional life on the line during Watergate; they didn't. I was in Afghanistan; they weren't. And I'm here and they aren't. I'm here. Where are the back shooters?"

Many people inside and outside CBS believed that Rather's Hussein interview had quieted questions about his credibility and his value to the network, questions that had dogged him since the mess in Miami and the boondoggle with Bush. "I think seeing Dan in the sands of Saudi Arabia in an open-necked shirt reminds everyone why he got where he is," said Broadcast Group president Howard Stringer. "Dan in action is pretty hard to beat. This helps him. We can build on this."

To be fair, Rather in the field *was* pretty hard to beat, his strange encounters notwithstanding. During the brutal tribal wars in Somalia, Rather and producer Larry Doyle chartered a plane from Mogadishu to a tiny, lawless village called Baidoa. The place was a free-fire zone, but Rather wanted to tape his standups there, a desire that Doyle, an ex-Marine and a pretty gung-ho type himself, considered crazy.

"I was in the street waiting for him to finish take four or five," Doyle told me, "and I was scared to death. I just wanted to get the hell out of there! And he'd say, 'Just one more.' I'd say, 'Oh, come on, already! I don't want to get my just desserts in this dump!'"

Doyle reflected on his many trips with Rather, which included several visits to Iraq. He said that while Rather was more than willing to take risks, he also heeded the advice of people he knew and trusted from other treacherous assignments. If they told him some location was simply too dangerous, Rather would not risk his own life and that of his crew. But if the advice was a "maybe," he just might.

"There were times that I used to think he wouldn't have minded if his legacy was being killed somewhere. Like the Last Intrepid Reporter in the most dangerous place in the world. That would have been a tough decision for me to make if I was out in the field with him and I thought he was being reckless. You don't want to walk away from somebody and be a chicken, but you don't want to be stupid either," Doyle said.

But despite Rather's efforts, CBS News was seriously outmanned and underfunded to cover the Gulf War properly, and it was criticized for a slow start once the shooting actually began, at least partly due to technical problems in transmitting its signal out of the Middle East.

As Ed Siegel of the *Boston Globe* put it, "Rather and CBS have not been particularly better or worse than ABC or CBS since the Gulf War began. They were even a bit better in the months leading up to the war, as Rather's stint in Jordan and Iraq led to more time for Arab perspectives as well as his prime-time interview with Saddam Hussein. The problems began long before the war; one could argue they began long before Dan Rather, when CBS founder William Paley decided to leave his legacy in the hands of bean counters." Indeed, in the middle of the war, CBS affiliates held a meeting in Washington in part to express their displeasure with the ratings at CBS News and the *Evening News*.

"The affiliates took the opportunity to vent their frustration with the declining ratings, the apparent lack of viewer empathy for our anchorman, and the general sense that things needed to change on the newscast," said the head of the affiliates board. "We're not asking them to do anything more than to fix it."

ABC News had now moved firmly into first place among the evening news programs, with CBS often finishing third. ABC's *Nightline* had become an institution. Thanks in no small part to its round-the-clock coverage of the massacre in Tiananmen Square, CNN had finally established itself as a hot place to go for breaking news. Commenting on CBS's lower ratings during the Gulf War, former president Ed Joyce said, "You can't hold Dan Rather personally responsible for the fact that CBS News has fewer resources. The Tiffany network looked like it was being outgunned by CNN." The *Los Angeles Times* reported that CBS had about 40 staffers covering the war while ABC and NBC had about 100 each and CNN 130. Walter Cronkite's old warning to Larry Tisch and the CBS board that when a fire breaks out, "You'll wish you had thirty guys instead of ten," had to no one's surprise been proven correct.

"It's a very depressing time here," said one CBS employee. "We're losing viewers and nobody seems quite sure of what to do about it. We're at war with ourselves trying to figure out what to do."

CBS began by replacing Tom Bettag, who had been Rather's executive producer for five years. In a statement, Rather called Bettag "the best broadcast news producer of his generation and one of the greatest ever." Why did they replace him? No one would say. But five years is an eternity in that position and with the ratings sagging, Bettag reportedly knew he was on the way out. (Bettag would have a second life as the award-winning executive producer of ABC's *Nightline*. Both he and anchor Ted Koppel left ABC in November 2005 to form their own news production company.)

An unnamed source at CBS said that the Bettag move "is just the peeling of one more layer from Dan Rather's authority. The budget has been cut and it will be cut again when the war ends, and what budget is left seems to be going to new programs. Rather doesn't like that, but he's not getting his way in these things anymore."

Two other firings received much less attention. Bill Crawford, senior producer and a longtime Rather ally, was let go as was Lee Townsend, who had been at CBS News for twenty-four years, fourteen of them as news editor of the *Evening News* for both Cronkite and Rather. "It happened in a very strange way," Townsend told me. "Dan was in Saudi Arabia and for four days we had been doing a one-hour newscast covering the war. At the end of Friday's show, I was told to see [Vice President] Joe

Peyronnin. And he just said, 'You're leaving.' Just like that. Now. Tonight. After twenty-four years. Turn in your ID and clean out your desk. I never got an explanation. When Dan came back, we had breakfast at the Carlyle Hotel. He didn't say much about it; he just wanted know if he could help me. I was still in shock. I never got to say good-bye to anyone. He had just lost Bettag and Crawford, and I guess he just felt defeated."

He had reason to. In April 1991, CBS announced a 73 percent drop in first-quarter earnings, mostly due to a dismal advertising market. Four hundred more jobs had to be cut and many producers and correspondents were being pressured to accept pay cuts. *Newsday* reported, "It is no secret that Rather, who is also the newscast's managing editor, is extremely unhappy with the cutbacks and with his diminished power. Rather has not been consulted on any of the news division's changes, and the reassignment or firing of key producers was handled without his approval."

Among those dropped was thirty-year veteran Bert Quint, who was told to close the Rome bureau on his way out the door. "Today," he complained to the *Los Angeles Times*, "there's no reason to believe that the person telling you the foreign story has been within 3,000 miles of where the story happened. (On one typical evening, a report on a soccer game turning violent in Bosnia was 'reported' by David Martin from the U.S. State Department in Washington and a report on neo-Nazi violence in Germany was 'reported' by Allen Pizzey from London.) Except of course for The Big Story, like Somalia, which we suffocate, with Dan Rather and his fellow suffocaters going in. And then we drop it. Look, Rather is an excellent journalist, but he's putting on a crappy program. A few years ago, he told me, 'Bert, things are changing and we have to learn new dance steps.' Well, Rather learned them. I know I didn't."

Rather was being hammered in the press, which had begun to smell blood in the water. Dick Williams of the *Atlanta Journal-Constitution* was typical: "Mr. Rather's leadership of the network's war coverage didn't help. His quirky manner, his phony cheerleading and on-air salutes, his country sayings all combined to make him a curiosity, not an anchor. . . . The disarray at CBS News is well documented. Its ratings tail off, the executive producer is fired, budget consciousness stirs internal turmoil, and Mr. Rather is said to be soon acquiring a coanchor, Connie Chung, say insiders, if she relinquishes her 'aggressive pursuit' of pregnancy."

To many people at CBS News, the Chung rumors, which had floated around ever since Diane Sawyer had left the network for ABC, seemed preposterous. Chung's only success in network television had come on morning shows. She was not a proven ratings-grabber in prime time unless one counted phony NBC News "specials" with titles like "Scared Sexless," "Life in the Fat Lane," and "Stressed to Kill." More important, she had a reputation at CBS as someone who was not terribly interested in the news and was not especially hardworking.

Rather was believed to have a clause in his contract that could veto any coanchoring scheme. The announcement by CBS that Chung would join Rather as coanchor effective June 1, 1993, came as more than a mild surprise. This had disaster written all over it. Was Dan Rather truly defeated? Had he simply decided to give up?

Richard Threlkeld, who was at ABC News at the time, was as astonished as everyone else. "The ratings were tumbling and Jennings was doing better and Howard Stringer was about to go to the annual CBS affiliates meeting and they were in a rebellious mood. He just felt he had to do something. So he figures, what the hell—Connie Chung is cute and it'll be fine. I don't think anyone knew how unprepared Connie was for a job like that. I know Connie very well and she's smart, but she's just not interested in the news that much. She doesn't read newspapers and she had been doing Channel 2 out in L.A., which was all happy talk and reading a teleprompter."

Threlkeld recalled the early returns from the experiment. "She had been sitting in the chair for about a week and there was an anniversary of *Roe v. Wade*. They did a live thing in which she was interviewing various correspondents and she obviously didn't know anything about the story. Susan Spencer, the White House correspondent, had to save her ass. That was the first indication that this was a mistake."

Rather's agent, Richard Leibner, said that his client agreed to the move because he was a "team player" and would go along with anything that would help the broadcast. In fact, Rather wrote in *The Camera Never Blinks Twice* that he was actually partially responsible for the idea: "Maybe my experience with my brother Don, and sister Pat, gave me the confidence that made me one of the people who came up with this plan. Others have said they'd have thrown a fit and refused to go along with it. Maybe they lack my willingness to try something new. Co-anchoring is our combined effort to be more flexible, more relevant, more ready. . . . Cooperation builds character. And Connie's professional attitude and winning personality make her a grand partner."

Others took a different view. In a vicious piece in *Rolling Stone*, former CBS News executive Jon Katz wrote that the heir to Walter Cronkite had now become Connie Chung's "sidekick" and was now debasing himself. "Once confident and in command, his guileless face became an open window into the person, conflict and unease raging inside him. He turns abruptly teary, pedantic or patriotic. The one thing he never appears to be is at ease. The newscast is often too painful to watch, sometimes too compelling not to. Having just signed a long-term contract Rather has now damned himself to anchor hell, joined at the hip to a companion who has no other role than to be warm and friendly and with whom he has nothing in common."

While on the air, Rather treated Chung with courtesy — unlike Harry Reasoner's open disdain for Barbara Walters more than a decade earlier. What Rather did behind the scenes was another matter.

"Now here we see Dan at his most duplicitous," the *Post*'s Tom Shales told me. "He was being a good soldier on the surface, going along with it and saying he was pleased as punch, while backstage he was doing whatever he could to scuttle the ship and get Connie out of there. I think the minute the partnership was announced, his goal was to break it up. It was insulting to have asked him to do it in the first place — and so visibly. I mean, it was demeaning to him."

The official reason given for Chung's ascension was that it would free Rather to do more out-of-studio reporting. But it's difficult to believe that the decision, aggressively pushed by longtime Chung fan Howard Stringer, was not ratings-driven despite the fact that Chung had no positive track record with prime-time audiences. She consistently scored high in so-called Q ratings in which sample viewers are asked if they can identify pictures of news personalities. But as virtually the only Asian American woman on network news at the time, she would be hard to miss. The Qs used at that time revealed nothing about how the viewers felt about the person they correctly identified. Indeed, the acerbic *Newsday* critic Marvin Kitman pointed out that "between the half of the people who can't stand Dan Rather, and the other half who can't stand Connie Chung, CBS is in for an expensive experiment in coed TV journalism."

The campaign to sell the Rather/Chung news team featured TV spots that many people at CBS believed were the worst and most embarrassing ever seen for a news program. The spots featured Rather in jeans and boots, the boots up on a desk, sipping from a mug of coffee while saying wonderful things about Chung. Then a cut to Chung, similarly garbed with her shoes up on the desk, sipping coffee and saying wonderful things about Dan. If you'd turned the sound off, you would have sworn it was a spot for Folger's, not the *CBS Evening News*. Being a good soldier was one thing, but agreeing to such a phony, mawkish sales pitch for a news show made Rather seem like nothing more than some local anchor guy who thought he might someday have a career in the movies.

It was with more than a bit of cynicism that many people greeted Rather's highly publicized speech that fall to the Radio and Television News Directors' Association in Miami. There he scolded the heads of the local stations for having "gone Hollywood." "Thoughtfully written analysis is out; 'live pops' are in. 'Action Jackson' is the cry. Hire lookers, not writers. Do powder puff, not probing, interviews. Stay away from controversial subjects. Kiss ass, move with the mass, and for heaven and ratings' sake, don't make anybody mad. . . . Make nice, not news."

Recalling the Van Gordon Sauter years in which "moments" were the key to making the broadcast and still stunned by that Rather/Chung ad campaign, I sent Rather a note that read: "Great speech. Too bad you didn't give it eight years ago." I received a form letter thanking me for my interest in the *CBS Evening News*.

This straddling of two worlds had become a real problem for Dan
Rather. I believed and still do believe he is sincere about his feelings for
the House of Murrow and all that it stands for. But at the same time he
was very much aware that the playing field had changed. Paley was gone,
as were Leonard Goldenson of ABC and David Sarnoff of NBC. Huge
conglomerates were now in charge and even more would join the mix
soon. This was a dilemma Rather could never really resolve. On those
occasions when he had tried to score points for substance over style, the
Miami walkout and the Bush shouting match, he had been bruised and
battered. He knew he had to play along with his corporate masters to a
point, but how far was he willing to go before it ceased being worth it?

Many aspects of Rather's personality always seemed in conflict, but
this is not unusual among the famous and the obscure. I recall Jim
Bishop's description of the various Jackie Gleasons he had met while
researching the comedian's biography: "Gleason the businessman does
not admire Gleason the playboy. Gleason the Catholic is not fond of
Gleason the connoisseur of blondes. Gleason the fine actor has little
respect for Jackie the drinker. Gleason the lonely brooder has no affection
for Gleason the wit." Likewise, Rather the hugely skilled, smooth, and
steady field reporter had little respect for Rather the uptight, ill-at-ease
anchorman. Rather, the courteous, mannerly gentleman, had no love for
Rather the hair-triggered, easily threatened, tightly wound coil. And
Rather, the do-anything-for-the-good-of-the-club trouper, had no affection for the Rather who allowed management to act against his own interests and who worked behind the scenes to undercut anyone he found
threatening.

By the end of 1993, the *CBS Evening News* with Dan Rather and
Connie Chung was in third place, despite the fact that the pair had been
voted "favorite TV couple" in a poll of satellite dish viewers. Second place
went to Beavis and Butt-Head, followed by Amy Fisher and Joey Butta-
fuoco, Loni Anderson and Burt Reynolds, and Woody Allen and Mia Far-
row. This was now becoming something worse than an embarrassing
failure; this was the stuff of comedy and derision.

Behind the scenes, Chung's agent, Alfred Geller, was badgering CBS management to give his client meatier stories, not just celebrity interviews. Even those interviews she had trouble with, as evidenced by her painful-to-watch stalking of bad-girl skater Tonya Harding and her vapid interview with Faye Resnick, the publicity-seeking friend of the murdered Nicole Brown Simpson.

Don Decesare, then vice president for News Gathering, told me that he repeatedly drew frowns at executive meetings for saying Chung was not anchor material. "She's not a hard-news interviewer; she's never going to be a hard-news interviewer. It is not how the public perceives her. And if you go that far against type, it's not going to work. Dan was incredibly uncomfortable—you could see it on his face. I thought he was a really good trouper about it, but it was obviously a terrible mistake and you could see it from day one."

The final act came in April 1995 with the horrific bombing of the Murrah Federal Building in Oklahoma City, in which 168 people, including many children, perished. It was, at the time, the worst terrorist act on American soil in history.

Rather was on vacation in Texas, but only about an hour and a half away by chartered jet. At the first news of the bombing, shortly after 11 A.M. EDT, executive producer Andrew Heyward claimed that he made a split-second decision to send Connie Chung all the way from Sacramento, where she had been doing promotional work. It is difficult to believe that such a decision on such a huge story was not first greenlighted by then News Division president Eric Ober and even by Broadcast Group president Howard Stringer, who had hired Chung in the first place.

In any event, Rather was stunned to hear that Chung was being flown in for that evening's coverage. So was producer Larry Doyle, who was at the scene of the bombing. "I was told to get from Miami to Oklahoma City to be Connie Chung's producer," Doyle recalled. "And I worked with her the first day. Then I was told Connie was leaving and Dan Rather was coming in. And I thought to myself, 'Now this should be fascinating.'"

Chung's performance on her first day in Oklahoma City played precisely into her weaknesses. Most CBS producers felt that she couldn't ad-lib and couldn't think on her feet. Even Dan Rather's most caustic critics always admitted, however grudgingly, that when it came to fast-breaking, running stories, without scripts or prompters, Rather had few if any peers. Fairly or unfairly, Chung was perceived as talking down to local officials and being overly critical of their response to the tragedy. The *Boston Globe* reported that locals were selling $11 relief fund T-shirts with the message "Who the hell is Connie Chung?" across the front. The *Globe* added that that was one of the more printable slogans.

"I figured management knew what they were doing," Doyle told me. "There must have been a reason why Dan wasn't there. When he arrived he was furious, I mean absolutely furious. I think it was on his third night there that we had dinner together and he was still beside himself. He was as angry as I'd ever seen him. He told me he was going to tell management in New York that within one month either he or Connie Chung would not be working at CBS News."

Sure enough, about a month later CBS announced that Chung would no longer coanchor the *Evening News*. She rejected management's offer to be the *Weekend News* anchor and took the offensive, suggesting that sexism was behind the move. Why, many wondered, did she think she had been hired in the first place? Her prime-time newsmagazine *Eye to Eye* was on life support, making management look even more foolish for having canceled *Street Stories with Ed Bradley*, which had been gaining steadily in the ratings, so that Chung could take over the hour. Her show did not survive the season.

In a blistering piece on the Chung failure, Jeff Simon of the *Buffalo News* basically took Chung's side: "Men, in the ancient mythology, do the hard work of reporting and analysis. Women do the smiling, the celeb handholding, the sob-sistering and the lifestyle thing. Put the two together as CBS tried idiotically to do, and you have a nice little sitcom: 'I Love Connie' with bombings in Oklahoma City and hostages in Sarajevo. 'Honnnnnnneeeee, I'm home. And you'll never guess what those Serbians are up to.' This was never a Connie vs. Dan issue. . . . The issue is CBS vs. CBS, by now the longest running assassination in TV history in which a once-great network does everything within its power to dismantle its own greatness. Wherever you find ambition the size of Rather's, you also find a killer anxiety level and, hence, a willingness to suck up which is always pleasing and flattering to bosses but which is the exact opposite of the solidity and credibility CBS has desperately needed. There is no Dan Rather. You watch him each night and you know it. He's making himself up as he goes along."

The conservative Rupert Murdoch's New York Post ran the headline "Dan's Dirty Double Cross" and published a column by tabloid gossip columnist Andrea Peyser called "How Dan Put the Knife in Connie." Chung herself was quoted as having told a friend, "My twenty-six years of credibility have been trashed."

Rather, countering every volley, had reporters over for breakfast during which he said of Chung, "Two trips to the Middle East do not make you a foreign correspondent." He added, "I did on several occasions encourage her, not in a patronizing way, that to be really connected with the news you have to read more."

Rather also told Claudia Dreifus of the New York Times Magazine that the Oklahoma City episode was not the only reason he felt something or someone had to give. He said that he learned from sources that Geller, Chung's agent, had met with management to discuss Chung's role in the upcoming 1994 election coverage. According to Rather's moles, Geller said, "You know, it's time for Dan Rather to step aside."

"Now, I didn't take kindly to that," Rather told Dreifus. "You know I was supportive of her. I worked hard to make it work. I gave much more than I got. I believed it would continue indefinitely until I found out about election night and what happened in secret . . . until it was made very clear to me that there was a push on not for me to share, but to give up."

Mr. Geller was not shy about firing back: "His statements are bald-faced lies, following many that have been made by Dan Rather over an extended period of time. . . . One would think that within the bounds of good taste, human decency, and gentlemanly behavior that he would stop attacking Connie Chung. It's time for him to enjoy his 'victory,' however tainted, and leave Ms. Chung alone."

Spoken like a true supportive agent—except there were just too many people around CBS who had seen and heard Geller hounding management to make his client number one. Rather no doubt made his views known behind the scenes, but there is no record of him publicly trashing Chung or treating her on the air with anything less than courtesy.

So, Dan Rather had won—but what exactly did he win? CBS was last in prime time, last in news, last in sports, last with its owned stations, and it was now about to be sold to Westinghouse. It had lost NFL football to FOX, causing a defection of affiliates across the country. CBS was forced to switch stations in Baltimore, Boston, Detroit, Phoenix, Dallas, Tampa, and Kansas City, in addition to many in smaller markets. The situation in Detroit was so bad that CBS was forced to align itself with WGPR, Channel 62, a UHF station with a weak signal and no news department, meaning that until the station could be upgraded, the CBS Evening News would have no local lead in Detroit, a top-ten market.

Shortly after the Westinghouse deal was completed in 1995, the News Division's president, Eric Ober, was ordered to clean out his desk. He took the fall for the pairing of Rather and Connie Chung, since the architect of the fiasco, Howard Stringer, had already left for greener pastures with a telecom startup. Peter Lund replaced Stringer as Broadcast Group president, and Ober was replaced by Andrew Heyward, a move that had seemed inevitable since the day Heyward arrived at the network back in 1980. Heyward was a witty, fast-talking Harvard graduate—a fact that seemed to appear in every story about him—who had a gift for working the room. He had been a competent if not spectacular producer, but it was his people skills, his ability to generate enthusiasm and excitement among staffers, that made him popular. Everyone wanted to work for Andrew and as time went on he rewarded his top loyalists with executive producer jobs and a few vice presidencies. Most important, Rather considered Heyward one of his guys, someone who would pretty much stay out of his way.

By 1996, Rather had spent fifteen years in the anchor chair. He had signed a new long-term contract two years earlier, confounding media watchers who had predicted that 1994 would be it for him as anchorman. The *Detroit Free Press* ran a lengthy piece by Marc Gunther about how Rather had changed over the years, bringing up the Miami walkoff and the Bush shouting match.

"I wasn't as mature as I should have been," Rather told Gunther. "My own confidence in my abilities as a reporter never wavered. But with the intense press pressure, and the house divided, there were moments when I doubted my abilities as an anchor. The ratings made a statement." He pointed out that there had been triumphs such as CBS's coverage of the massacre in Tiananmen Square and his exclusive interview with Saddam Hussein just prior to the Gulf War. Given the many staff firings over the years and the fallout from the loss of pro football, Rather said, "It's one of the miracles of journalism that there still is a CBS News."

Newsday columnist Verne Gay had a more psychological take on Rather's anniversary. He mentioned in his column a photograph taken about ten years earlier. Seated around a table were all of the remaining legends of the House of Murrow, including Cronkite, Sevareid, and a stiff, uncomfortable-looking Dan Rather. "In that one snapshot," Gay wrote, "you get an inkling of the quintessential Rather. He is the outsider, the loner, the kid from Texas who battled the Brahmins and finally got a membership to their exclusive club. But there's just this little nagging problem, and it's always been a problem that has dogged Rather. It is this sense that maybe he doesn't belong. Maybe he never did measure up to Cronkite. Well, rest easy, Dan. You can finally banish all your demons. You are one of TV's great newsmen. You not only belong in the club. You *are* the club."

In an interview in the *Los Angeles Times*, Rather was asked if he expected to remain until his contract ran out in 2000. "I'd love to," he responded, "but that's not going to happen. You can sooner expect a tall talking broccoli stick to offer to mow your lawn for free. Television is a young person's game, and I'm living on borrowed time."

The borrowing would continue for another eight years and would breach the new millennium. The company would be sold again—this time to Sumner Redstone's media behemoth Viacom. CBS News had

little to crow about. Heyward would string together a disastrous list of
on-air hires, including Bryant Gumbel, ex-congresswoman Susan
Molinari, and ex-Senator Bill Bradley, all of whom flopped. The News
Division was so woefully late in getting on the air with the news of Princess
Diana's death that Heyward issued a formal apology to the affiliates and
fired a vice president, Lane Vernardos, who had been a close friend.

Through it all, Heyward's relationship with Rather never appeared
strained even as the combined audiences for the three network evening
news programs continued to decline, with CBS now mired in third place.
The company began talks about merging news operations with CNN,
which no doubt would have resulted in more firings at CBS. Fortunately
for both companies, the talks went nowhere. CBS, thanks to the intransi-
gence and short-sightedness of Laurence Tisch, made a too-late attempt
to enter the cable news market and was effectively shut out, while NBC
successfully launched two cable news channels, MSNBC and CNBC,
to offset its overhead and develop new talent.

As the 1990s came to an end, about the only good news for CBS was
that it had regained an NFL football package at a cost of $500 million.
When one staffer was told that some of that would probably result in further cutbacks in the News Division, the employee responded, "Great.
That will leave us with Dan Rather and a mop."

About the only good news for Andrew Heyward was that after much
arm-twisting and mud wrestling, he and the network's new programming
chief, Les Moonves, had convinced Don Hewitt, Mike Wallace, Morley
Safer, Ed Bradley, Lesley Stahl, and Steve Kroft to give their blessing to a
weeknight prime-time spinoff of *60 Minutes* to be called *60 Minutes II*.
ABC had already done the same thing with *20/20*, and NBC was running
Dateline seemingly every night of the week. But this was *60 Minutes*, the
gold standard—the most successful broadcast in the history of television.
You do not clone the Mona Lisa. You can copy it, yes, but the copy would
be virtually worthless. Reproducing *60 Minutes* was not an easy sell.

"I initially opposed it," Morley Safer told me, "because I felt they
were cynically trying to use the brand, the logo, the ticking clock. They
were 'branding,' all these unfamiliar words now being applied to what I

thought was the noble profession of journalism. That's what bothered me. We thought it was just the first shot across our bow—*60 Minutes Wednesday*, then *60 Minutes Thursday*, and on and on, essentially just selling the cover. That's what appeals to network brass. You get some people liking something, then it's 'Hey, let's put a lot of other stuff on that has the same brand.'"

At a meeting at CBS headquarters, Safer and his colleagues were assured that no such scenario would happen. Management promised to appoint as executive producer someone the *60 Minutes* gang knew and trusted, agreed to give him his choice of available correspondents, and promised to allow him total freedom to choose the stories the broadcast would report.

"When that happened," Safer said, "I didn't see how we could oppose it. We didn't have grounds to grumble. I had other concerns—obviously, when you start competing from within your own shop for stories it doesn't make for a healthy culture, but it happened. And it was okay."

Management chose Jeff Fager, a well-respected veteran of *60 Minutes*, who was then executive producer of the *Evening News*. He and Heyward in turn chose veterans Bob Simon, Scott Pelley, Vicki Mabrey, and PBS's Charlie Rose as the correspondents and Dan Rather as the chief correspondent. The plan was for Dan to continue his anchor duties, continue to host *48 Hours*, and contribute whenever he could to *60 Minutes II*.

Once again, Rather was making himself indispensable. As an exec from another network said, "If Dan gets hit by a car, who else does CBS have?" It was a question CBS had ducked for years. Was Rather being spread too thin? Was his desire to be a part of everything at CBS News unrealistic if not downright dangerous? "Suddenly, you have a guy whose head is too big for his own good, believing his press to a certain degree and all the bullshit he was getting from elsewhere that he could do all these things," Verne Gay of *Newsday* said to me. "So while he's trying to add to his persona as anchorman, he's also given this huge management responsibility to remake the News Division not only in own image but in an image that would suit a succession of bosses. It was just nuts."

The broadcast premiered on a Wednesday night in January 1999, and Rather had the lead story. The reviews were glowing: "*60 Minutes II* is the very essence of *60 Minutes*," wrote the *Boston Herald*. "For all the hand-wringing, the fretting about protecting the precious franchise, *60 Minutes II* does serious justice to the genuine article."

Tom Shales in the *Washington Post* wrote, "It instantly became the second-best magazine show on network TV. . . . It had the quality touch for which its progenitor is justifiably celebrated."

Rather and CBS News were also praised for their reporting on a far more important event, the attack on the United States on September 11, 2001. Of course, all three anchors stayed on the air from the morning when the planes hit the World Trade Center until the wee hours of the following morning, as the full horror of the attacks was revealed under the rubble.

"I heard about the attack while I was in the shower," Rather said. "I said a quick 'Our Father.' I thought about rushing down to the scene and being a reporter. But then I wondered where could I do the most good?" For Rather, it was his usual dilemma during a crisis: whether to be the reporter or be the anchor. "I thought about Murrow during the Blitz and I just kept thinking of the word *steady*. That's what I had to focus on."

Recalling the mistakes that had been reported on election night 2000 and the wild rumors that had circulated after President Kennedy's assassination, Rather wanted to make sure the network reported only what it knew, what it did not know, and what may be true but had not yet been confirmed. When Tower Two collapsed, Rather was speechless. "I couldn't talk," he said. "There weren't any words. That's one thing that shouldn't happen to any anchor. But when I thought about all those people . . . I must have called home a half dozen times to check on my wife and make sure the kids were accounted for."

Rather stayed on the air for fifty-five hours between September 11 and 14. He had anchored marathon coverage before, including the *Chal-lenger* explosion. "You have to pace yourself. Keep your energy up. And in my experience, the first thing you hear is likely to be wrong. There was a story about a car bomb going off at the State Department. The source for that was a high official, not just someone passing by. We questioned it, reported it, and as soon as it became clear it was wrong, we said so on the air," Rather told *Texas Monthly*.

He spent days at Ground Zero in Manhattan and even beneath it, getting a frightening tour of the carnage below the massive buildings in what used to be an underground shopping mall and train station. And he conducted insightful interviews with experts like consultant Fouad Ajami about just who this Osama bin Laden was, why he and his followers had declared war on the United States, and whether President Bush's plan for retaliation against terrorists on a worldwide scale was feasible and realistic. It may well have been the finest work of his career as an anchorman/reporter.

Looking back on it, Rather told former CBS News senior foreign correspondent Tom Fenton that they all blew a big chance after 9/11 to convince their network bosses to reverse years of decline and cost cutting on foreign news. "We should have gone with our boldest, most aggressive, most integrity-filled pitch for rebuilding our international coverage in a significant and dramatic new way. And I include myself in that. We may not have made the case strong enough and quick enough in the wake of 9/11. Because I remember that very quickly after 9/11 they were saying, 'What do you need? Bring it to us and we'll try to arrange it.'"

A week later, Rather appeared on David Letterman's *Late Show*, which had not aired for a week since the attack. While describing the time he'd spent with rescue workers, Rather began to weep. Letterman grabbed his hand and called for a commercial. Coming out of the break, Rather actually apologized, saying, "I'm a professional. I get paid not to do that." To which Letterman replied, "But you're also human." Rather then said of President Bush's plan to fight terrorism, "Wherever he wants me to line up, tell me where. He'll make the call." Toward the end of his segment, Rather said that the song "America the Beautiful" would never sound the same to him. "Oh beautiful for patriot's dream," he began to sing in a quivering voice, "that echoes through the years/Thine alabaster cities gleam/Undimmed by human tears." His voice broke at the last line.

The Late Show received more than thirty-five hundred e-mails in support of Rather and Letterman. Even Walter Cronkite, not known for kind words about Rather, defended him. "I wouldn't want an anchor who couldn't show human emotion." But the *Pittsburgh Post-Gazette* mildly chastised Rather's "tell me where to line up" remark: "Extraordinary times may require extraordinary patriotism, but not at the expense of the Fourth Estate's integrity. Perhaps Mr. Rather should follow the lead of Tom Brokaw and stay away from interviews where maintaining one's composure would be difficult. We need our newsmen and newswomen to have their wits about them so that the public truly knows what's going on."

While conceding that all the networks did an honorable job of keeping a terrified public informed, Tom Shales singled out Rather. "I never needed more reassurance," Shales said. "The role of anchor was critical in nonjournalistic ways. In such a time of horror, I wanted the most human anchor, the anchor with the most warmth. Rather's that man; there's no competition. If it looks like the world is coming to an end, I want Dan Rather to be the one to break it to me."

What a metamorphosis — Dan Rather, considered too hot for the cool medium, the man considered most likely to explode while on the air, the man of whom radio star Don Imus once said, "I want to be watching when he finally cracks," was now being saluted for his steady, calm, reassuring demeanor during the worst attack in American history.

The attacks seemed not only to reenergize Rather — although he is a person who has never really required more energy — but to call into question the widely held belief that anchormen and network news no longer mattered, that cable and the Internet were now the preferred source of information. The entire week put the lie to all that. Ratings for the three broadcast networks shot up; the viewers had returned en masse.

"I never doubted it," Rather told Frank Rich of the *New York Times*. "The viewer must have a sense that the anchor has seen enough of life, enough of news, to be trusted in this storm, this hurricane of fact, rumor, information, misinformation, interviews, new reports coming in to sort through. On the big breaking news, there's no place to hide. It's where experience is leveraged."

Rather believes that he and his colleagues are at their best when trying to convey a shared experience to the country. "I've never liked the metaphor, but people are looking for a national hearth. And if the anchor does his best, he has the ability to do that. It took me a long time to come to grips with the symbolic nature of the job. But, like it or not, people key off you. If in your inner core you think of yourself as the holder of a trust, not in any arrogant or conceited way, then I think that gets through the glass. It's the very essence of being an effective anchor."

In the U.S. invasion of Iraq that followed 9/11, CBS News was again crippled by a lack of resources, although Rather snared another interview with Saddam Hussein shortly before the attack. Once American troops arrived, the Pentagon made the journalist's job even tougher than it has been during the Gulf War. Now, correspondents were required to be "embedded" or cocooned with troops, ostensibly for their own safety, but in reality so that the Pentagon could better manage where reporters went, what they were allowed to see, and who they could talk to.

Former executive producer Sandy Socolow was apoplectic when he heard about the embedding scheme. "The major media had to sign twelve-page documents that the Pentagon produced on the rules of doing this coverage. *You had to sign a contract!* I couldn't fucking believe it! The proper response, given our history and our traditions, would have been to say to the Pentagon, 'Look, you go out and do your job, and we'll go out and do ours.' That's the way it was in Vietnam."

For his part, Rather took a firm but more moderate tone in his attitude toward rules of engagement for reporters in battle. In an essay in the *Harvard International Review* just prior to the Iraq invasion, Rather wrote, "An overemphasis on censorship and control of information does not necessarily benefit the military; indeed it presents a danger to our country. People may say the truth is the first casualty of war, but I don't believe that has to be. It had better not be, not when the United States has fighting men in the field. I believe that in war, truth is our best weapon. Even the tough truths. Even if the truth is that U.S. troops are getting the hell kicked out of them. I am not proposing that every commander tell every reporter the truth, the whole truth, and nothing but the truth. I am saying it is best not to lie."

But, of course, the reality is that the Defense Department did lie. They lied about the circumstances surrounding the death of former football star turned soldier Pat Tillman; they lied about why ten marines were blown up in Fallujah in early December; and they lied outrageously about the story of Private First Class Jessica Lynch, whose injuries were actually sustained in an auto accident and not during a heroic gun battle with Iraqis. Before even knowing the details of the incident, CBS, among other networks, offered her a book deal, a TV show, magazine cover stories, and other inducements in exchange for an exclusive interview. CBS vice president Betsy West, who drafted her network's proposal, vehemently denied that this was checkbook journalism.

Rather, Brokaw, and Jennings rose above the rubble on 9/11 and during the war that followed. In different ways and for different reasons, it was the last time they would compete on a story that would forever be etched in history.

10

Blinded by the Light

I am wounded, but I am not slain. I may lay me down and
bleed awhile but then I shall rise and fight again.
> —Dan Rather, quoting Dryden, in an e-mail to a friend

A
lthough *60 Minutes II*, or *60 Minutes Wednesday* as it came to be
known, had been airing since January 1999, by the fall of the
2003–2004 season it was considered in jeopardy as far as renewal
was concerned. While it had aired some reports as compelling as any on
the original *60 Minutes*, it was struggling in the ratings and attracting an
audience too old for the taste of most advertisers. As management told
staffers, what saved the show and won a renewal for another season was
a Dan Rather report on conditions inside the Abu Ghraib prison in Iraq.
By any measure, it was a genuine, 100 percent, solid-gold scoop, a story
worth fighting for because it revealed how poorly trained and largely
unsupervised American soldiers could become as brutal and sadistic as
the enemy they had been sent to fight. The report, which showed photographs of naked Iraqis being tormented by their American captors,

horrified viewers the world over, but especially in America where such behavior by our troops was believed to have been unthinkable.

The Abu Ghraib story produced an international uproar. CBS had agreed to a Defense Department request to hold the story for several weeks because the impact would obviously be explosive, but there was no delaying the inevitable. That story led to further revelations about secret prisons spread out in various parts of the world where torture was a fact of life. As of this writing, Congress and the press have still not been able to detail the breadth and the scope of these operations, and the president, while condemning torture, had to be shamed into signing a bill that would not exempt the CIA from this practice.

The Abu Ghraib story was produced by Mary Mapes. It won a well-deserved George Foster Peabody Award, but even before that, producer Mapes had been on a roll. She had located the illegitimate black daughter fathered by segregationist Senator Strom Thurmond and after much hounding, persuaded her to give a first-ever interview.

Producers can get hot, just like baseball players. When a hitter is "in the zone," the baseball looks more like a beach ball. One feels imbued, omnipotent. That's when things get dangerous, because in journalism you're only as good as your next story. So perhaps Dan Rather's enthusiasm for the next piece Mary Mapes had in mind was understandable. For some time Mapes had been looking into the story alleging that George W. Bush had ducked the Vietnam draft more than thirty years ago and then ducked his obligations to the Texas Air National Guard. This story had been floated about for years. During the 2000 presidential campaign, some Democrats stumping for Al Gore, including John Kerry and Max Cleland, raised the Bush-National Guard issue at rallies and in interviews. Vice President Gore did not, perhaps because of reports that his family had used its influence to secure for him a relatively cushy assignment as a journalist/photographer for the army during Vietnam. While Gore flew over some hot spots from time to time, there is no record of his being involved in actual combat.

Once again, Dan Rather was blinded by the light of a scoop with a hot producer. Never mind that he had two political conventions to anchor, plus doing the *Evening News*, plus working on other stories for *60 Minutes Wednesday*. Never mind that he was also covering a hurricane in Florida. Never mind that the story would air just two months before the presidential election and that no matter how the story ended up, it would once again involve a member of the Bush family and would look like a Rather vendetta. He wanted in. Mapes had delivered for him before and was certain she would again.

In fact, Mary Mapes had not set out to simply rehash the Bush–National Guard allegations. The focus of at least part of her research team was on what George W. Bush was doing while he was supposed to be in the Guard flying jet planes. What the team found were individuals, some Bush supporters and some not, who claimed to have firsthand knowledge of serious criminal activity on the part of the future president, matters that, if true, were far more serious than his skipping Guard duty. The problem was that no one was willing to go on camera to tell his story. But after weeks and weeks of cajoling, it appeared a few might agree.

Investigations require time and patience, but those two requirements flew out the window when Mapes was given photocopied documents concerning Bush's National Guard record. Suddenly, the documents were driving the story. As is well known now, she was handed the photocopies, first two pages, and later four more, by a man named Bill Burkett, who was familiar to many journalists and considered something of a zealot. Burkett, a former Guardsman, had a long-standing beef with George W. Bush, the Guard, and the Veterans' Administration in part over a dispute about benefits. That in and of itself did not disqualify him as a source, but when he later changed his story about where the documents had come from, it definitely damaged his credibility. The documents purported to show that Bush had refused to take a necessary physical, that the commander of the Guard unit had disapproved of Bush's transfer to another unit in Alabama, and that pressure had been exerted to make Bush's performance record appear better than it had been.

In an effort to extract more documents from Burkett, Mapes agreed to put him in touch with the Kerry campaign so that he could impart his advice on how Kerry should respond to criticism of his war record. That call to one of Kerry's top lieutenants, former Clinton press secretary Joe Lockhart, amounted to nothing. But Mapes's critics used it later as proof that she had a political bias.

Burkett had given Mapes the documents shortly before Labor Day weekend. She then set about hiring document experts to examine the photocopies and draw conclusions. Mapes said that she had been planning a story for Wednesday, September 29. The broadcast would be preempted by other programming on the Wednesdays of September 15 and 22, which left only September 8 and 29 as possible airdates. Since it was already September 4, the notion of throwing together such a politically charged story in just four days seemed ludicrous, but that is what Mapes convinced the new executive producer, Josh Howard, had to be done. They knew that other news organizations had the same photocopies and could run their stories at any time. It is not clear when Rather was informed of this airdate. The team moved into round-the-clock mode, pulling Rather out of hurricane coverage and flying him back and forth between New York and Texas for hurried interviews.

The decision to go for September 8 meant that Mapes was forced to assemble whatever she had, not necessarily whatever made the best story. What she had, basically, was a bunch of photocopies and several rushed interviews with people who had already been heard from, at least in print. Ben Barnes, the former Texas lieutenant governor who said he had made calls on behalf of Bush to get him into the Guard, had told his story to the *New York Times* in the fall of 1999. As for the documents, only one of the four experts hired by CBS was willing to stake his reputation that the signature on two of the documents had been made by Bush's National Guard commander, who had been deceased for some time, and that the documents could have been produced on certain typewriters available at the time. The authenticity of the four documents shown in the report was certainly not bulletproof, to put it generously.

Mapes believed that the content of the documents "meshed"—a word she used a lot in explaining her reportage—with the known facts about Bush's term in the Guard. What she seemed to be saying, and would later continue to maintain, is that the content or gist of the documents was more important than the issue of whether or not they were fake. The end justified the means, and the means is what journalists call "the process." "Process is just as important as content," Phil Scheffler told me. "You have to do it right or the content falls apart. Of course, process matters. How you got the story matters. Did you steal the documents? Did you pay somebody off for them? All of that matters. Sure, the story may be right, but you have to get it the right way or you'll end up screwed in the end. That was part of the reason why Mike Wallace used to call me 'Dr. No,' because I was always questioning how he got the story. The process is part of the story, and I don't think Mapes understood that. She was still riding the wave from Abu Ghraib—she was a hero. But if I had been sitting in that editing room, I would have said, 'Where did this Texas guy get the documents?' And if she had said she wasn't sure, I would have said, 'Well, then you can't use them.' It's not even a difficult call."

How much was Dan Rather wired into this story? According to some members of the Mapes team, he did occasionally question her about how much of what she had was genuine, but in general he was not considered tough enough on his producers. "He didn't oversee his producers the way Mike Wallace and Morley Safer do," said one 60 Minutes veteran. "But he was a good judge of talent and he surrounded himself with good producers who didn't need much overseeing. In and of itself, there's nothing wrong with that unless you're trying to portray a picture of being a hardworking journalist when you're not."

As for the political implications of going with the story, most colleagues agreed that Rather did not jump on the train just because the story was about George W. Bush. "He would have done the same thing if the story had involved John Kerry," correspondent Richard Wagner told me. "He wasn't trying to throw an election. He just thought he had a great story and he wanted it to be true. It was also another example of Dan's loyalty to people he trusted. He believed in Mary Mapes and he wanted the story to be true."

"Would he have gone after the same story if it had involved a Democratic-liberal instead of a Republican-conservative?" asked former executive producer Bud Lamoreaux. "Yes, he would have, but he probably wouldn't have been excoriated as much. I mean, Dan is just an animal reporter. He'll bite you in the ankle to get a story and he just won't let go."

To that point, the freelance producer Lucy Scott, who had been brought in to help on the story, recalled an incident that occurred during one of the team's frantic late-night chartered flights between New York and Texas. "I was sitting in the front of the Lear jet, and Dan was in the back with an unlit cigar in his mouth, dead on his feet," she told me. "And I said something to someone else about Bush, and from the back I heard Dan say, 'Lucy?' I turned around and he said, 'Look, I just have this thing and I just have to tell you this: he is the president of our country, and as long as we are working together I don't want you to refer to him as Bush. You call him President Bush or the president.' And I said, 'Okay. I'm sorry.'"

Throughout that Labor Day weekend of madness, neither Rather nor the rest of the team got much sleep in their quixotic attempt to beat an unreasonable deadline. Mapes admitted, "I felt crushed by the press of time." One wonders why no one in authority stepped forward, took one look at the zombies trying to make the story happen, and said, "Stop. Just stop. This is not worth it. The payoff is not worth the risks. Stand down and go for September 29. If someone else runs with these documents first, then find a way to advance and broaden the story."

In fact, the senior management of the broadcast, Josh Howard, senior producer Mary Murphy, and Vice President Betsy West, did not even come to the office on Labor Day, with just two days remaining before the air date. Was this story important enough or not? Said one team member, "By the time the grownups had returned from the beach, the train had already left the station."

On Wednesday, September 8, another bizarre incident occurred. Howard, Murphy, and West, now joined by two CBS lawyers, another staff member, and Mapes, decided to screen the finished piece. They were crammed like rush-hour straphangers into a tiny editor's room with nary a seat or a square foot of floor space available. When Rather arrived, he opened the door and saw that the piece was already halfway through. Not one person except for Mapes offered to give Rather a seat. No one suggested that the editor stop the piece and re-run it from the beginning. It was as if Rather were some visitor who had opened the wrong office door. According to someone who had witnessed the moment, Rather closed the door and walked slowly down the hall. "He was crestfallen," the staffer told me. "We sat down in another office and he was really emotional. I said, 'I'm so sorry, Dan. I don't get what just happened. I'm really sorry.' And he just looked at me. I mean, they really fucked him. And this was before we even knew that anything was wrong and that we were about to go off a cliff! These people wouldn't make a space for him in the room. It just broke my heart because they felt that he didn't need to be part of the process—that his opinion didn't really matter."

The tape was later shown to CBS News president Andrew Heyward, who approved it for air. Heyward would later claim that his subordinates, mainly Betsy West, had misled him about whether proper checks had all been made on the overall veracity of the report as well as the authenticity of the documents.

"Andrew Heyward could have stopped that broadcast from airing," correspondent Phil Jones told me. "He was the last person to see it. And where was he when the shit hit the fan? Boy, you never saw him again."

When the broadcast ended that night, the team members returned to their hotel, had a few celebratory cocktails, and went to sleep believing they had accomplished something heroic. And as they slept, critics of the report were wide awake and flooding the Internet. At least one blogger had fired his first salvo even before the broadcast had gone off the air. Much of the critics' "proof" that the documents were fake, specifically arguments over typeface and proportional spacing, later proved to be wrong, but this so-called proof was picked up without question by the mainstream media. Rather said, "There are bloggers who the mainstream press seems to take delight in our dilemmas. They picked up pretty quickly on those who were partisan and politically motivated and who had an ideological axe to grind. We had a story that had thermonuclear potential in its reaction. And instead of saying we have to be prepared to respond quickly to any and all criticism, we were remarkably unprepared to do that."

In the end, what had aired was a six-year-old story supported by documents of highly questionable validity on an issue of little consequence. As Mark Laswell wrote in *Broadcasting & Cable* magazine, "What they found was precious little information that qualified as news. In the sprint to the finish line, they failed to notice that their scoop—even if legitimate—didn't really add up to much."

"I was covering the campaign in 2000," Phil Jones told me, "and Mary Mapes was spending all her time then trying to run that story down and she never could. Then she spends three more years on it? Let me tell you that if there was anyone out there who hadn't concluded that George W. Bush used influence to get into the Guard and did not fulfill the spirit of his commitment, I don't know who they are. And most people had already decided either it didn't make a goddamn bit of difference or they weren't going to vote for the little bastard anyway."

That such a huge uproar had been produced by such a thin story also came as a surprise to producer David Gelber. He and correspondent Ed Bradley had another story that was supposed to air that night but was bumped by the Rather piece. "My story had been vetted by so many people that even the Brooklyn Board of Rabbis signed off on it," Gelber told me. "We knew how the forged Niger documents had gotten into circulation. The documents purported to show that Saddam Hussein had attempted to buy yellowcake uranium in Africa to build his nuclear plant but the documents were fake. And we had it all nailed down."

Forged documents again. Only this time, the documents in question were used by the Bush administration as one of the justifications for going to war. It was the claim that Saddam was attempting to restart his nuclear program that led former ambassador Joseph Wilson to publicly criticize the Niger-nuclear connection as phony. That in turn had led some members of the administration to "out" Wilson's wife, Valerie Plame, as a covert CIA agent. Gelber's story was supposed to air on September 8, 2004, and had it aired on schedule, it would have put CBS News way ahead of a major story that so far has led to the indictment of Vice President Cheney's aide I. Lewis "Scooter" Libby for being one of the leakers.

"I was told our piece had to wait because I heard Rather had this great piece that was going to break new ground on George Bush," Gelber said. "And I remember seeing the story and saying, What's the big deal here? I mean, it just didn't seem like a new story. Then later, Andrew Heyward issued a statement that my piece was too controversial to air so close to the election. So that was the standard that he was establishing. It was unbelievable! I've never seen censorship here before, but we were censored. I regarded Heyward's decision not to air the Niger piece as censorship, and that's how I see it now."

A revised Gelber-Bradley piece aired a year and a half later.

By the next morning, the storm created by the documents reached a hurricane force that not even Rather had ever experienced. During a conference call to discuss how CBS should respond, Andrew Heyward is said to have screamed, "If someone fucked this up, they'll be phoning in from Alcatraz!" This from the president of the News Division who had approved the story prior to air.

In an effort to respond to the critics, the team was dispatched to try to find someone, anyone, who would support the documents. They found an octogenarian who had been the late commander's secretary and flew her on a chartered jet from Texas to New York. She said on camera that the documents were probably not authentic because she had not typed them and they did not follow the form she generally used. But she added that the content accurately reflected what Lieutenant Colonel Killian thought about young Lieutenant Bush at the time. Bill Small, watching at home, asked the same obvious question that had occurred to just about everyone else: "Why didn't they have her on the original show? It would have been so easy to do, and it would have helped what they were trying to tell on the show."

Rather, Mapes, and West then rushed to revisit Burkett, who had given Mapes the documents and who had since changed his story about where he had gotten them. Heyward had issued orders to make Burkett the heavy, to make it seem as though his single fib about the origin of the documents was to blame for the entire fiasco. Rather repeatedly asked the old man, "Then you lied to us, didn't you?" until even Rather couldn't stomach it anymore. Burkett's wife was beyond angry. She screamed at West and Mapes that they had made her husband "crawl" on camera and that they were trying to pin the mess on him, which, of course, is precisely what Andrew Heyward wanted them to do.

It was a shameful exercise and Rather and Mapes knew it. These "follow-up" reports defending the broadcast began to turn up almost nightly on the *Evening News*, much to the consternation of the show's executive producer, Jim Murphy, who wondered, since this had happened on *60 Minutes Wednesday*, why they didn't use their airtime to defend their story instead of tainting his broadcast.

"It's the same failing I had seen with Rather over and over again," Ed Joyce told me. "'I want this so much that I will suspend my belief here and there—suspend the process.' I guess what stunned me was the defense by Rather. The switch went on in my brain and I said, 'Uh, oh. He's in trouble here.' It's the same thing he did over and over again. You know, 'Don't tell *me* I'm wrong.'"

After a week and a half of "we stand by our story," Heyward finally ordered an on-air apology delivered by Rather on the *Evening News*, and a concession that the documents could not be authenticated and should not have been used. If the apology wasn't the low point of Rather's career, it had to be in the top three.

In interviews Rather continued to maintain bravely if not foolishly that the documents could be authentic, telling one reporter, "If they prove to be fake, I'd like to break that story" (to which one columnist replied, "Who would he interview . . . himself?").

Heyward was dispatched to the White House to personally apologize to the Bush administration. After all, there were wider political implications to this episode. Viacom chief Sumner Redstone had publicly stated the obvious: Republican administrations favored less government regulation than Democrats did and Viacom had big plans ahead to further broaden and widen its entertainment empire through acquisitions and other maneuvers. Heyward wanted to make clear that CBS was not anti-Bush, and his personal apology was publicly accepted by a White House spokesman.

CBS management also announced that an "independent" panel would investigate how the report was produced and that its findings would be made public. Their choice of former attorney general Richard Thornburgh and former Associated Press executive Louis Boccardi to head the investigation was seen by most of us at CBS News as a recipe for another disaster. Thornburgh had been a longtime Bush family friend and Boccardi hadn't been inside a newsroom in years. Neither man had any experience in broadcast journalism. Neither man had a clue as to how television news reports were put together or about the relationship between producer and correspondent. Where was the impartial TV news veteran—a man like the retired Bob Chandler who as vice president of CBS News was famous for his rapid-fire questioning of producers whose stories he had screened?

"The panel was all wrong," Morley Safer told me. "I don't know what on earth Thornburgh was doing on there. They had no one with any television experience. That's a major error. And there are plenty of people out there who are no longer working who would at least be open-minded and who would understand the process. They should have included a senior trusted person from this network or formerly from this network."

CBS also hired a private investigator, a former FBI agent, ostensibly to track down the origin of the documents. When it was later revealed that he had spent most of his time looking into the personal life of Mary Mapes, it was not only Mapes who was outraged. "The fact that CBS had a private investigator looking into its own employee," wrote the *New York Observer*, "suggests that well before the panel issued any findings, network management had begun to shift its focus away from solving the mystery behind the documents and toward placing the blame for the decision to air the segment."

The investigation took more than three months; the results were finally released in early January 2005. The widely quoted headline was that the Rather-Bush story had been driven by "a myopic zeal" on the part of Mapes and the rest of her team. If there was any villain in all of this, said Thornburgh, "it was haste."

Executive producer Josh Howard, senior producer Mary Murphy, and

Vice President Betsy West all took hits for not having done their oversight jobs very well, but criticism of Heyward was mild. After firing Mapes and demanding the resignations of Howard, West, and Murphy, Moonves said that he had spared Heyward because "He had asked the right questions— he did his job; his lieutenants didn't do theirs." That explanation did not sit well with most people at CBS News. Producer David Gelber's complaint was typical: "How can Heyward keep his job? I think the fact that he's still working here is stunning. Because this is a guy with no honor. Josh Howard had told them to fold their cards, but Heyward was orchestrating the cover-up and leaving the impression that his lieutenants had screwed up. I'm just crazed about this."

I asked Morley Safer if he thought the firings were appropriate and necessary. "Heads had to roll," he said. "You could not just say 'Mea culpa, we made a mistake.' They had to fire people. But did they fire the *right* people? No. And that's all I will say about that."

More than nine months later, Heyward finally was fired. Most likely, he had cut a deal with Moonves that allowed him to remain on the job until his fifty-fifth birthday, October 29, so that he would be eligible for early retirement benefits. Rather had seen that one coming. "Heyward won't last a day beyond his fifty-fifth birthday," he reportedly told a friend. In fact, Heyward was gone less than a week later.

One CBS veteran who had not been involved in the affair said that she had been willing to wait for the Thornburgh-Boccardi report before making a judgment. I allowed her to vent not for attribution because of the sensitive nature of her position. "I wanted to cut them some slack. But when I heard that Mary Mapes had called Joe Lockhart, I just snapped and said, 'Fire her ass!' I was looking for mitigating circumstances in that report but I read all two hundred and twenty-four pages and there's not one mitigating moment. They were all asleep at the switch. Didn't they think there was something weird? We'd been looking for these documents for five years and we got them on day one and they're on the air on day six, with Labor Day in the middle? And it's a white-hot election? I mean, this thing was so radioactive. And you know Karl Rove [Bush's deputy chief of staff] is going to eat our nuts. I'm really mad at Dan. He's a political reporter. That's his pride; he's one of the best political reporters in America and this is a story involving his home state. Where the fuck was he in all this? I don't care how tired he was. I don't care how hard he was working. You're only as good as your last story."

As for Rather, the report concluded that he should have been more involved in the piece. Moonves added that since Rather had already apologized and had "voluntarily" announced that he was stepping down as anchor, "any further action would not be appropriate." The report also concluded that there was no evidence of political bias as a motive for pursuing the story and that the panel could not prove or disprove the authenticity of the documents. Both Mapes and Rather used this last point as something of a major concession, with Mapes repeatedly telling interviewers that no one had conclusively exposed the documents as fake and that proving their authenticity had not been part of her job. Whose job was it then — Sotheby's?

Bernie Birnbaum's conclusion was shared by Rather's supporters at CBS. "Dan was not well served. I don't think his producer served him well and he sometimes puts too much faith in his producer. When you're dealing with this kind of material, you can't be ninety-nine percent pure. There's no gray area. It's either black or white. But he's always driving, always trying to be first. So he said, 'Let's do it.'"

"One supporting pillar of that story has been called into question," Rather told Marvin Kalb at the National Press Center in Washington. Of course, that "supporting pillar," the documents, turned out to be a load-bearing wall. "Yes, I stuck with the story. Yes, I stuck with my people. I've made every mistake in the book. But my attitude is we go into the story together, we ride through whatever happens, and we come out on the other end together. I didn't give up on our people. I didn't and I won't."

Speaking on a panel at FOX News, Carl Bernstein said that although he didn't know anything about Mary Mapes or her politics, news organizations, including the *Washington Post*, were going to make mistakes for a variety of reasons. "CBS should be held accountable by its viewers, particularly in terms of its response, which was belated. Now they've cleaned house to some extent, but I think there are really huge problems, especially in television news, of which political bias is about the least. Our failures of reporting are mammoth, and they rarely have to do with the question of political bias. There's enough available airtime to do real reporting like you used to see or still do in newspapers, but none of the networks want to do it."

Rather said he believed that the larger truth of the story still managed to get through to most of the audience despite what he believed were partisan attempts to deflect attention away from the substance of the story and onto the tainted documents. "The public at large, they got it," Rather told Kalb. "They understood that the story still hasn't been denied. They understood that on the documents, I wish we had done it better. No excuses. And that gives me hope that something is turning in this country when it comes to journalism. Now, if you're wrong, they'll nail you. But people understand that many of the politicians of both parties have gotten so good at what I call hidden hand pressure that the public is waking up to it. And if we have an increase in the integrity of journalism, it will start with the public demanding it."

Once again, though, a reasoned assessment of the gist of the report would have led any reasonable person to conclude that the mess hadn't been worth it from the beginning. Had Mapes's team kept going on the larger story—the far more serious allegations against young George W. Bush—it might have led nowhere, but it might also have led to a bigger scoop than Abu Ghraib. Saying the ingredients might not be kosher but the dish is pure is simply not good enough.

"Sometimes we have to be saved from ourselves," Phil Jones told me. "Sometimes our strengths become weaknesses when you have weak management. Andrew Heyward could have saved Dan from this. And if Andrew Heyward and the rest of that gang had spent any time in Washington and understood the sensitivity of the politics, they would have never rushed this on. Somebody had to save Dan from this and say, 'No—you do not want to do this.'"

Interestingly, Van Gordon Sauter, the original Mr. Anti-Washington, agreed with Jones that if you put your anchorman out in front on a story, especially a politically charged story, the least you can do is cover his rear. "I kept trying to figure out who in the fuck was protecting the anchorman? He needed to be protected and nobody was doing it. *He is the asset.* And it doesn't matter whether the producer is badgering anybody to get it on. They can badger all they want. But when things go sour, someone has to ensure that the anchorman is behind a thick wall and doesn't get any shit on him. CBS was flailing away out there and people in Texas were out there telling lies and Rather was saying things that were not appropriate and were damaging to himself. Someone should have said, 'No, you're not going to say that. You're not going to talk at all.'"

Should Rather have resigned along with his fired colleagues? Andy Rooney thought so, telling a radio interviewer that Rather's response should have been "If they go, I go." Former president Ed Joyce agreed. "Stick a fork in him. He's done. He sullied the reputation of that place and they've got to get over that. In my opinion he was guilty of journalistic malpractice. To go out on a limb with that sort of thin sourcing and then when you get caught, go on the *Evening News* defending it in such an arrogant fashion was wrong."

At a forum sponsored by Court TV, Don Hewitt was asked if Rather should have been fired. "Yes," he replied. "I have a built-in bias against reporters who have axes to grind. I think that's a crime against journalism." No one asked whether Hewitt also had a built-in bias against employees who accuse their bosses of sexual harassment. In 1998, CBS offered a female *60 Minutes* employee a half-million dollars plus a transfer and a promotion to keep her from going public with her well-documented charges against Hewitt. She took the deal.

In another gratuitous shot at Rather, Mike Wallace appeared on FOX's *The O'Reilly Factor* in November 2005 to promote his book. During the interview he said, "I was there the weekend they were putting the [Bush] story together and it was chaos." No one working on Mapes's team that weekend recalled seeing Mike Wallace. The edit rooms for *60 Minutes Wednesday* were not even on his floor in the building. Wallace also said, "Dan acknowledged to me that he had not seen the finished piece before it went on the air."

"Is that right?" O'Reilly asked. "Too busy?"

"Yeah," Wallace replied. "Busy. One thing or another."

That was not the reason, but Wallace said it anyway. He also went on NBC to tell Katie Couric that he thought Rather should have quit. "He would have been seen as a hero."

"The moment that report came out, he should have said, 'I'm outta here,' a longtime staffer told me. 'It's my fault and I'm gone.' He was already so old, why not just go? Why take those other people down with you? Why? It's so typical of Dan—make it look like it's somebody else's fault. For once in his life he should have folded his hand. But it's a game to him, and staying in the game is everything to him."

That remark reminded me of a conversation Rather once had with producer Richard Cohen years after Cohen had left the network. The two hadn't seen each other for a long time but decided to get together for what proved to be an awkward lunch. "I remember saying to him, 'The business is gone, Dan, it's gone south,'" Cohen told me. "'You don't need money anymore and you're way past proving anything to anybody. Why don't you get out? Get out on your own terms and on your own feet?' And Dan said, 'I have to do this. I have to anchor the *Evening News* because that's all I am.' This story is Macbeth. It's about someone who was so seized by his own ambition that he forgot everything else. All he wanted to do was anchor the *Evening News*—in fact, he wanted to *be* CBS News."

Dan Rather was hanging on now for dear life. But if he needed to rationalize his refusal to do what some people felt was the honorable thing, he needed to look no further than the tenets of two men who had had a major impact on his life. His old nemesis Richard Nixon used to say, "A man is not finished when he is defeated. He is finished when he quits." And his late father, Rags, wanted this phrase etched on his tombstone: "Don't quit."

That would justify Rather's stance, both to himself and his supporters. He would not give his enemies, real and perceived, their final satisfaction. He would not allow the bloggers, the right-wingers, the turncoats at his own network, to dance around with his scalp. But he knew that hanging on for one more season would mean a cruel reprise of that episode as the eager child on the baseball team. He knew it would mean sitting on the bench, game after game, until he was allowed to take the field with the season virtually over.

His old manager didn't want him back then. His new manager didn't want him right now.

11

Edward R. Murrow Is Dead

If Roosevelt were alive today he'd turn in his grave.
— Samuel Goldwyn

Finally, in May 2005, *60 Minutes Wednesday* was formally canceled. Les Moonves insisted that the Bush affair had had no bearing on his decision, that ratings and only ratings were to blame. Although the broadcast was known to have been in trouble, the announcement clearly came as a shock to at least some of the more than eighty producers, associate producers, broadcast assistants, and editors who had worked on the show. At a hastily called meeting outside the staff's ninth floor offices across from the CBS Broadcast Center, executive producer Jeff Fager, the show's original boss who had been brought back after his successor, Josh Howard, resigned in the wake of Memogate along with two other senior staffers, told the group that the only villain in this sad story was the audience—that not enough people were willing to watch a broadcast that would not succumb to the entertainment mania that had infected the rest of television.

Dan Rather, his lower lip quivering and his eyes moist, thanked members of the group for their hard work and dedication and gave them hope that many of their jobs would be saved. Staffers were told that airtime might be set aside for a series of "specials" anchored and reported by Rather and that those specials would need to be staffed. More than a few graybeards in the audience—veteran producers and editors who had spent decades in the company—knew that this fantasy life preserver was just that, fantasy. The last situation CBS wanted to create was a new forum for Rather. CBS had stopped producing documentaries years ago, and the only news "specials" they were now airing concerned Britney Spears's pregnancy and the acquittal of Michael Jackson.

So dozens of associates, assistants, producers, and editors, including me, walked the plank a week later, each being informed in person or by telephone that his or her services were no longer needed. The show's demise left CBS News management with a myriad of problems, not the least of which was what to do with Dan Rather. With correspondents Bob Simon and Scott Pelley moving to the Sunday show to pick up the slack for the eighty-eight-year-old Mike Wallace, who would retire in March 2006, and the seventy-five-year-old Morley Safer, and with the young South African Lara Logan taking the place of CNN's Christiane Amanpour, whose contract for occasional reports was not renewed by CBS, the Sunday broadcast would now have eight correspondents. Dan Rather would make nine. The weekly fight for airtime, or "face time" as it is known in the business, as well as the intramural tug of war for the best stories, promised to be bloody. And it would be bloodier still for Rather, whose scheduled return to the broadcast on which he had appeared before succeeding Cronkite was treated with ill-concealed resentment by some of the weighty veterans.

Mike Wallace, the master of the left-handed compliment who could always be relied on for a swipe at Rather while pretending to praise him, did not relish the idea of sharing the spotlight with yet another star on what used to be *his* program.

"I'm the one who suggested that Dan come here the first time back in the seventies," Wallace told me. "But now, it's tough. Come on, he was here [he raised his hand up to the sky and then dropped it down to his knees] and then all of a sudden he's down here. He's taken quite a beating, and that's why I said to him, 'Dan, for Chrissakes, if you had just resigned at the time, you would have been a hero. If you had just said, 'I quit—these are the people I work with, they got fired, so I ain't gonna stay.'"

Morley Safer has not been a friend of Rather's for years, since their days in Vietnam. Rather had replaced Safer not long after Safer's now-famous report about the burning of a Vietnamese village by a platoon of U.S. Marines. While reluctant to discuss Rather, Safer would say only that "When Rather replaced me in Vietnam, he went to a group of marines and said, 'If I were you guys, I would have shot him.' Or words to that effect. And that my report should never have gone on the air."

"Was this to get on their good side?" I asked.

"Who the hell knows why? Have I ever confronted him about it? No. Now we just have a polite relationship."

There was also the matter of the gun—the .38 caliber Smith and Wesson that Safer swears Rather was wearing when the two first met in a hotel in Saigon, along with the battle fatigues and combat boots. "I could not imagine who he might have to shoot at the Caravelle," Safer wrote. "The service was usually pretty good." To this day, Rather angrily denies that he ever wore a sidearm in Vietnam. "Would he like me to get witnesses?" Safer laughed.

After Memogate, the relationship between the two *60 Minutes* staffs was anything but polite, with some people on the Sunday broadcast self-righteously insisting that the Rather report had sullied their show's reputation and that such a fiasco could never have happened on their show.

In fact, it had, twice in a four-month period. In April 1999, Lesley Stahl delivered an on-air apology for a Mike Wallace story that accused a U.S. Customs official of being connected to a Mexican drug cartel. The story was based in part on a memo that later turned out to be bogus. The previous December, executive producer Don Hewitt apologized on air for a June 1997 report based on a British documentary about smugglers who swallowed heroin in latex gloves to get past authorities. An investigation later showed that the film's producers had staged the whole thing, faking locations and paying actors to portray the smugglers.

Safer did not feel that the issues were comparable. "It's not the same. Did the executive producer know the names of the sources? Nobody's suggesting he didn't. Did everybody sign off on these stories with full knowledge? Yes. Were we had? Obviously. I'm sorry, but they're not parallel. Memogate was a totally different thing, especially since it involved the holder of the highest office in the land. That demands extra scrutiny."

It was now time to pile on Dan Rather. Don Hewitt, at this point out of the picture but never out of the earshot of anyone with a microphone or a notepad, gave his take on Rather's personality. "The *Evening News* is like Miss America, only it's Mr. America. If you're in a three-network race and you come in third, then the public is against you."

Like *The Flying Dutchman*, Rather was coming back for the year remaining on his contract, whether *60 Minutes* liked it or not. He got a taste of what life would be like during the summer of 2005, when Hurricane Katrina blasted the Gulf Coast and took apart the city of New Orleans. Here was Dan Rather, Mr. Hurricane himself, forced to sit out what would become the biggest story of the year. Despite his repeated requests to at least join in the coverage, he was repeatedly told that CBS News had it under control.

Appearing as a guest on *Larry King Live* on CNN, Rather watched several correspondent reports about the approaching Hurricane Rita. King then turned to Rather in the studio and asked, "Do you miss this?"

"Sure, I miss it," he replied. "How could I not miss it having grown up with the lore of hurricanes at my grandmother's knee on the Texas coast and [having] covered hurricanes for a long time?"

King then asked Rather if he was bitter about being left out.

"No, there might have been a little at the beginning."

"Why not?" King asked.

"Well, because I'm a pro and I don't say that in any self-serving way. But you know, I have a passion for journalism and over the years I've gotten credit for a lot more than I ever deserved. I've had more come to me than I deserved. And so when the bad times come, by this stage of my life, I'm able to put it in some perspective."

Rather went on to praise the network's coverage of Katrina, saying that it represented the best of "the next generation of reporters."

Actually, a lot of people questioned just how brilliantly the next generation had covered the storm and its aftermath. Apparently, reports of widespread looting and rapes in the New Orleans area were flat wrong. Reports of deaths in the thousands turned out to be wrong as well. FOX issued a "news alert" about the situation at the Superdome, where some twenty thousand evacuees were struggling to survive. "There are robberies, rapes, carjackings, riots, and murder. Violent gangs are roaming the streets at night, hidden by the cover of darkness." While the pain and suffering of the evacuees was plain and obvious, the ineptitude of the federal, state, and local response deplorable, and the failure of the president to immediately leave his Texas ranch just plain stupid at best, there was virtually no evidence to support the notion that the city had become a Mad Max film. According to state officials, of the 841 recorded deaths related to Hurricane Katrina, 4 were from gunshot wounds. No incident of rape at the Superdome was confirmed.

Biographer and former *New York Times* television industry reporter Sally Bedell Smith was appalled by the coverage. "Those people down in New Orleans basically got the story wrong, over and over and over again. They were misreporting. They were reporting rumor. They were all hot and bothered. They didn't know what they were doing. I didn't see any reporter weeping on camera over seventy-nine thousand people dying in the Pakistan earthquake. It was all self-dramatizing."

Rather's characterization of the Katrina coverage as among "television news's finest moments" was no doubt his nod to the men and the women who had to slog through the muck and the rushing water to get the pictures and the interviews. But the reporting was by almost any measure atrocious.

Would Katrina and its aftermath have been covered more accurately if Tom Brokaw, Peter Jennings, and Dan Rather had been at their anchor desks as they were for 9/11? There is little doubt it would have, and Katrina was perhaps the first example of how much television news has lost with their departure.

F or Dan Rather, award ceremonies were nothing to get excited about– Lord knows he had been to enough of them. But this one, the 57th Annual Emmy Awards, which aired in September 2005 on CBS, would be different in more ways than one. This was not about having been voted the best in some arcane category; this was more of a hail and farewell.

The final hour of the broadcast featured a tribute to the three major TV news anchormen who had delivered the news to Americans for the past quarter century: Tom Brokaw, who had retired the previous year; the recently deceased Peter Jennings; and Dan Rather, who had been forced to leave his anchor chair in March.

Alan Alda, one of the presenters, said, "They were solid. They illuminated our darkest hours with insight and they reflected the warm light of our sunniest days. They helped us know who we were, and through that, maybe who we could become. They were a kind of electronic Mount Rushmore on our journalistic landscape. And now the contours of that mountain have changed. Tom Brokaw and Dan Rather have left their evening news desks, and my friend Peter Jennings has said his last goodnight. But the standard of excellence they have left us with—the will to get it right—those things will never go away."

This was followed by a brief film of highlights from the trio's careers, ending with each of their final signoffs. The most wrenching, of course, was Jennings's hoarse revelation that he had lung cancer. It was the last time he would ever appear on the air. When the house lights came up and Brokaw and Rather walked to center stage, with a photo of Jennings on the large screen behind them, they received a sustained standing ovation. The elite of Hollywood stood and saluted what used to be the elite of television news, Brokaw tall and dashing as always and Rather stiff and uncomfortable as always.

As Brokaw and Rather praised their friend Peter and thanked the Academy for its gesture of recognition, the CBS TV director twice cut to a man in the audience whom most viewers probably did not recognize—Les Moonves, the CEO of CBS, a man who was playing a major role not only in the departure of Dan Rather but also in the radical reshaping of network news.

"Using this medium for good journalism comes with undeniable challenges," Rather told the audience. "But there are times, as we've been most recently reminded with Hurricane Katrina, when the immediacy and images that television provides are not only the best way to convey a breaking news story, but are also an essential part of the story itself."

Following his appearance on the Emmy Awards in Los Angeles, Rather took the red-eye back to New York. He had a busy schedule that included appearances in which he could defend his reputation and attempt to shore up his legacy. The next morning, he appeared at Fordham University's School of Law along with HBO Documentary president Sheila Nevins; both were to receive Lifetime Achievement Awards that evening at the TV Academy's News and Documentary affair.

Occasionally fighting back tears, Rather told the assemblage that "a new journalism order" had been created in which politicians "of every persuasion" used their power to pressure the conglomerates that now owned the TV networks to do their bidding. These pressures, he claimed, had created a climate of fear in newsrooms more insidious than anything he had ever experienced in his career, along with "the dumbed-down and tarted-up" priorities of ratings-driven managements.

That night, in a hotel ballroom in Manhattan, many of Rather's colleagues rallied around him. Host Ted Koppel praised Rather as a man of "honesty and integrity and decency." He added, "I would simply urge your most vociferous critics to take a page from the White House's own playbook. When one of their own makes a mistake, they stress the importance of 'looking to the future' and of 'not playing the blame game.'" When he appeared to receive the award, Rather received a thunderous standing ovation. The award was inscribed, "For a distinguished career of outstanding television reporting. Known as the hardest working man in journalism, Dan Rather is a fearless reporter who has kept Americans informed about the world's most defining moments for over half a century."

The president of MSNBC, Rick Kaplan, a former CBS News wunderkind, mounted a rhetorical attack: "Dan was meticulously careful to be fair and balanced and accurate. When did we stop believing that this indeed is how we all perform our jobs, or try to? When did we allow those with questionable agendas to take the lead and convince people of quite the opposite? It's shameful. Dan's legacy is the gold standard journalists today have struggled to live up to. And working to serve the needs of his fellow citizens as admirably as he has is how he deserves to be spoken of."

A s 60 *Minutes* geared up for the start of the season, Rather was given an office at the opposite end of the floor, the space vacated by the old 60 *Minutes Wednesday*. What he wasn't given was the co-editor title held by the other correspondents. Between September and the end of the year he appeared only three times, with one of his reports airing on Christmas night and another airing on New Year's night, two of the worst nights on the TV schedule in terms of viewership.

Actually, he didn't appear but was mentioned on another 60 *Minutes* story, ironically reported by Mike Wallace: an exclusive interview with Russian president Vladimir Putin.

PUTIN: Don't you know that some of the American journalists were fired because of their positions on Iraq or the presidential election campaign?

WALLACE: Were you talking about Dan Rather at CBS News?

PUTIN: Yes, exactly. . . . On our TV screens we saw him resigning. We understood that he was forced to resign by his bosses at CBS. This is a problem of your democracy, not ours.

WALLACE: He still works at CBS News. He continues to work, as a matter of fact, on 60 *Minutes*.

Yes, barely.

"I think he's largely responsible himself for what happened," Sandy Socolow told me. "I mean, he's unwelcome at 60 *Minutes*, absolutely unwelcome. Nobody wants to have anything to do with him at all."

Rather brooded publicly about the same concerns that weigh heavily on the minds of professionals who have worked against obstacles of every variety to maintain some sense of honor, dignity, and respect for their craft and for the responsibilities that come with it.

"Some people conclude that the sun is rapidly setting on what was once considered broadcast journalism," Rather told the *Washington Post*. "And what makes some people concerned about it is bloggers, paid political operatives posing as White House journalists, paid hucksters hustling political programs all lumped together in a soup that's served up as professional punditry. I confess that I am concerned that we may be reaching the point where too many members of the press fear being labeled unpatriotic or partisan if they challenge the actions or decisions of political leaders of any persuasion. What the country doesn't need, particularly just now, is a press that's docile—never mind obsequious or intimidated. I don't agree with those who say, 'Dan, it's already happened,' but I do recognize there's some danger."

There are signs, albeit few, that not everyone in the mainstream press has been cowed or intimidated by the current administration. NBC's White House correspondent David Gregory, whom some view as a Rather-in-the-making, became a major irritant to White House press secretary Scott McClellan and has been targeted by Bush supporters on firedavidgregory.com. After calling McClellan a "jerk" during a daily news briefing, Gregory apologized and added that he had no personal animus toward the president.

"Like Dan Rather, Gregory just does his job but does it in a way that irritates some people," said Robert Lichter of the Center for Media and Public Affairs. "He's not trying to stand out; he just does so normally. He has to recognize that as a weakness as well as a strength."

Dan Rather still doesn't see it that way. In speech after speech, crisscrossing the country, Rather told audiences that journalists needed "a spinal transplant" and he admitted on C-SPAN that he faulted himself for not being more aggressive during the debate over going to war with Iraq. "I wish I had had more courage to ask more and tougher questions and not to confuse my role as a patriotic journalist with the role of trying to protect your popularity, your ratings, your demographics, and all that stuff that doesn't matter in the big picture of what's best for the country."

One of the hot movies of 2005, a movie that garnered six Oscar nominations, was a film about Rather's hero, Ed Murrow, titled *Good Night and Good Luck*. Director and cowriter George Clooney had arranged for a piece about the film, which concerns Ed Murrow's clash with anticommunist bully Senator Joseph McCarthy, to appear on the NBC newsmagazine *Dateline*. But the piece was dumped at the last minute in favor of a profile of Eva Longoria, one of the stars of the hit show *Desperate Housewives*.

"Why do we keep talking about Murrow?" Rather asked in a Marvin Kalb interview. "Because he knew the public can pick out whatever is phony. Every time we cower, every time we say, 'I know the tough questions, but I'm just gonna sit here on my duff because I don't want to face the bloggers, I don't want to face the political machine that's gonna come down on me'—every time we do that, we lose. And we deserve to lose."

To be sure, the mainstream press in the misguided throes of post–9/11 patriotism asked few tough questions about such subjects as the Patriot Act, the reliability of intelligence concerning weapons of mass destruction, and why so much of the Islamic world seems to hate America. Even the *New York Times*, it turns out, knew about President Bush's executive order allowing widespread domestic wiretaps without court orders but agreed to hold it—in the interest of "national security"—*for one year*.

"When reporters do what is in the best traditions of journalism," Rather said at the National Press Club, "the public responds positively. When the public begins to get a whiff of 'Hey, these guys think they walk on water,' or worse, 'They're in the pocket of politicians and they're scared because they think their access is going to be cut off, or they don't have the spine they once had,' then the public isn't surprised when we say we're going to dumb it down and sleaze it up because if we don't, our competitors will. The public gets that. In our arrogance, we sometimes think we're fooling them, but we're not. When our bosses say, 'Hey, we've done market research and we know people don't want to hear about poverty in Africa, they don't want to hear about AIDS in China, they want to hear about Michael Jackson and whatever murder case is going on in California.' When we succumb to that, when we don't speak *truth to our own power*, that's when the public says, 'I don't think much about these guys anymore.'"

The power now—at least, at CBS—is Les Moonves. He initially expressed a desire to "break the mold" of television news, with ideas ranging from "blowing up the CBS News building," a remark not particularly amusing given the times in which we live, to some version of the British TV show *The Big Breakfast*, in which women in lingerie read the news, or *Naked News*, which is as billed. "Of course," he told the *New York Times*, "you could have two boring people sitting behind a desk. Our newscast needs to be somewhere in between."

Moonves is a failed actor who became a hot executive picking TV shows for Warner Brothers. At CBS, he has parlayed two shows, *Survivor* and *CSI* (which begat *CSI New York*, *CSI Miami*, *NCSI*, and no doubt others), into a first-place finish among households and frequent weekly victories among the eighteen-to-forty-nine demographic most coveted by advertisers. Moonves thought nothing of involving himself in the content of news broadcasts despite having no journalistic credentials of his own. To him, there really was no distinction between news and entertainment—it was all "content," subject to the same programming and marketing laws.

So he had no pangs of conscience about having Dan Rather, the network's top reporter, host a *48 Hours* broadcast that was no more than a blatant advertisement for *Survivor*, CBS's big reality hit. "Is there anything people won't do for fame?" Rather said at the opening. Moonves thought nothing of having CBS newscaster Julie Chen (now Mrs. Moonves) host a reality show called *Big Brother*. He is also having success with a radio format called the Jack. "We have no deejays, we have no news, we have no sports, and we have no weather," he boasted. "Programming costs are considerably down." Not bad for a man whose reported compensation last year was $52 million. He and his boss, Sumner Redstone, are said to covet CNN, which would allow CBS to close virtually all of what's left of CBS's foreign operations where CNN is strongest and fire most of the older, more experienced, and more expensive CBS news personnel on the domestic side. "Americans do not like dark," Les Moonves has said. "There's a way to fix news, just as there's a way to fix prime time."

"He says Americans don't like dark news?" asked a veteran producer. "So the biggest story of the past forty years is a war we're losing in the Middle East that's costing a hundred billion dollars a year and more than two thousand kids dead. We don't cover that war aggressively. Why? Is that in keeping with Les's view of lighter, happier news? This is precisely why I feel in my gut that whatever Dan Rather's limitations, and God knows he's made huge mistakes, compared to the people who have been running the news at this network, he's the height of integrity."

"I've been told by people on the inside," Bob Pierpoint commented to me, "that Moonves said, 'Edward R. Murrow is dead' and that his era is over. And I was told he said it as a *threat.*"

Murrow . . . Murrow—that pain in the ass Murrow. As the frustrated King Henry once said of Thomas Becket, "Will no one rid me of this troublesome priest?"

After reading Moonves's philosophy in a *New York Times* magazine cover story, former CBS News president Ed Joyce told me, "Jesus—that was terrifying. He should be arrested for indecent exposure of his brain. This is the end of civilization as we know it."

The youth market is now driven by technology and technology drives the youth market. Video can be streamed through cell phones. Anyone with a computer can be a "journalist"; anyone can have his or her own radio talk show. Anyone can publish a book without the tiresome interference of fact checkers and editors. This, we are told, is empowering. This is true democracy. This is what the authors of the Communications Act of 1934 must have meant when they wrote of their desire for "a multitude of voices." This multitude, however, is based more on technological convenience than on craft—what a miracle that we can now hold a tiny video gizmo in the palm of our hands and find celebrity poker on every channel!

While citizen journalists are sprouting like crabgrass, the professionals are being mowed down. In a single week in September 2005, the *New*

York Times announced that it would be laying off forty-five employees from its newsroom and thirty-five more from the *Boston Globe*, which it owns. The Knight-Ridder chain announced a hundred firings from its newspapers in Philadelphia before selling off its entire empire. The *San Jose Mercury News* announced that it would be paring its staff by sixty, including fifty-two in the newsroom. The *Los Angeles Times* later announced eighty-five newsroom cuts. At NBC News, CEO Jeff Zucker told employees there would likely be News Division cuts to offset the cost of retooling the network's disastrous prime-time lineup.

CBS has now started a blog of its own, which, one producer told me, "is like Pat Boone covering a Little Richard record—it's a corporate 'me-too.'" Moonves has begun a video-on-demand scheme to stream programs on Google. He called the venture "a truly historical meeting of the established and the new media." One techie publication called the Web site "a piece of crap" and "a shambles." Former CBS executive and now CNN president Jonathan Klein saw the future, too, and it didn't even involve human beings. "Within five years," Klein proclaimed, "people will be saying, 'I want the news about Jordan,' and they'll type *Jordan* into their handheld device and up will pop the news about Jordan that they want, nothing else. There won't be anchors. There won't be people introducing stories. Consumers won't have the time or the need for that. They'll just be getting the news they want, when they want it, in whatever form they want it."

Klein left it unclear whether the consumer in question wanted the news about Michael Jordan, Vernon Jordan, Barbara Jordan, the great tenor sax man Louis Jordan, or the entire country of Jordan—but that's the consumer's problem. As a corollary, this new on-demand news means that the consumer gets to see and hear only what he or she wants and nothing else. It is narrowcasting—*narrowminding* might be a better term—in its most unadulterated form, leaving out all other news that might be considered important to an informed public.

Dan Rather, writing in *Nieman Reports*, foresees an "on demand" age in which everyone is wearing blinders and earpieces. "With the Internet comes the potential to act as one's own managing editor, one's own gatekeeper. Well, it's a double-edged sword. And we ought to recognize that this trend could contribute to the balkanization of our society and of our lives, public and private. In a way, sure, the Internet is the realized ideal of a town meeting. But no one foresaw a town meeting where you wouldn't have to listen to everyone in the room."

While careful not to trash the new technology and the potential profit that is driving it, Rather was quick to register his belief that at some point, especially in times of crisis, someone will have to act as the clear voice of reason.

"Les Moonves, whom I respect as a person and a leader, has said he does not want one person to become the new all-purpose center for a revised *Evening News*," Rather told Larry King. "Now I can see some difficulties with this concept, which isn't to say it won't work. But when big news breaks, unexpected news—9/11, Oklahoma City, Hurricane Katrina—somebody has to step into the chair and lead."

Apparently, Moonves began to see things the same way—or at least the marketplace made him see things the same way. He abandoned his unconventional musings and launched a very public wooing of NBC's Katie Couric, whose *Today* show contract would expire in May 2006. It seemed that while the Voice of God approach was unappealing to Moonves, the Voice of Goddess had distinct possibilities. The numbers being tossed about were truly staggering, even by television standards. Twenty million a year?

Andy Rooney, never reluctant to take a stiff shot at his network, pointed out to Larry King that since Bob Schieffer had taken over, the *Evening News* had been up an average of two hundred thousand viewers per week compared with the same period the previous year. "He's embarrassing the hell out of CBS. His ratings keep going up and they're still talking about giving $20 million to Katie Couric. I say take that $20 million and buy forty reporters and make CBS the best news report in the world."

"Hiring her just shoots fireworks over a graveyard," said Tim Goodman of the *San Francisco Chronicle*. "It looks pretty and all, but what's needed is a paradigm shift. Yet that's a brave new world nobody is ready to build."

"Yeah, that's just what CBS News needs," former congressional corre-spondent Phil Jones told me sarcastically, "a liberal Democrat who is so in love with Hillary Clinton she can't have her on the *Today* show enough. And here we're headed into a campaign where Hillary is an obvi-ous nominee. This sounds like a disaster in the making."

Dan Rather, meanwhile, continued his barnstorming tour, playing to packed houses from Maine to Los Angeles. In Hartford he told the audi-ence, "We cannot afford to ignore the world beyond our borders. We know little about Iraq, less about Iran, and almost nothing about North Korea." At the University of Maine, Rather, referring to bloggers, asked, "Is more better? And is all that calls itself news really news?" In Oregon he told a Portland audience that if there is another war, it would likely ignite in the North Pacific instead of in Europe. "North Korea, China and Russia have nuclear weapons and all three have ambitions for greater influence. This is increasingly a part of the world with high-tech weaponry and the most deadly weaponry of all."

In Seattle he said, "Whether you are talking about the 21st century economy, or, God forbid, a new world war, a great deal of the pages of this century will be written on the axis of Seattle-Vancouver to Tokyo, Pyongyang, and Beijing." Before a group of students in Seattle's McCaw Hall, he urged journalists to "do more digging and cut down on sensa-tionalism." Of Memogate, he would say only, "I've had a lot of time to think about that story, and I've learned a lot."

In a two-night appearance in which he sold out the Dorothy Chandler Pavilion in Los Angeles at $50 to $75 a pop, Rather answered questions screened for him by the speaking tour's producer and by what the *Los Angeles Times* called "a member of Rather's entourage. 'American jour-nalism needs a spine transplant [now obviously becoming part of his stump speech] and they need it quickly.' Obliquely referring to Rather's troubles, one audience member asked what role bloggers played in his career. 'Their influence was less than perceived,' he said, equally obliquely. 'Some bloggers have found it to be a good way to further a par-ticular political agenda. It's not a crime, but the public should recognize there's a new opportunity here to manipulate public debate.'"

Screened questions? No direct questions allowed about Memogate? When George W. Bush and other politicians pulled that trick at staged "town meetings," Rather was among the first to point it out and call it for what it was. Once again there was more than an echo of Richard Nixon being heard—not in substance but in the eerie parallel. After resigning, Nixon spent several years in silence except for his paid interviews with David Frost and then embarked on a feverish attempt to recast himself as America's elder statesman. He wrote more than a half-dozen weighty tomes on world affairs with titles like *Victory without War*; his views on foreign policy were frequently sought by the press and were offered obligingly in many op-ed columns and magazine essays. It was called his "rehabilitation." He knew the nation would never forget Watergate and his sad departure from the White House, but it was critical to him to let the world know he was still watching the game, if not as a player than as an expert commentator.

Of course, Memogate was a summer squall compared to the tsunami that was Watergate, but given Rather's makeup, he seemed to be adopting yet another persona—the conscience of the broadcast news business. Fred Friendly, Ed Murrow's alter ego, played that role for the last thirty years of his life, railing against the "sellout" of the press to corporate interests and warning the nation of its consequences. (Friendly's old enemy, Don Hewitt, used to ask, "Who died and left him in charge of the First Amendment?")

Even Walter Cronkite, who had been criticizing TV news and CBS in particular for the last twenty years, caused barely a ripple when he publicly challenged all the news anchors to call for the withdrawal of U.S. troops from Iraq, saying that his "editorial" against the Vietnam War "was one of the moments I am most proud of." Then, of course, he mattered. Now he is eighty-nine and much of the population doesn't even know who he is or who he used to be.

For once, Dan Rather does not want to follow Walter Cronkite. He wants another chance at the plate, another try at the big swing—that Ted Williams swing—to remind any and all that he can still hit if only given the chance.

"He's miserable, I know that for a fact," said columnist Verne Gay. "I wrote a column saying CNN should hire him. They said they had no interest. It's just killing him and he's miserable."

M ost of us want to go out when we feel like it. Some people actually pull it off. Salinger wrote his book and just said adios. Jim Brown, the greatest running back in history, walked away from pro football at the height of his powers and never looked back. Schubert never finished his Eighth Symphony but plunged straight ahead and wrote his Ninth, which many consider his greatest work. Johnny Carson put in his thirty years, said his farewell while still number one and appeared only once on live television again. There is something admirable, even heroic, about leaving the scene in one's prime. The public's appetite is insatiable, even gluttonous, and it is the sage who finally says *enough*—I've given all of you enough.

Others tempt fate and stay a bit too long on the stage, as some of Rather's friends and foes believe he has. But there is something noble about people who remain in the arena despite fading skills, dark clouds of self-doubt, and the incessant threat of young ones staking new turf. Sir John Gielgud continued acting into his nineties because he felt he still had something to offer and still had an audience more than willing to receive him. The vision may be dim, the reflexes stiff, the gut instincts not quite as solid, but the passion remains. Those who choose to soldier on and who are not dogged by alimony payments or IRS threats do so because they must—it's what they know; it's what they do.

Tom Brokaw walked away on his own terms. Good for him. Ted Koppel is setting up shop somewhere else. Bully for him, too. Dan Rather remains, or is at least trying to, because he believes in his soul that reporting is why he was put on earth. Yes, he has a wife who is a successful painter, and children—Robin runs her own high-tech business and Danjack is an assistant district attorney—and two grandchildren who give him joy and pleasure. But in 2006, he still suits up for every game, just the way his coach had told him to, knowing full well he probably won't get to play.

In April 2006, CBS announced that the *Today* show's Katie Couric would become the first female solo anchor in network TV history, prompting right-wing commentator Lowell Pointe to denounce the move: "Couric's politics are apparently even further to the left and more partisan Democratic than Dan Rather's." Pointe quoted conservative pinup Ann Coulter's description of Couric as the "affable Eva Braun of morning TV. . . . She hides behind her Girl Scout persona in order to systematically promote a left-wing agenda." Apparently learning nothing from the Dan Rather experience, CBS also gave Couric the managing editor title.

For Les Moonves, the Couric hire is a major roll of the dice. A *TV Guide*/AP poll found that 49 percent of those questioned said they would prefer to see Couric in the morning, with 29 percent voting for the evening. Andy Rooney cast his vote with this remark on the Don Imus radio show: "I don't know of anybody at CBS who's happy she's coming here." Both Walter Cronkite and Bob Schieffer praised the move. Dan Rather was either not asked or had nothing to say on the day of the announcement.

On the evening of Rather's final broadcast as anchor, CBS presented a one-hour retrospective of his career. It was edited in the now common quick-cutting MTV style, and one caught snippets of overlapping audio as the pictures whizzed by: *"This convoy* (gunfire blaring in background) *is trying to move out of the area."* . . . *"On the main campus of the University of Alabama, Governor George Wallace is standing in the doorway and appears to be giving a message of capitulation."* . . . *"In this building, perhaps from one of those open windows, is where the assassin who killed President Kennedy is believed to have fired."* . . . *"If any or more of what is believed to have gone on is true, how high up in the White House did it go?"* . . . (Nixon) *"Are you running for something?"* (Laughter) . . . *"No sir, Mr. President, are you?"* . . . *"The documents purported to show that President George W. Bush received preferential treatment during his years at the Texas Air National Guard. After further investigation, we can no longer vouch for their authenticity."*

Television captures moments. It cannot capture a life, especially not in a forty-five-minute hour. But what those moments do capture is a man out there on the front lines—taking risks, some of them foolish . . . showing loyalty, some of it misplaced . . . extending himself often beyond reason and common sense . . . doing his job just the way Rags had taught him, doing what he loves.

Rather said, "One can have too much zeal. One can have too much passion. And sometimes I've had too much passion for loving this work and that has led me to make mistakes."

Now, at seventy-four, Dan Rather must be tempted to finish packing those boxes and ship them right back to Texas where it all began for him.

"Jean Rather and I did discuss it," he told a reporter. "She fixed some of her famous Texas prison chili and we had about two spoonfuls' worth of time discussing it. And that was pretty much it."

Epilogue

Picking Up the Pieces

Take me out of contention,
I surrender my crown
So, somebody pick up my pieces
It's just me comin' down
— Willie Nelson, "Pick Up the Pieces"

E ven now, with years still to go in his presidency, George W. Bush is being asked about his legacy. Judgment comes quickly these days; a singer gets lucky with one song and the next album is called *Greatest Hits*. But when a figure has been on the public stage for as long as Dan Rather, there is an irresistible tendency to take stock, to add up the perceived pluses and minuses of the person's life and draw conclusions about whether he really has mattered in the long run, and what effect his career might have on those who follow him.

As for Dan Rather and network anchormen in general, some people believe that any talk of legacy is misplaced and foolish, even laughable. After all, anchormen don't cure cancer or teach children morals and math, or work with the poor and the downtrodden to make the world a better place. They are not among the Mozarts or the Picassos or the Duke Ellingtons whose bodies of work will shape generations for decades and even centuries. Anchormen read the news, period, or so that argument goes.

"I don't think Dan has a legacy," former producer Richard Cohen told me. "I don't think Peter [Jennings] has a legacy. He was well liked and respected, but the idea of legacy is preposterous. What's Cronkite's legacy? The Most Trusted Man in America. That's a legacy? He was an anchorman. You sit there and you read the prompter for years and you have a legacy? I think we should go to the BBC system of newsreaders and stop all this bullshit about how these people are speaking with authority. I'm sorry, but you're not going to browbeat me into believing that anchormen should have legacies."

Former correspondent Richard Wagner, noting the parallel between Rather's rise and fall and the power of network news, agreed. "I don't think people will be talking or writing about him years from now. I think from the 1960s through the end of the century, we saw the beginning of network television and we saw its rapid decline. A hundred years from now, no one will know who Dan Rather was because network news, which was so huge to you and to me and to our country, will have long disappeared."

But what about the argument that the anchors—Cronkite, Huntley, Brinkley, Chancellor, Reasoner, Brokaw, Rather, Jennings, and others—by their very presence guided the nation through difficult times, through wars and domestic upheaval, through political scandals and abuses of power, that they were the people's ombudsmen and had the authority and the audience to address the issues and ask the questions we would ask if we could?

All that, of course, was when they were the only game in town. "I scarcely watch the evening news anymore," biographer Sally Bedell Smith told me. "I still read three newspapers every morning, and I check things throughout the day on the Internet. I've turned away from evening newscasts because even when they try to do things in a longer form, it's just not enough. You either get the news from the Internet, or you get interviews on NPR, or you watch people scream at each other on cable."

If it is fair to say that the Murrows and Cronkites and Huntleys and Brinkleys were useful in their time and that they used the medium effectively while they had the audience to themselves, can the same be said of Rather, who took the anchor chair just as cable was beginning and the Internet was being formed? Setting aside for the moment the peculiar nature of his personality and the many controversies in which he found himself, did he matter for at least the time the stage lights were mainly on him and him alone?

Sandy Socolow, first and always a Cronkite man, doesn't think so. "From a historian's point of view, if you were writing twenty years from now or fifty years from now, he was not very important. I mean, Cronkite was very important, partly because of the era he lived through—Vietnam, civil rights, Watergate, and a series of assassinations. The Cronkite-Huntley-Brinkley years were crammed full of really important, revolutionary news. Fortunately or unfortunately for Rather, he lived through a relatively quieter period. And with the competition, he never had the dominance that Cronkite had and I don't think anyone else ever will. Rather was nothing compared to Cronkite and Huntley and Brinkley, and, of course, Murrow—God, yes—Murrow."

But former vice president Don Decesare saw in Rather's work a reinvention of the anchorman's traditional role. "I think for his time, from the mideighties and around there, I don't think there was anyone who communicated better. I think if you have a true evaluation of the stories that he put an imprint on, I don't think there's anybody who matches up and I would include Cronkite in that. I mean, the Gunga Dan stuff was much more like him. Sure, the outfit looked silly, but it was much more like him to be there. God knows, I spent a ton of the company's money making sure he got there plenty of times. But I actually believe Jennings and Brokaw went on the road a lot of times just because Dan was doing it. And so in that sense, he created the genre of the late-twentieth-century anchorman."

Correspondent Morton Dean, who had switched networks during the Rather years, told me, "When I was at ABC, I had to go to some of the worst places in the world. I'd see Dan there every now and then, more often than I saw the other guys. And I used to think, here's one guy who doesn't have to be here. And he might be quirky and strange, but at least he's out there getting the story."

On the subject of his treatment by the press, most of the critics who followed Rather's long career are fulsome in their praise.

"I think Dan was one of the greats, period," said Verne Gay, who covered the TV beat for *Ad Age*, *Variety*, and *Newsday*. "The first Gulf War, Dan got on that plane and got a knock in the middle of the night and got to interview Saddam Hussein. Tom Brokaw's attitude was, 'Hey, I've got a life.' Tom would get on a plane, but what he really wanted to do was go whitewater rafting or climb a mountain. I mean, when all is said and done, I miss Dan. I miss seeing him on the air. I miss covering him. I miss all his bullshit and his head games and his toadying to the *New York Times*. He was just a wonderful part of this beat."

"I found him to be baffling at times, as everybody did," Bedell Smith told me. "I mean, some of the things he would come out with—you always wondered whether these things were spontaneous or studied. But the images of Dan, both good and bad, are what endure. You think of Gunga Dan, you think of the Carla thing, you think of the exchange with Nixon—yeah, he made a difference."

Of course, the writers could see only what Rather chose to show them. The evidence and the comments from many people who worked most closely with him suggest that his primary motive was not so much building a legacy of greatness but escaping from all-too-human fears: fear of being judged unworthy, fear of failure, fear of not being accepted, fear of being left with only a wood block to play in the band. Ultimately, Dan Rather did not believe that just being himself would be enough in a business in which image is often more important than reality.

"I've always felt sorry for him, but in a way he probably wouldn't imagine," says former correspondent Richard Threlkeld. "He is one of the two most self-conscious people I have ever met . . . the other being Richard Nixon. Dan was Mr. Outside. He was on the outside when he came to the Washington bureau, and they didn't really accept him because he was from some jerkwater station in Texas. He's been Mr. Outside his whole life, and he'll never have a moment's peace. I don't think he ever felt he really belonged. Not as an anchorman, not as a White House correspondent, not as anything. I just don't think he's a very happy guy, and I don't believe he ever will be."

What remained of the old CBS News came together in Manhattan on February 1, 2006, at the Museum of Radio and Television, just a few doors down from CBS corporate headquarters. It was a memorial service for Artie Bloom, who had died over the weekend from cancer at the age of sixty-three. Artie was the first and only director *60 Minutes* had ever had, and he had handled the big events as well—the election nights, the inaugurals, the special coverage of disasters, the complex, multicamera, largely unscripted events that separated the great directors from the wannabes. The public at large had never heard of him but within CBS, he was a little giant who went from gofer to go-to guy over his forty years with the company.

I had been to these memorials before—for Charles Kuralt, for Eric Sevareid, for Douglas Edwards, for Burton Benjamin—men who at least in my mind had left true legacies. Memorials were not just about paying respects; they were also a chance to see CBS veterans—even those you really didn't want to see—who had retired or gone off to other networks. Like family funerals, whether you liked it or not, you would have to make nice with that cousin you had avoided for twenty years, and promise to do lunch at some unspecified time and place. I usually sat in the back, leaving the front rows to the big shots and the big names, preferring instead the company of grunts like myself. For the Sevareids, the Kuralts, and the like, Dan Rather was always among the speakers. He was, after all, the figurehead of the News Division. And the talk was always about how the death of so-and-so had made the organization smaller in ways too painful to contemplate, how another piece of what CBS used to be had broken off and could not be pasted back on.

This event was different. For openers, the guests arrived somewhat in shock. That morning, John Roberts, the handsome young correspondent whom CBS News had been grooming for several years to replace Rather, had resigned and bolted to CNN. After having done everything CBS had asked of him, including substituting for Rather during weeknights, anchoring on the weekends, going off to cover the war in Iraq, and covering the White House, he was being passed over in favor of rumors of Katie Couric.

The foyer of the museum was alive with the buzz.

"You mean he just quit?"

"Yup. He's been taken off the air effective immediately."

"But he was just on last night for the State of the Union!"

"Well, he's gone now."

Now John Roberts, seduced and abandoned, would try to build his legacy somewhere else.

A quick glance at the program revealed that—yes, indeed—Dan Rather would be speaking, that he would follow Mike Wallace and Don Hewitt to the podium. Hewitt and Wallace kept their remarks brief, warm, and funny, with only Hewitt creating a bit of a stir when he said, "And that ticking stopwatch, which was my idea, Artie lit and framed so beautifully that it's now in the Smithsonian."

Many of the old-timers in the audience looked at each other quizzically. Hey, how's that again? Wasn't that stopwatch *Artie's* idea? Perhaps Hewitt was still freshening up his own legacy for the time when he would be the subject of one of these gatherings. Then Dan Rather walked slowly and stiffly up the stairs, onto the stage, and up to the podium. The audience knew that he would speak much longer than the others and at some point emotions would overtake him.

Sure enough, midway through his address, Rather said, "When Artie first got the diagnosis that he dreaded, he passed by while I was watching a football game. He stopped and said, 'You know, I love it when a team has third and long. I love the drama of those moments.' [Voice cracking] He never backed up, never backed down, and never gave in. We will remember him any time we enter any television control room. We will remember him when the *60 Minutes* stopwatch starts ticking [voice cracking badly now]. We will remember him when there are just seconds to go before a big broadcast [breaking up now] and we will remember him any time in life when we are third and long or fourth and goal. We will remember him when the full moon glows and the North Star rises over the Hudson. We will remember Artie for what he was and for what he stood."

Applause enveloped Rather as the spotlight shone down on him. Now the chatter from the exiting guests was no longer about John Roberts's sudden defection or Don Hewitt's subtle rewrite of history. Now it was all "So, what did you think of Rather?" and "Geez—what did you make of Dan?" Any competent reporter who had to write a story about Artie Bloom's memorial would have had to make Rather the lead.

Once again, intended or not, planned and practiced or not—as he folded his script, walked out of the spotlight, and left the stage—Dan Rather became the story.

Notes

Prologue

2   "We weren't attending"   Boyer, *Who Killed CBS?* p. 8.

4   "With Dan, you just never knew"   Interview with the author, 10/26/05.
    "I am not—never have been"   *The Camera Never Blinks*, p. 274.
    "transparently liberal"   *Larry King Live*, 7/28/02.

5   "This race"   Transcript, CBS News, election night 2000, 11/7/2000.
    "If we could be one-hundredth"   CBS affiliates meeting, 6/27/93.

6   "I never watched him"   Ed Gordon radio show, NPR, 3/9/05.
    "Keep in mind"   *The Camera Never Blinks*, p. 18.

7   "In a little over a year"   Interview with author, 12/23/05.

8   "We keep saying"   Ibid., 11/2/05.

9   one anonymous executive   Howard Kurtz, "Stopwatch Ticking for Dan Rather," *Washington Post*, 6/15/06.

9   "They talk about wanting to break with the past"   Jacques Steinberg, "Moving Ahead, Rather Throws Sad Look Back," *New York Times*, 6/17/06.

1. Thanks for the Memories

13   "Dan Rather holds the dubious"   teevee.com, posted 11/7/96.
    "Not long after"   Transcript, *CBS Evening News*, 3/9/05.

14   "The Independence"   michellemalkin.com, posted 3/7/05.
    "Why is Dan Rather"   *National Review*, 10/11/05.
    "He's a superb reporter"   Ken Auletta, "The Long and Complicated Career of Dan Rather," *New Yorker*, 3/7/05.
    "Mike, may all your foxholes"   Dennis Duggan, *Newsday*, 3/2/05.
    "It surprised quite a few"   CNN, Wolf Blitzer Reports, 3/7/05.

15   Rather as a "victim"   Glenn Garvin, "Cronkite Urges News Anchors to Push Withdrawals," *Miami Herald*, 1/16/06.

15   "You can take your CBS"   Tim Goodman column, *San Francisco Chronicle*, 3/9/05.

"Yes, Dan Rather and his"   "Where Rather Was Right," *The Nation*, 10/11/04.

"He's ninety-eight years old"   Interview with author, 12/7/05.

"Dan Rather is guilty"   Column, *New York Daily News*, 11/24/04.

16   "an institutional failure"   *FOX News Live*, 1/10/05.

"They haven't even asked me"   Transcript CNN, *Larry King Live*, 6/02/05.

17   "Be thou a soul"   Tom Shales, *Washington Post*, 3/9/05.

2. Never Stay Down and Never Quit

20   "our Champs-Elysées"   *I Remember*, p. 13.

"In a boxing match"   Ibid., p. 27.

21   "Father's marathon"   Ibid., p. 155.

22   "I had an optimistic"   Academy of Achievement Interview, 5/5/01.

23   "My identity"   *I Remember*, p. 115.

"We turned on the radio"   Academy of Achievement Interview, 5/5/01.

24   "He meant it as"   *I Remember*, p. 112.

"All those opposed"   Ibid., p. 203.

"Daisy is a"   Ibid., p. 201.

25   "a handsome, proud"   Ibid., p. 51.

"the greatest speech"   Ibid., p. 144.

26   "They pointed to something"   Ibid., p. 197.

"Standards have changed"   Ibid., p. 75.

27   "Those papers had"   Ibid., p. 83.

"There he stood"   Ibid., p. 88.

28   "In Liberty"   Ibid., p. 121.

"What makes you think"   *The Camera Never Blinks*, p. 30.

29   "I polished them"   *I Remember*, p. 253.

"Son, I watched you"   Ibid., p. 250.

"And that was it"   *The Camera Never Blinks*, p. 33.

30   "I possessed a kind of"   *I Remember*, p. 256.

"Have you listened"   *The Camera Never Blinks*, p. 37.

31 "She was a pretty"   Ibid., p. 53.

"It helps," he once wrote   Ibid., p. 273.

32 "Oh, that's Dan"   *The Camera Never Blinks*, p. 305.

33 While doing a radio weathercast   Ibid., p. 54.

"Charles Collingwood"   Academy of Achievement Interview, 5/5/01.

34 "I had never heard"   *The Camera Never Blinks*, p. 61.

"The first day on the job"   Interview with author, 10/27/05.

"They all arrived late Thursday"   *How Many Words Do You Want?* p. 74.

36 "The interesting thing"   Interview with author, 11/21/05.

"I told my friends"   Ibid., 11/3/05.

37 "Look at the white institutions"   "Away, Dixie," *The Nation*, 4/11/94.

3. From Big D to D.C. to the VC

39 "I had to go everywhere"   Interview with author, 10/20/05.

40 "The NBC station"   Ibid., 10/24/05.

"I had to hotfoot it"   *The Camera Never Blinks*, p. 115.

41 "I'm Dan Rather"   Ibid., p. 117.

"So I went with it"   Interview with author, 10/24/05.

42 "I'll tell you one thing"   Ibid., 10/20/05.

"This has been one of"   *The Camera Never Blinks*, p. 134.

43 "We said, 'We're just feeding"   Interview with author, 11/21/05.

44 "public relations ploy"   Smith, *In All His Glory*, p. 166.

45 "So, Stanton tells Dan"   Interview with author, 11/21/05.

"He had done such a good job"   Ibid., 12/07/05.

46 "As country as I am"   *The Camera Never Blinks*, p. 147.

"You did a good job"   Halberstam, *The Powers That Be*, p. 437.

47 "Once a politician"   *The Camera Never Blinks*, p. 158.

"Johnson could say"   Ibid., p. 158.

48 "Three things could have happened"   Ibid., p. 159.

"What is it with you?"   Ibid., p. 161.

"Collingwood was the only guy"   Interview with author, 11/21/05.

49 "This war isn't going to be over"   *The Camera Never Blinks*, p. 195.

"I think we were the first"   Interview with author, 12/27/05.

50 "He stepped off the plane" Ibid., 11/21/05.
"I hit the ground" *The Camera Never Blinks*, p. 197.
"My first reaction was" Ibid., p. 200.
51 "I felt I should spend" Ibid., p. 205.
According to Rather Ibid., p. 212.
52 "They might be mistaken" Ibid., p. 213.

4. Nixon and Gunga Dan

55 "Naturally, I think too much" Tony Schwartz, *Playboy* interview, 1/84.
"Here was a kid who" Interview with author, 11/5/05.
"When that was over" Ibid., 10/20/05.
56 "Rather wanted to do" Ibid., 10/27/05.
"He was a straight reporter" Ibid., 10/20/05.
57 "Rummy used to get even" "Tape Runs as Brokaw Knocks Rather," *Albany Times Union*, 10/17/96.
"It was October third" Interview with author, 10/20/05.
"The print reporters" Crouse, *The Boys on the Bus*, p. 141.
"Rather often adhered to" Ibid., p. 310.
59 "What can the president do" Transcript, *CBS News Special Report*, 6/17/73.
"I totally disagree with the conclusion" Transcript, *CBS News Special Report*, 5/1/74.
60 "In fact," Jones said Interview with author, 12/27/05.
61 "I went up to Dan" Ibid., 1/9/06.
"He had a more dramatic" Ibid., 10/20/05.
"He stood up to" Ibid., 10/24/05.
"In answering back Nixon" Ibid., 11/2/05.
62 "They had chosen" *The Palace Guard*, p. 361.
"The White House is not" *The Camera Never Blinks*, p. 278.
"I tried to fight against" Ibid., p. 297.
63 "In the course of the past" *The Palace Guard*, p. 369.
"We got to trust him" Buzenberg, *Salant*, p. 267.
64 "The Cuban premier" *CBS Reports: Castro, Cuba and the USA*, 10/22/74.

66 "We had to work very hard" Interview with author, 10/26/05.
    "I said to Dan" Ibid., 1/09/06.
68 "we distrusted the least" *The Camera Never Blinks Twice*, p. 57.
    "Some of the locals" Ibid., p. 66.
69 "After the niceties" Ibid., p. 67.
    "We were told" Interview with author, 11/13/05.
70 "The Afghans with us" *The Camera Never Blinks Twice*, p. 99.
71 "I was doubled over" Ibid., p. 102.
    "This is why you paid" Ibid., p. 133.
72 "It made little sense" Interview with author, 11/13/05.
    "As usual, *60 Minutes*" "Gunga Dan," *Washington Post*, 4/7/80.
    "I was probably too critical" Interview with author, 11/2/05.

5. Life without Walter

75 "It's one of those jobs" Tony Schwartz, *Playboy* interview, 1/84.
76 "Come on, Dick" Salant, *Memoirs*, p. 267.
    "Walter wanted to retire" Interview with author, 9/24/05.
77 "When I was there" Ibid., 12/07/05.
    Mudd strongly denied Interview with author, 12/16/05.
    He corrected the misperception Cronkite, *A Reporter's Life*, p. 351.
    "I must confess" Interview with author, 9/24/05.
78 "I'm telling you" Ibid.
    "I wouldn't do it" Leonard, *In the Storm of the Eye*, p. 22.
79 "He said, 'There are people" Tony Schwartz, *Playboy* interview, 1/84.
    Arledge said he was so smitten Arledge, *Roone*, p. 252.
80 "You told me" *The Camera Never Blinks*, p. 273.
    When Arledge asked Mudd Arledge, *Roone*, p. 255.
    "I honestly believe" Interview with author, 12/26/05.
81 "I'm a journalist" Quoting Houtrides, interview with author, 12/26/05.
    "There was a sense that" Interview with author, 11/3/05.
    "I can't say what Roger" Ibid., 1/23/06.
    "If you pick Mudd" Quoting Morton Dean, interview with author, 12/23/05.

82   "It was Dan and Roger"   Ibid.

83   "With Walter"   Interview with author, 10/24/05.

"He could find something nice"   Leonard, *In the Storm of the Eye*, p. 29.

"We've kept Dan Rather!"   Ibid., pp. 29–32.

86   "I was mystified"   Interview with author, 10/11/05.

87   "There are rocks under"   Boyer, *Who Killed CBS?* p. 50.

"He was being told too many things"   Interview with author, 10/24/05.

88   "It's fair to say"   Tony Schwartz, *Playboy* interview, 1/84.

"I'll never forget the day"   Interview with author, 1/9/06.

"I remember the snafu"   Ibid., 10/26/05.

90   "Rather's bombing"   Boyer, *Who Killed CBS?* p. 54.

"He was always looking for something"   Interview with author, 1/23/06.

6. Seduced and Abandoned

93   "Van wanted the job"   Boyer, *Who Killed CBS?* p. 83.

"I was the general manager"   Interview with author, 10/19/05.

94   "They said the job"   Ibid., 10/24/05.

95   "Then Van did that interview"   Ibid., 10/19/05.

"I gave him the title"   Boyer, *Who Killed CBS?* p. 245.

"Dan was really the guy"   Interview with author, 12/27/05.

"I was running"   Ibid., 1/9/06.

96   "I remember Ernie Leiser"   Ibid., 9/24/05.

97   "No. Which may be one reason"   Tony Schwartz, *Playboy* interview, 1/84.

98   "It was terrible"   Joyce, *Prime Times, Bad Times*, p. 240.

"Rather asked Martha"   Interview with author, 10/19/05.

"Well, that's just fucking obnoxious"   Boyer, *Who Killed CBS?* p. 121.

"Rather thinks you guys"   Joyce, *Prime Times, Bad Times*, p. 44.

"I don't know"   Interview with author, 10/24/05.

99   "The kind of thing we're looking for"   Ron Rosenbaum, "The Man Who Married Dan Rather," *Esquire*, 11/82.

99 "It's all sob sister" Peter Kerr, "Cronkite Now Critical of Network News," *New York Times*, 12/7/83.

100 "They say I took the news soft?" Interview with author, 10/24/05.
"They've copied our whole format" Tony Schwartz, "The Tumult in TV News," *New York Times*, 12/7/83.
"Van wants stories" Ron Rosenbaum, "The Man Who Married Dan Rather," *Esquire*, 11/82.

101 "We fought about it" Boyer, *Who Killed CBS?* p. 140.
"He certainly has not been shunted" *Playboy* interview, 5/84.
"The idea that Walter" Interview with author, 9/24/05.

102 "Walter could do a smaller" Joyce, *Prime Times, Bad Times*, p. 407.
"What did Dan want?" Interview with author, 10/19/05.

103 "I went steaming down" Ibid.
"Howard Stringer was" Ibid., 9/24/05.

104 The *Washington Post* reported Tom Shales's column, *Washington Post*, 6/28/83.
"Know this" Joyce, *Prime Times, Bad Times*, p. 199.
"I flew over to London" Interview with author, 10/19/05.

105 "They were accusing me" Ibid., 9/24/05.
"Rather came to me" Ibid., 10/19/05.

106 "One line from a song" Joyce, *Prime Times, Bad Times*, p. 426.
"In order to pay these" Interview with author, 10/19/05.
"Yeah, there's a logic to that" Tony Schwartz, *Playboy* interview, 1/84.

107 "Yeah, right." Interview with author, 10/19/05.
The Rathers arrived last Joyce, *Prime Times, Bad Times*, p. 503.

108 "Yeah, it hurt" Interview with author, 10/19/05.
"Oh, that's bullshit" Ibid., 10/24/05.
"Didn't like him!" Ibid., 10/27/05.

109 "That is absolutely" Peter Kaplan, "CBS News in Turmoil after Year of Trauma," *New York Times*, 10/23/85.
"None," he told me. Interview with author, 10/24/05.
"Larry Tisch looks to me" Steve Daley, "Dull Declaration of Independence," *Chicago Tribune*, 10/3/86.

110 "Hey, man" Boyer, *Who Killed CBS?* p. 159.

7. What Is the Frequency?

128   "I never said to Howard"   Peter Boyer, "CBS's Tisch Responds," *New York Times*, 3/10/87.

"I want people to know I care"   Ibid.

"'From Murrow to Mediocrity'"   Peter Boyer, "How CBS News Got Tisched," *Business Month*, 6/88.

"self-serving, breast beating"   Editorial, "Dan Rather and the Small Screen," *Arkansas Democrat*, 3/17/87.

129   "My God"   Peter Boyer, "How CBS News Got Tisched," *Business Month*, 6/88.

"Now Rather's getting his"   Peter Boyer, "As the Wheel Goes, So Goes TV Profits and Careers," *New York Times*, 5/8/86.

The *Washington Post's*   Tom Shales, "He'd Rather Be Rather," *Washington Post*, 8/12/87.

"I keep hearing"   Ibid.

130   "I'll do whatever"   Jonathan Alter, "Dan Rather's Struggle," *Newsweek*, 8/24/87.

"I don't know much about"   Interview with author, 10/25/05.

"It was about 6:22"   Ibid., 10/26/05.

131   "What I remember is they"   E-mail to author, 10/26/05.

"It said about 6:29"   Interview with author, 11/28/05.

132   "I don't know"   Ibid., 10/25/05.

"We were in Miami"   *The Camera Never Blinks Twice*, p. 166.

"The network is in black."   Ibid., p. 169.

133   "They may have made"   Interview with author, 11/28/05.

"Maybe I deserved it"   *The Camera Never Blinks Twice*, p. 172.

"I fault myself"   Ibid., p. 173.

"After the second show"   Interview with author, 11/27/05.

134   "There's no excuse for it"   Interview with the *Daily Texan*, 10/14/87.

"Walter's a great journalist"   Tom Shales, "The Anchor and the Angst," *Washington Post*, 1/12/88.

"Is Dan Rather"   Editorial, *Times of London*, 9/17/87.

"'My God'"   Interview with author, 11/5/05.

135   "Tom Bettag should have"   Ibid., 12/27/05.

"So Dan got on his high horse"   Ibid., 10/26/05.

136   "We were in Belgrade"   Ibid., 10/20/05.
       "He just has this ability"   Ibid., 11/2/05.
137   "We all surmised"   Ibid., 10/19/05.
       Spy magazine published a story   Charles Pooter, *Spy*, 2/88.
       "He and his wife are"   Tom Shales, "The Anchor and the Angst,"
            Washington Post, 1/12/88.
       A forensic psychologist   Paul Limbert Allman, "The Frequency, Solv-
            ing the Riddle of the Dan Rather Beating" *Harper's*, 12/01.
138   But author Paul Limbert Allman   Ibid.
139   "a failed ghost-buster"   *TV Guide*, 2/25/89.

8. Live Fire

142   "Dan shared almost nothing"   Interview with author, 10/6/05.
143   "I honestly believed"   *The Camera Never Blinks Twice*, p. 181.
144   "I was in the control room"   Interview with author, 10/6/05.
       "And so I find this"   Transcript, *CBS Evening News*, 1/25/88.
146   "The bastard didn't lay a glove"   *The Camera Never Blinks Twice*,
            p. 207.
147   "I made some mistakes"   *The Camera Never Blinks Twice*, p. 209.
148   "These kinds of interviews"   David Hoffman, "Bush Revels in Reac-
            tion to Faceoff," *Washington Post*, 1/27/88.
       "I don't see any upside to this"   Diane Mermigas, "Affiliates Scruti-
            nize Rather," *Electronic Media*, 2/1/88.
       "I'd never seen brother"   Associated Press, "Sevareid Assails TV
            News," *New York Times*, 2/25/88.
149   "I feel comfortable with Rather"   Richard Stengel, "Bushwacked!"
            Time, 2/8/88.
       "This was an effort to deal with"   Eleanor Randolph, "Counterattack-
            ing the Messenger," *Washington Post*, 1/27/88.
       "Bush was shocked?"   Howard Rosenburg, "Whose Ambush Was It
            Anyway?" *Los Angeles Times*, 1/27/88.
       "Their contretemps was not just a"   Richard Stengel, "Bushwacked!"
            Time, 2/8/88.
150   "Now a personal word"   Transcript, *CBS Evening News*, 1/26/88.
       "Look, I think Dan made"   *Des Moines Register*, 2/8/88.
151   "By this time"   Interview with author, 10/6/05.

152   "We want to allow freedom"   Peter Boyer, "CBS Drops Outspoken
         News Official," *New York Times*, 3/15/88.
      "If we spent more time"   Ibid.
      "called two reporters"   Howard Kurtz, "The Producer and His Break
         with Rather," *Washington Post*, 4/8/88.
      "I really loved"   Interview with author, 10/6/05.
153   *Final Report of the Independent Counsel for Iran-Contra Matters*,
         8/1/93.
154   "What's in and what's out"   *TV Guide*, 12/31/88.

9. Surviving

156   "brave souls"   Tom Shales, "The Anchor, the President and War and
         Peace," *Washington Post*, 9/10/90.
      "I said to myself"   Verne Gay, "The Resurgence of Dan Rather,"
         Newsday, 9/10/90.
      "The only action"   Tom Shales, "The Anchor, the President and War
         and Peace," *Washington Post*, 9/10/90.
157   "Steve Friedman said that."   Michael Ryan, "Dan Rather
         Unleashed," *Time*, 8/27/90.
      "That's fucking outrageous!"   Ibid.
      "I think seeing Dan"   Bill Carter, "A Resurgent CBS Moves to
         Regain the Edge in News," *New York Times*, 12/3/90.
      "I was in the street"   Interview with author, 11/5/05.
158   "Rather and CBS have not"   Ed Siegel, "Rather Enough of Rather,"
         Boston Globe, 2/6/91.
      "The affiliates"   Diane Mermigas, "CBS News Move Hailed by Affil-
         iates," *Electronic Media*, 2/18/88.
159   "You can't hold Dan Rather"   Jane Hall, "CBS Brings Up the Rear in
         Gulf Coverage," *Los Angeles Times*, 2/11/91.
      "It's a very depressing time"   Ibid.
      "the best broadcast news producer"   Press statement by Rather, 2/13/91.
      "is just the peeling of"   James Warren and Kenneth Clark, "CBS
         Trouble Spots," *Chicago Trubune*, 2/14/91.
      "It happened in a very strange"   Interview with author, 10/26/04.

160 "It is no secret"   Verne Gay, "CBS Pulls the Purse Strings Tighter," *Newsday*, 4/9/91.

"Today," he complained   Howard Rosenburg, "Reporter's Love Is Not Extinguished," *Los Angeles Times*, 2/24/93.

"Mr. Rather's leadership"   Dick Williams, "Gunga Dan Still Doesn't Get the Frequency," *Atlanta Journal-Constitution*, 3/7/91.

161 "The ratings were tumbling"   Interview with the author, 11/3/05.

162 "Maybe my experience"   *The Camera Never Blinks Twice*, p. 31.

"Once confident"   Jon Katz, "Over to You, Dan . . . How Cronkite's Heir Became Chung's Sidekick," *Rolling Stone*, 12/93.

"Now here we see Dan"   Interview with author, 11/2/05.

163 "between the half of the people"   Marvin Kitman, "Courage, Dan," *Newsday*, 5/19/93.

"Thoughtfully written"   Radio and Television News Directors' Association speech, 9/29/93.

164 "Gleason the businessman"   Bishop, *The Golden Ham*, p. 13.

"favorite TV couple"   Marisa Leonardi, "The Morning Report," *Los Angeles Times*, 1/1/94.

165 "She's not a hard-news"   Interview with author, 10/25/05.

"I was told to get from"   Ibid., 11/5/05.

166 "Who the hell is Connie"   Frederick Biddle, "Chung in the Hot Seat," *Boston Globe*, 5/10/95.

"I figured management"   Interview with author, 11/05/05.

"Men, in the ancient mythology"   Jeff Simon, "The Real War Isn't Chung vs. Rather," *Buffalo News*, 6/11/95.

167 "Two trips to the Middle East"   Howard Kurtz, "Here's Mud in Your Eye," *Washington Post*, 5/24/95.

"Now, I didn't take kindly"   Claudia Dreifus, "The Survivor," *New York Times Magazine*, 9/10/95.

"His statements are baldfaced lies"   Ibid.

169 "I wasn't as mature"   Marc Gunther, "Rather Relaxed Dan Rather," *Detroit Free Press*, 3/4/96.

"In that one snapshot"   Verne Gay, "Welcome to the Club, Dan," *Newsday*, 3/7/96.

"I'd love to"   Jane Hall, "Rather's Reality Check," *Los Angeles Times*, 3/9/96.

170   "I initially opposed it"   Interview with author, 10/27/05.

171   "Suddenly, you have a guy"   Ibid., 1/23/05.

"*60 Minutes II*"   Monica Collins, "60 Minutes II Is Worthy Successor," *Boston Herald*, 1/15/99.

172   "It instantly became"   "A Chip Off the Old Clock," *Washington Post*,
1/14/99.

"I heard about the attack while"   Alicia Mundy, "In Dan We Trust,"
Media Week, 10/29/01.

"You have to pace yourself"   Gary Cartwright, "Dan Rather Retort-
ing," *Texas Monthly*, 3/2005.

173   "We should have gone with"   Fenton, *Bad News*, p. 17.

"I'm a professional"   *Late Show with David Letterman*, 9/17/01.

174   "I wouldn't want an anchorman"   Michael Hamersly, "People,"
Miami Herald, 9/26/01.

"Extraordinary times"   Editorial, "To Everything, a Season," *Pittsburgh Post-Gazette*, 9/22/01.

"I never needed"   Interview with author, 11/2/05.

"I never doubted it"   Frank Rich, "The Weight of an Anchor," *New
York Times*, 5/19/02.

175   "The major media had to sign"   Interview with author, 12/24/05.

"An overemphasis on censorship"   *Harvard International Review*,
2001.

10. Blinded by the Light

180   Ben Barnes, the former   Jim Yardley, "Former Texas Lawmaker Says
He Helped Bush Get into Guard," *New York Times*, 9/27/99.

181   "Process is just as important"   Interview with author, 10/27/05.

"He would have done"   Ibid., 1/9/06.

"Would he have gone"   Ibid., 12/27/05.

182   "I was sitting in the front"   Ibid., 11/13/05.

"I felt crushed"   Mapes, *Truth and Duty*, p. 188.

183   "Andrew Heyward could have stopped"   Interview with author,
12/26/05.

"There are bloggers"   Kalb interview, 9/26/05.

184   "What they found was precious little"   *Broadcasting & Cable*, 1/17/05.

184 "I was covering"   Interview with author, 12/27/05.
     "My story had been vetted"   Ibid., 10/11/05.
185 "If someone fucked this up"   Mapes, *Truth and Duty*, p. 16.
     "Why didn't they have her"   Interview with author, 12/7/05.
     "Then you lied to us"   Mapes, *Truth and Duty*, pp. 228–29.
186 "It's the same failing"   Interview with author, 10/19/05.
     "If they prove to be"   Bryan Curtis, "The Anchor as Madman," *Slate*,
          9/21/04.
187 "The panel was all wrong"   Interview with author, 10/27/05.
     "The fact that CBS had"   Tom Scocca, "CBS News Reports," *New
          York Observer*, 1/17/05.
     "a myopic zeal"   *Report of the Independent Review Panel*, 1/5/05.
188 "He had asked the right"   Press statement by Les Moonves, 1/10/05.
     "How can Heyward keep his job?"   Interview with author, 10/11/05.
     "Heads had to roll"   Ibid., 10/27/05.
189 "any further action"   Press statement by Les Moonves, 1/10/05.
     "Dan was not"   Interview with author, 11/21/05.
     "One supporting pillar"   Kalb interview, 9/26/05.
     "CBS should be held"   *FOX News Live*, 1/10/15.
190 "The public at large"   Kalb interview, 9/26/05.
     "Sometimes we have to be saved"   Interview with author, 12/27/05.
191 "I kept trying to figure out"   Ibid., 10/24/05.
     "If they go"   Rooney, prior to appearance on *Imus in the Morning*,
          3/1/05.
     "Stick a fork in him"   Interview with author, 10/19/05.
     "I have a built-in bias"   Transcript, Court TV, 2/9/06.
     "In 1998, CBS offered a female"   Conversation with author; also
          sourced in *Tick . . .Tick . . . Tick*.
     "I was there the weekend"   *The O'Reilly Factor*, 11/28/05.
192 "I remember saying to him"   Interview with author, 10/6/05.

11. Edward R. Murrow Is Dead

196 "I was the one who suggested"   Interview with author, 10/7/05.
197 "If I were you guys"   Ibid., 10/27/05.
198 "It's not the same"   Ibid.

198   "The *Evening News*"   Ken Auletta, "The Long and Complicated Career of Dan Rather," *New Yorker*, 3/7/05.

     "Sure, I miss it"   *Larry King Live*, CNN, 9/20/05.

199   "There are robberies"   Susannah Rosenblatt and James Rainey, "Katrina Takes Toll on Truth," *Los Angeles Times*, 9/27/05.

     "Those people down in New Orleans"   Interview with author, 10/26/05.

201   "I would simply urge"   NewBusters.org, posted 10/4/05.

202   "Dan was meticulously careful"   Ibid.

     "Don't you know that some"   *60 Minutes*, 5/9/05.

     "I think he's largely responsible"   Interview with author, 9/24/05.

203   "Some people conclude"   Tom Shales, "Dan Rather Leaving by the High Road," *Washington Post*, 3/9/05.

     "Like Dan Rather, Gregory Just Does His Job"   David Bauder, "Gregory Gets Caught in Political Battle," Associated Press, 3/19/06.

     "I wish I had had more courage"   Kalb interview, 9/26/05.

204   "Why do we keep talking about"   Ibid.

     "When reporters do"   Ibid.

205   "blowing up the CBS News building"   Lynn Hirschberg, "Giving Them What They Want," *New York Times*, 9/4/05.

     "We have no deejays"   Robert Marich, "Succeeding with Generic Radio Content," *Kagan Insights*, 12/05.

206   "Americans do not like dark"   Lynn Hirschberg, "Giving Them What They Want," *New York Times*, 9/4/05.

     "I've been told by people"   Interview with author, 10/20/05.

     "Jesus—that was terrifying"   Ibid., 10/19/05.

207   "is like Pat Boone"   Ibid., 10/11/05.

     "a piece of crap"   *The Register.com.UK*, posted 1/11/06.

     "Within five years"   David Blum, "Anchor Roulette," *New York*, 11/29/05.

     "With the Internet comes"   *Nieman Reports*, vol. 54 (Winter 2000).

208   "Les Moonves, whom I respect"   *Larry King Live*, CNN, 9/20/05.

     "He's embarrassing the hell out of"   Ibid., 1/11/06.

     "Hiring her just shoots"   "No News Is Good News," *San Francisco Chronicle*, 12/5/05.

209   "Yeah, that's just what"   Interview with author, 12/27/05.

209 "We cannot afford" William Weir, "A Moment with Dan Rather,"
     Hartford Courant, 11/14/05.

"Is more better?" *NewsMax.com*, posted 11/3/05.

"North Korea, China and Russia" Dylan Rivera, "Dan Rather Points
     to Tensions," *Oregonian*, 1/24/06.

"Whether you are talking about" Kay McFadden, "Dan Rather on
     News, Himself and Seattle," *Seattle Times*, 1/20/06.

"American journalism" Lynn Smith, "Going Live with Dan Rather,"
     Los Angeles Times, 1/28/06.

210 "was one of the moments" Glenn Garvin, "Cronkite Urges News
     Anchors to Push for Withdrawal," *Miami Herald*, 1/16/06.

211 "He's miserable" Interview with author, 1/23/05.

213 "One can have too much zeal" *CBS News Special*, 3/9/05.

"Jean Rather and I" Tom Shales, "Dan Rather Leaving by the High
     Road," *Washington Post*, 3/9/05.

Epilogue

216 "I don't think Dan has" Interview with author, 10/6/05.

"I don't think people will be" Ibid., 1/9/06.

"I scarcely watch the evening news" Ibid., 10/26/05.

217 "From a historian's point of view" Ibid., 9/24/05.

"I think for his time" Ibid., 10/25/05.

"When I was at ABC" Ibid., 12/23/05.

218 "I think Dan was one of the greats" Ibid., 1/23/06.

"I found him to be baffling at times" Ibid., 10/26/05.

"I've always felt sorry for him," Ibid., 11/3/05.

Bibliography

Arledge, Roone. *Roone: A Memoir*. New York: HarperPerennial, 2003.

Auletta, Ken. *Three Blind Mice: How the TV Networks Lost Their Way*. New York: Vintage Books, 1992.

Barthelme, Donald. *Sixty Stories*. New York: Penguin Classics, 1981, revised 1982.

Bedell Smith, Sally. *In All His Glory: The Life and Times of William S. Paley and the Birth of Modern Broadcasting*. New York: Random House, 1990.

Benjamin, Burton. *Fair Play: CBS, General Westmoreland, and How a Television Documentary Went Wrong*. New York: Harper & Row, 1988.

Bishop, Jim. *The Golden Ham*. New York: Simon & Schuster, 1956.

Blum, David. *Tick . . . Tick . . . Tick: The Long Life and Turbulent Times of 60 Minutes*. New York: HarperCollins, 2004.

Boyer, Peter J. *Who Killed CBS? The Undoing of America's Number One News Network*. New York: Random House, 1988.

Buzenberg, Susan, and Bill Buzenberg, editors. *Salant, CBS, and the Battle for the Soul of Broadcast Journalism*. Boulder City, Colo.: Westview Press, 1999.

Cohen, Richard. *Blindsided: Lifting a Life above Illness*. New York: Harper-Collins, 2004.

Cronkite, Walter. *A Reporter's Life*. New York: Alfred A. Knopf, 1996.

Crouse, Timothy. *The Boys on the Bus*. New York: Random House, 1972, revised 1973.

Fenton, Tom. *Bad News: The Decline of Reporting the Business of News and the Danger to Us All*. New York: Regan Books, 2005.

Goldberg, Bernard. *Bias: A CBS Insider Exposes How the Media Distort the News*. Washington, D.C.: Regnery Publishing, 2002.

———. *100 People Who Are Screwing Up America*. New York: HarperCollins, 2005.

Halberstam, David. *The Powers That Be*. New York: Alfred A. Knopf, 1979.

Heller, Joseph. *Something Happened*. New York: Alfred A. Knopf, 1974.

Joyce, Ed. *Prime Times, Bad Times*. New York: Anchor Books-Doubleday, 1989.

Kendrick, Alexander. *Prime Time: The Life of Edward R. Murrow*. New York: Avon Books, 1969.

Leonard, Bill. *In the Storm of the Eye: A Lifetime at CBS*. New York: G. P. Putnam's Sons, 1987.

Mapes, Mary. *Truth and Duty: The Press, the President and the Privilege of Power*. New York: St. Martin's, 2005.

Midgley, Les. *How Many Words Do You Want?* New York: Carol Publishing Group, 1989.

Rather, Dan. *The American Dream*. New York: William Morrow, 2001.

——— (with Mickey Herskowitz). *The Camera Never Blinks: Adventures of a TV Journalist*. New York: William Morrow, 1977.

——— (with Mickey Herskowitz). *The Camera Never Blinks Twice: The Further Adventures of a Television Journalist*. New York: William Morrow, 1994.

———. *Deadlines and Datelines*. New York: William Morrow, 1999.

——— (with Peter Wyden). *I Remember: Growing Up in Texas*. Boston: Little, Brown, 1991.

———. *Our Times: Based on the Landmark Study by Mark Sullivan*, abridged edition. New York: Charles Scribner & Sons, 1996.

——— (with Gary Paul Gates). *The Palace Guard*. New York: Warner Paperback Library, 1975.

Safer, Morley. *Flashbacks: On Returning to Vietnam*. New York: Random House, 1990.

Schieffer, Bob. *This Just In: What I Couldn't Tell You on TV*. New York: Penguin Putnam, 2003.

Shales, Tom. *On the Air*. Washington, D.C.: Summit Books, 1982.

Talese, Gay. *Fame and Obscurity*. New York: Random House, 2003.

Wallace, Mike (with Gary Paul Gates). *Between You and Me: A Memoir*. New York: Hyperion Books, 2005.

———. *Close Encounters: Mike Wallace's Own Story*. New York: Berkley Books, 1985.

Credits

Music Credits

VII: Song lyrics from "Lone Star Blues," words and music by Delbert McClinton and Gary Nicholson © 2002 Nasty Cat Music (Carol Vincent & Associates, LLC) (BMI)/Gary Nicholson Music (Sony/ATV Tunes, LLC dba Cross Keys Publishing Co.) (ASCAP). Used with permission. All rights reserved.

199: Song lyrics from "Pick Up the Pieces," words and music by Willie Nelson © 1998 Warner-Tamerlane Publishing Corporation and Act Five Music. All rights administered by Warner-Tamerlane Publishing Corporation. Lyrics reprinted with the permission of Alfred Publishing Co., Inc. All rights reserved.

Photo Credits

111 (top): © The Hulton Archive/Getty Images
111 (bottom): © CBS Photo Archive/Getty Images
112: courtesy KTRH
113 (top): courtesy Bernie Birnbaum
113 (bottom): © Bettman/Corbis
114 (top): © Getty Images
114 (bottom): © Michael Edwards
115: © Time & Life Pictures/Getty Images
116 (top): © Getty Images
116 (bottom): courtesy Sandy Socolow
117 (top): © Steve Friedman
117 (bottom): © Corbis
118: courtesy Sandy Socolow
119: © John Chiasson/Getty Images Entertainment

Index

Page numbers in *italics* indicate photographs.